IMAGES
of America

ALEXANDER CITY

On the Cover: Groom Joseph Rhyal Watkins and bride Maggie Fletcher Thweatt are the first couple at left on the platform. According to the back of the photograph, "Attendants: Misses Zula Watkins, Bessie Whitaker, Lilla Street; Messers: F. L. Pearson, John Street, J.T. Sandlin; ushers: Messers: F.H. Leslie and T.S. Christian, Jr.; maid of honor, Miss Maggie Bloodworth; best man Mr. J.P. Watkins. After ceremony they entrained for Opelika where a dining in their honor was held" on March 7, 1894. The couple became the grandparents of William Odum Watkins. (Courtesy of Grady Lamberth.)

IMAGES
of America

ALEXANDER CITY

Peggy Jackson Walls
and Laura Dykes Oliver

ARCADIA
PUBLISHING

ISBN 978-0-7385-8804-9

Published by Arcadia Publishing
Charleston, South Carolina

Printed in the United States of America

Library of Congress Control Number: 2011927201

For all general information, please contact Arcadia Publishing:
Telephone 843-853-2070
Fax 843-853-0044
E-mail sales@arcadiapublishing.com
For customer service and orders:
Toll-Free 1-888-313-2665

Visit us on the Internet at www.arcadiapublishing.com

Alexander City *is dedicated to the 214th Company, Alabama Army National Guard, and to Jeremy and Zac Lynn, Tatum Knowles, and Tyler, Emma, and Sophie Walls*

Contents

ACKNOWLEDGMENTS

The authors wish to extend special thanks to Grady Lamberth, who provided the cover picture; Tim Phillips, who assisted with technical adjustments of the picture; and Richard Wagoner, director of the MainStreet Organization, who provided access to their photographic archives. Many thanks go to Avondale chief executive officers Marcus Tapley and Stephen Felker for making possible the use of the *Avondale Sun* pictures in this book through the gift of the Bevelle collection to Laura Dykes Oliver. Much gratitude is extended to Bill Walls, whose ongoing technical assistance made completion of the book possible, and to Troy Cruz at Radio Shack, who rescued the authors from a computer crash a few days before the book deadline. We are especially indebted to local historians Bob Saxon, Jennie Lee Kelley, and Thomas Byron Saunders, whose research, writing, and organization of materials in previous history projects laid the groundwork for this book. Appreciation is extended to Russell Lands for assistance with research and photographs regarding the Russell family and the lake area. We deeply appreciate the assistance of Brinkley Taliaferro, Southeast acquisitions editor, as we assembled *Alexander City*.

INTRODUCTION

In the early 1800s, pioneers who made their way into the area now known as Alexander City encountered Creek Indians living in scattered villages alongside rivers and streams. A few traders and backwoodsmen lived in notched log cabins and among Indians often residing in similar structures. A few Cherokee lived among them, but the land predominantly belonged to the Creek Nation. Travelers were required to carry passports for safe passage through the Indian Territory. The Creek Confederacy was divided into the Upper Creeks, who lived along the Coosa and Tallapoosa Rivers, and the Lower Creeks, who lived predominantly along the lower Chattahoochee and Tallapoosa Rivers.

The Creeks fished in the streams and hunted in nearby forests. They planted corn, sweet potatoes, pumpkins, and field peas. Wild plants, berries, and roots served as both food and medicine. Women sewed deerskin into clothing and moccasins to protect family members against the elements of sun, rain, and wind. The clothing, blankets, and skins were bartered with early traders, such as Scotsman Robert Grierson, who lived with his Creek wife, Sinnuge, on their plantation in the Hillabees. The Grierson plantation included Creek families and slaves who worked in the fields to grow and harvest food for the Grierson family and the Hillabee tribes. Henry Towns was the last trader to the Hillabees. After the Indians were removed, Towns joined the settlers.

During the Indian Wars of 1813–1814, Robert Grierson rode to Talladega to gain amnesty for the Hillabee tribes. Gen. Andrew Jackson granted Grierson's request, but before he could return to the Hillabees, a group of Tennessee militia passing by the village and commanded by Gen. James White attacked, killed, or captured many of the inhabitants. The massacre was mainly of women, children, and old men, since the younger men were away on a hunting foray into the forest. The Hillabee Massacre on November 18, 1813, embittered the Creeks and strengthened the warriors' resolve to attack and destroy the homes and lives of encroaching white settlers.

There were conflicts, such as the Battle of Enitachopco, on January 24, 1814, when Creeks attacked General Jackson, causing him to withdraw to Fort Strother. But the decisive encounter was the Battle of Horseshoe Bend on March 27, 1814, when Gen. Andrew Jackson and 3,300 men attacked 1,000 Creeks at Tohopeka. Jackson's troops sustained few casualties, while at least 800 Creeks were killed in battle. The overwhelming defeat of the Creeks at Horseshoe Bend broke the power of the Creek Nation. In 1819, Alabama declared statehood, absorbing the 23 million acres of Creek land relinquished in 1814 through the Treaty of Fort Jackson.

The state was heir to the Indian place names, such as Hillabee, Enitachopco, Tallapoosa, Coosa, and even the name Alabama. The names serve to remind each generation of the Indian Wars of 1813–1814, the smaller skirmishes that took place before the Indian Removal Act in 1832, and the final tragic Trail of Tears march to the Native Americans' new home in the West.

Out of this land, Tallapoosa County was formed in 1832. In 1833, settlers and speculators made their move to claim the newly vacated land that had been divided into 320-acre allotments by the federal government and given to the Indian families. Some settlers purchased land directly from the Creeks. By 1836, few Creeks remained in Tallapoosa County. The General Land Office sold numerous tracts in 1835 and 1836 to individuals and pioneer families. Among the influx of settlers was James Young, who purchased a 320-acre tract from the Creeks in 1835. His son Griffin Young measured off and sold lots in what, today, is the town square.

In June 1837, Griffin Young obtained an appointment as the settlement's first postmaster at a place he called Youngsville. The post office was located in the Georgia Store. The Young family was instrumental in establishing the town, and for a period of time, the settlement bore the names Youngsville and Georgia Store—the latter name derived from Griffin's ownership of the store.

The settlers came on horseback and in wagons loaded with household goods, pots, pans, farming equipment, shovels, axes, and hoes, prepared to build cabins, clear pastureland, and plant gardens. Though a small number of white and black settlers had lived in the area for 150 years, the Indian Removal Act made possible the transition from a Creek culture to an Anglo culture within half a dozen years.

During the land boom of the 1830s, gold prospectors came into the county, along with yeomen farmers, itinerant preachers, and land speculators. On Sundays, small groups met in a brush arbor for interdenominational worship services.

In 1874, the railroad came, altering the landscape with long, winding tracks and bringing with it opportunities for commerce, shipping, and travel. To honor railroad president Edward Porter Alexander, the name of the town was changed from Youngsville to Alexander City. People flocked to town on Saturdays to picnic and socialize as they watched the trains arrive and depart, some "running in fear for their lives" when they saw the train and heard the whistle blow. By 1902, Alexander City had a number of general merchandise stores, a post office, a bank, churches, and schools that met in private residences.

Tragedy struck hard in 1902, when sparks from a small fire in a business ignited and swept through the village, destroying the town. With the help of friends in neighboring communities, the residents immediately began to rebuild the town. The Alexander City Cotton Mill opened in 1898, survived the fire, and was still in operation when Russell Garment factory was built in 1902. In 1919, Avondale purchased the Alexander City Cotton Mill and opened the Bevelle plant. With two cotton mills operating in the city, life was centered around the mill work, gardening, church, and school. Other early businesses included a Ford dealership and a Coca-Cola Company.

Prior to 1928, people moved from lake communities to Alexander City in preparation for the opening of the floodgates of the newly constructed Martin Dam. With the dam to control and direct the water, the lake became a tremendous source of energy. Lake Martin became famous for hosting annual sporting events, musical concerts, sporting tournaments, and retreats at Children's Harbor.

Alexander City can boast of several sports celebrities and successful people in diverse, professional fields. The community spirit that fostered and supported the development of each generation remains the same devotion to the institutions of home, church, and family and the desire to continue to progress as a town.

One

SETTLEMENT DAYS

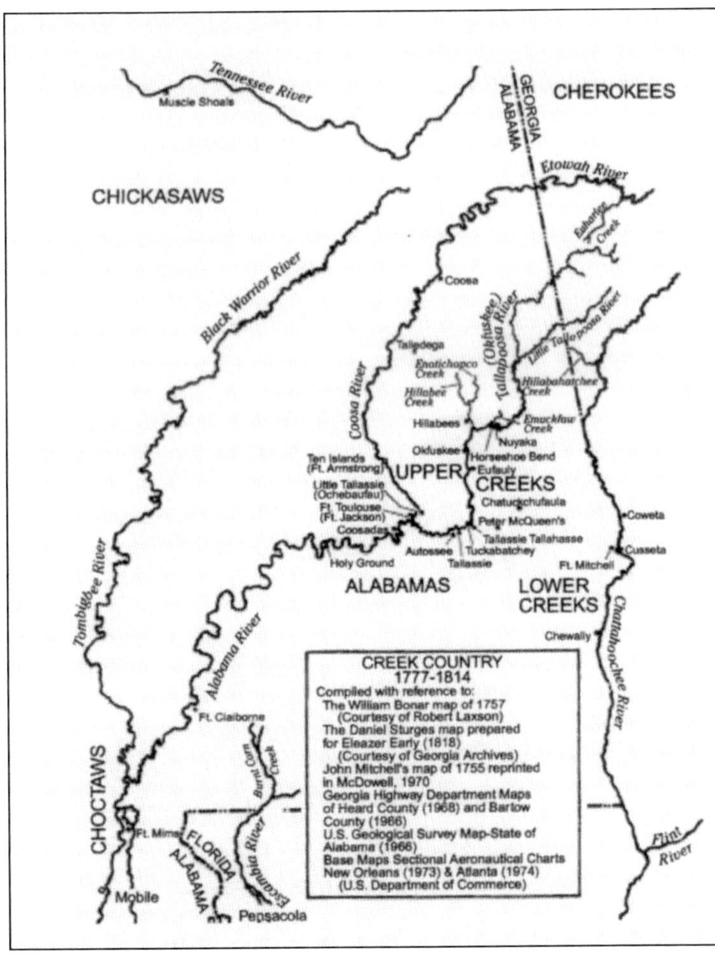

Before the early settlers moved into what was then the Old Southwest territory, the Creek Indians, known as Muskogee, inhabited the land. From 1777 to 1814, the great Creek Nation was divided into Upper Creeks and Lower Creeks. The Upper Creeks' territory included battle sites of Enitachopco, Hillabee, Okfuskee, and Horseshoe Bend. They supported Red Stick leaders William Weatherford, Pete McQueen, and Menewa and opposed the encroachment of white settlers on Creek land. (Courtesy of Horseshoe Bend Park.)

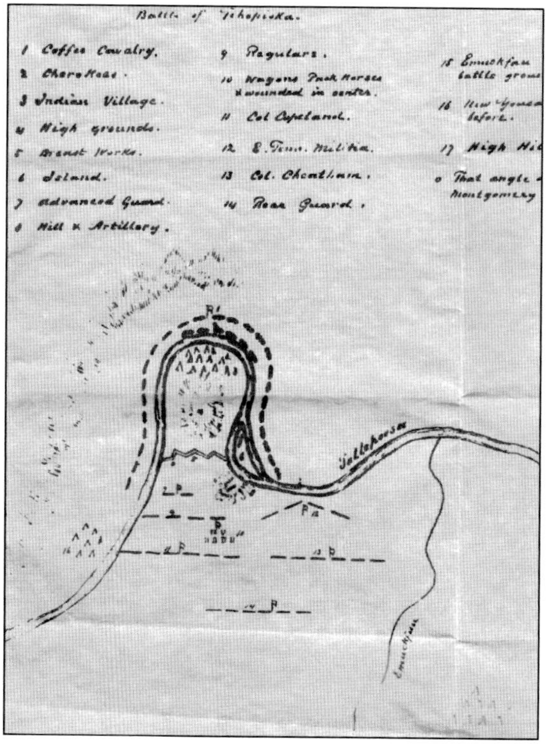

In this bend on March 27, 1814, warriors from Oakfuskee, Hillabees, Oakchaya, New Youka, the Fish Ponds, and Eufaula Indian towns waited to defend the Tohopeka village. Andrew Jackson, General Coffee, and their troops, along with friendly Cherokees, surrounded the village and river bend, preventing any Indians from escaping through the Tallapoosa River. At least 800 of the 1,000 Creeks were killed. Only 49 of Jackson's men were killed in the battle, but many died from wounds later. (Courtesy of Horseshoe Bend Park.)

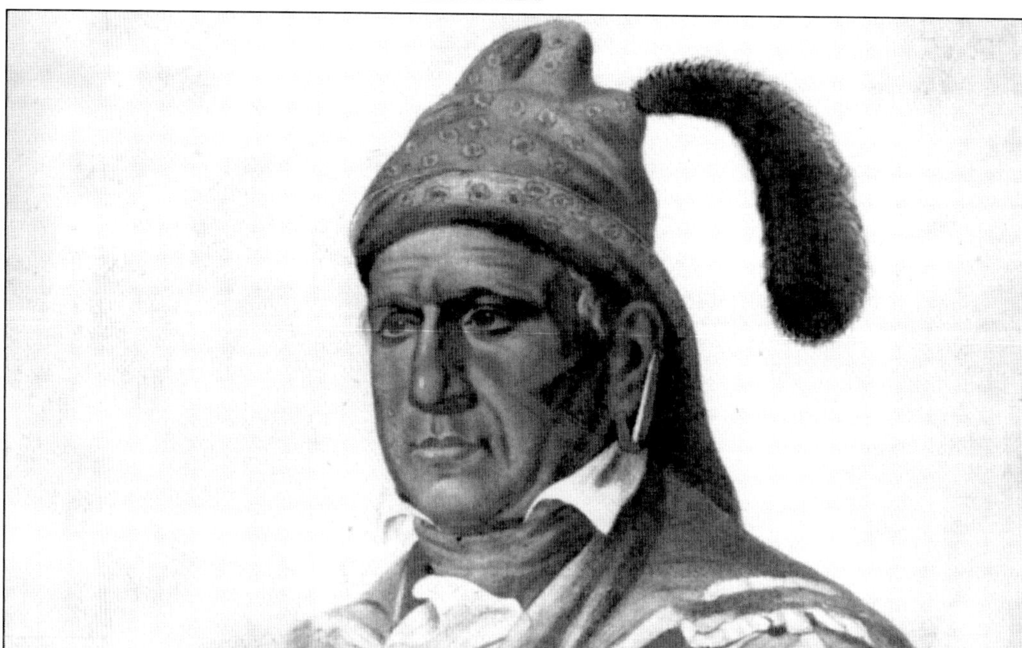

Menewa, formerly known as Hothlepoyar ("The Crazy War Hunter"), led the Red Stick warriors at the battle of Horseshoe Bend on March 27, 1814. The majority of his warriors were killed, but Menewa escaped. After being wounded twice and left for dead, he revived, crawled to the river, and escaped in a canoe. He regained his health and status as a leader. In 1836, Menewa joined the Trail of Tears march to Indian Territory in Oklahoma. (Courtesy of Horseshoe Bend Park.)

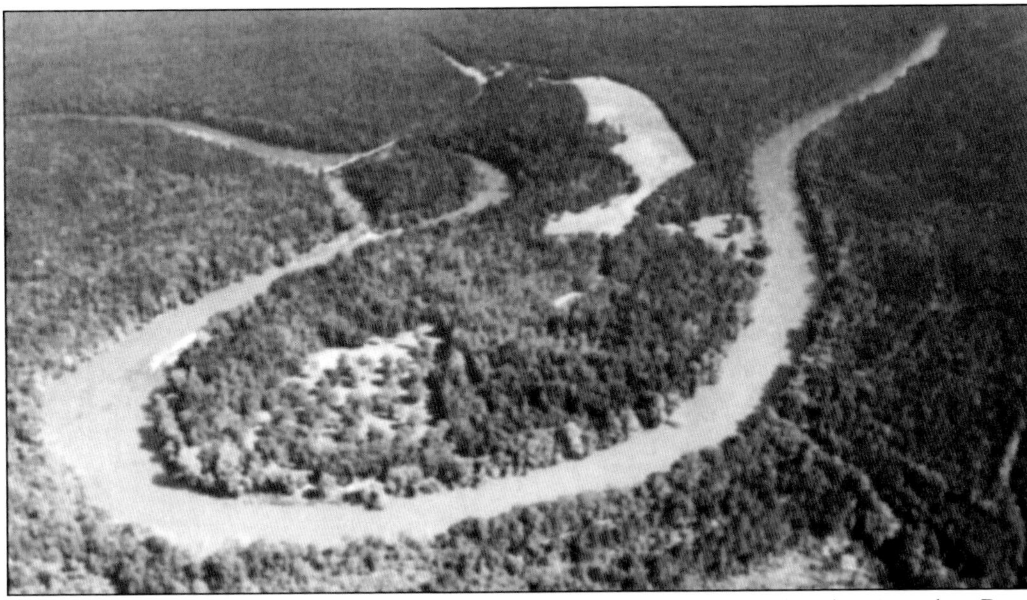

The site of the final battle of the Creek War of 1813–1814 was designated as the Horseshoe Bend National Military Park by an act of Congress in 1956. On August 11, 1959, a proclamation by Pres. Dwight D. Eisenhower reserved 2,040 acres for the park and a museum for preservation of artifacts. Key players in achieving this feat were C.J. Coley, Thomas Martin, and Thomas Russell. (Courtesy of Horseshoe Bend Park.)

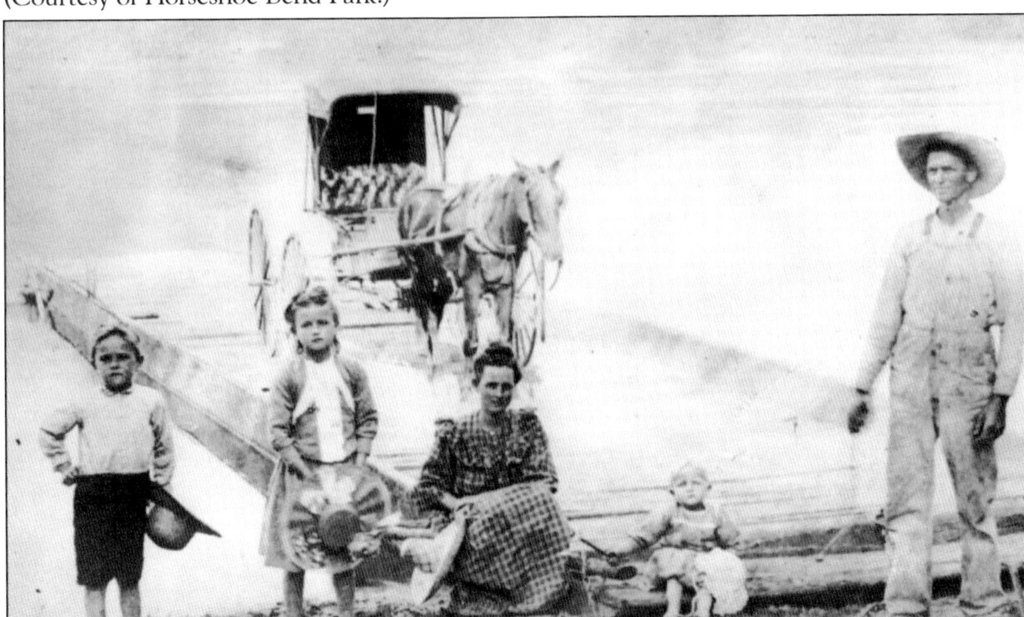

Settlers arrived on horseback and in wagons laden with household goods, primitive farming equipment, seed, and livestock and with large families to work crops and build notched log cabins. A number of ferries conveyed wagons, horses, and passengers into the newly gained federal territory, such as Young's ferry, which brought settlers across creeks. Pictured here in 1906 is ferry operator Martin Luther Vickers with his wife and children on a ferry similar to earlier ones. (Courtesy of Fletcher Adamson.)

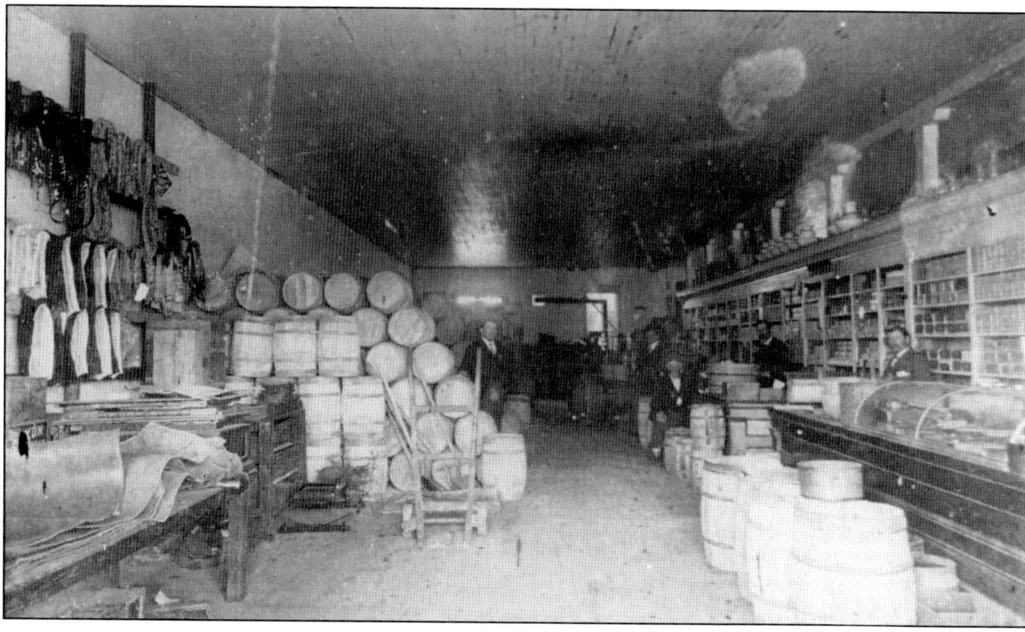

The interior of Chalmers Thomas Hardware Store was stocked with items farmers needed to maintain their farm, such as horse collars and harnesses, rolls of wire, and wooden barrels. Farmers traveled on mules or in wagons from outlying communities into town to purchase merchandise, such as building tools, nails, saws, rope, and plow stocks. They spent part of their day in the store and around the railroad depot, catching up on local news, politics, cotton prices, and cost of other goods. In the winter months, men gathered around the old potbelly stove to share stories of local events. Light filtered into the building through the windows and doors. (Both, courtesy of Bobby Martin; photographs by Robert Graves.)

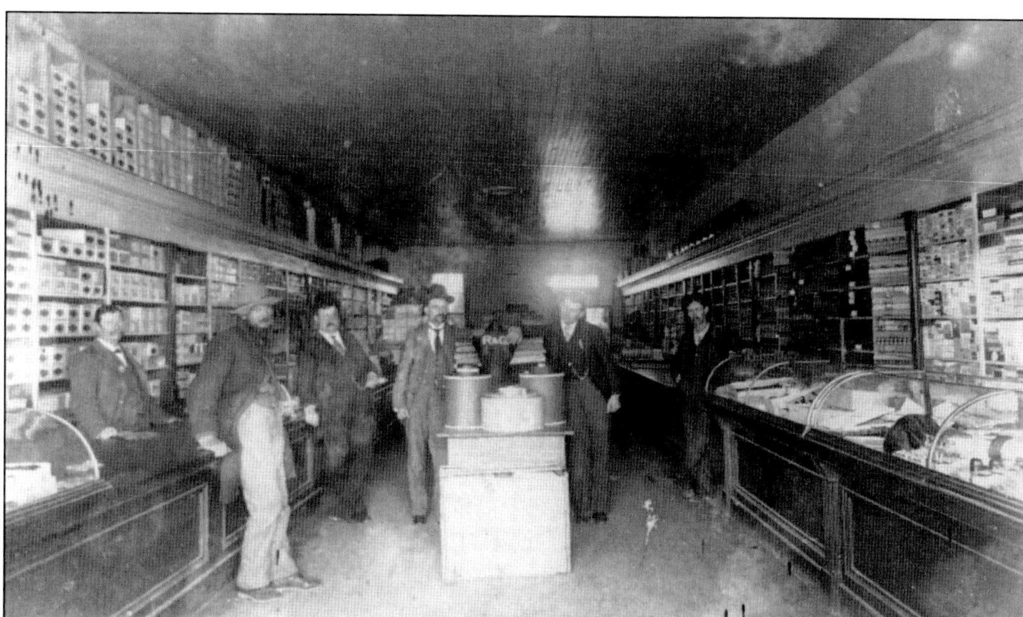

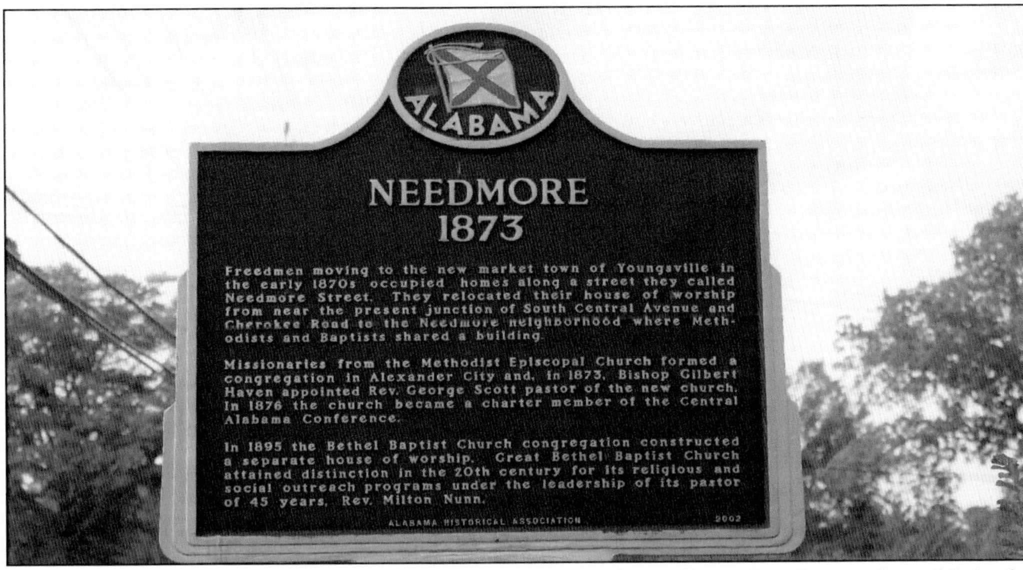

Following the Civil War, a number of freedmen moved to Alexander City and established a neighborhood along the street that they named Needmore. Methodist Episcopal missionaries helped the local group establish a church. In 1873, Rev. George Scott was appointed pastor of the church where Methodists and Baptists met. The Great Bethel Baptist Church grew out of this tradition and thrived under the leadership of Rev. Milton Nunn for 45 years. (Courtesy of Peggy Walls; photograph by Tammy East.)

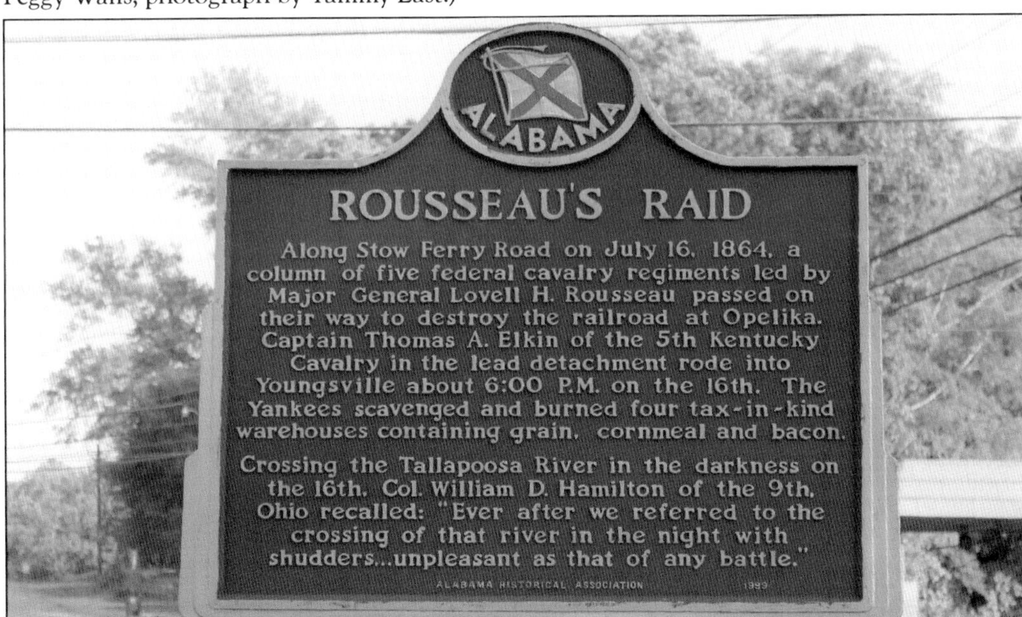

Plans for installing railroad tracks through Youngsville were postponed until after the Civil War. On July 16, 1864, Maj. Gen. Lovell H. Rousseau and his troops, known as Rousseau's Raiders, rode with Capt. Thomas A.E. Elkin and his 5th Kentucky Cavalry through the city on their way to destroy the railroad in Opelika. The troops burned four warehouses containing scarce war supplies. Tallapoosa's citizens voted against secession but volunteered to fight in Gen. Robert E. Lee's army. (Courtesy of Peggy Walls; photograph by Tammy East.)

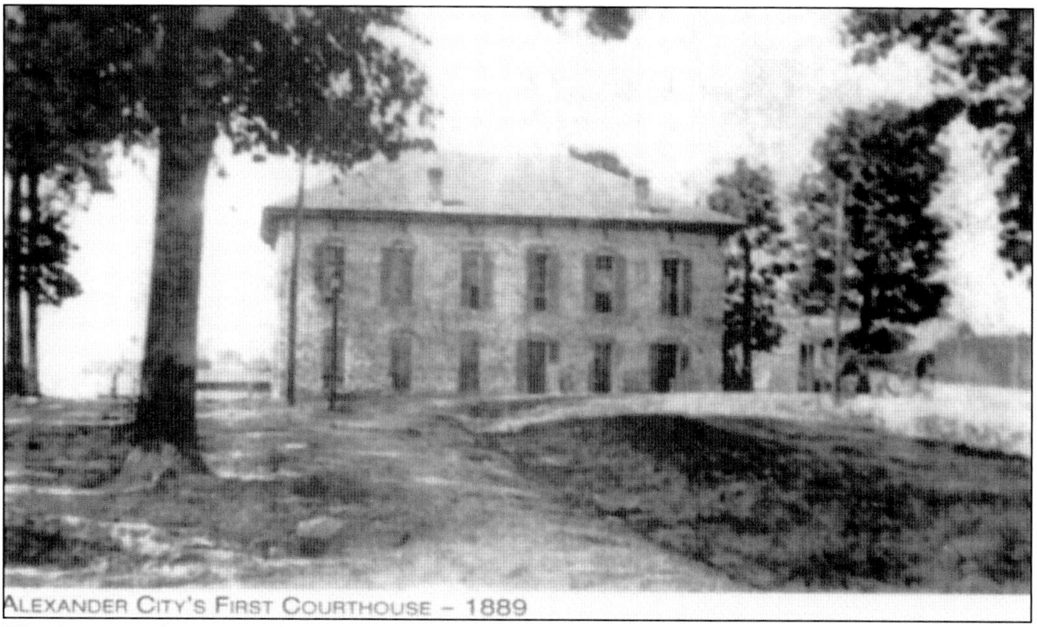

The first courthouse in Alexander City was built from contributions of the local people and was ready to begin court business in the spring of 1890. Lauded by the *Opelika Daily News* as "a house of justice as handsome as any in the state," the building burned in the 1902 fire. An office for the city clerk was set up in the home of the *Alexander City Outlook* editor to secure all records that were salvaged from the courthouse. (Courtesy of MainStreet Organization.)

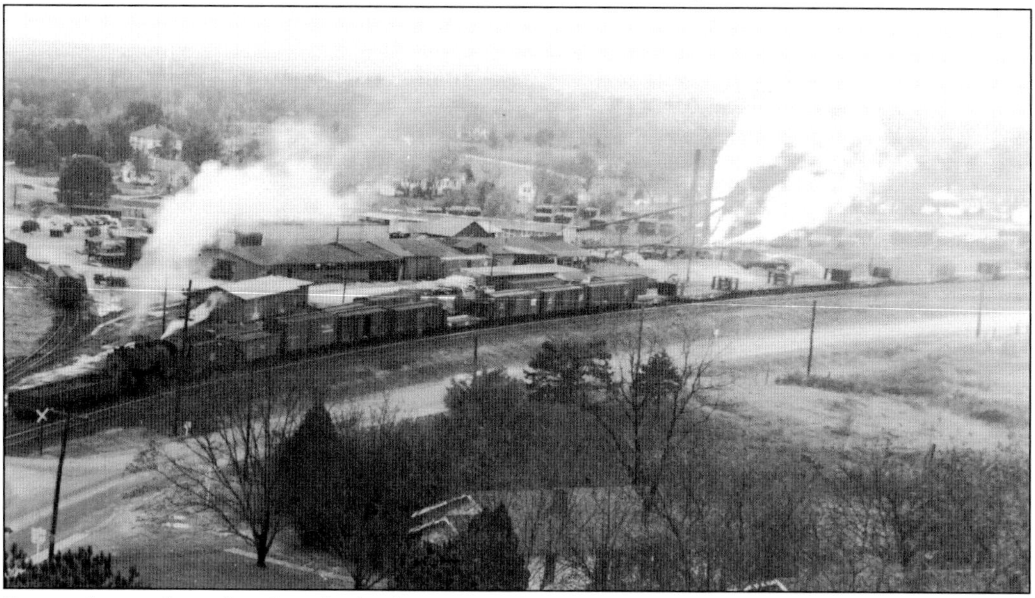

Prior to laying the railroad tracks for the Savannah & Memphis Railroad, a proposal was approved in Montgomery to change the town's name to honor E.P. Alexander, president of the railroad. On March 19, 1873, the town of Youngsville officially became Alexander City. On June 24, 1874, hundreds of folks arrived with picnic baskets to commemorate the arrival of the train. Many fled in fear when they saw the train and heard the loud whistle. (Courtesy of Robert Martin; photograph by Robert Graves.)

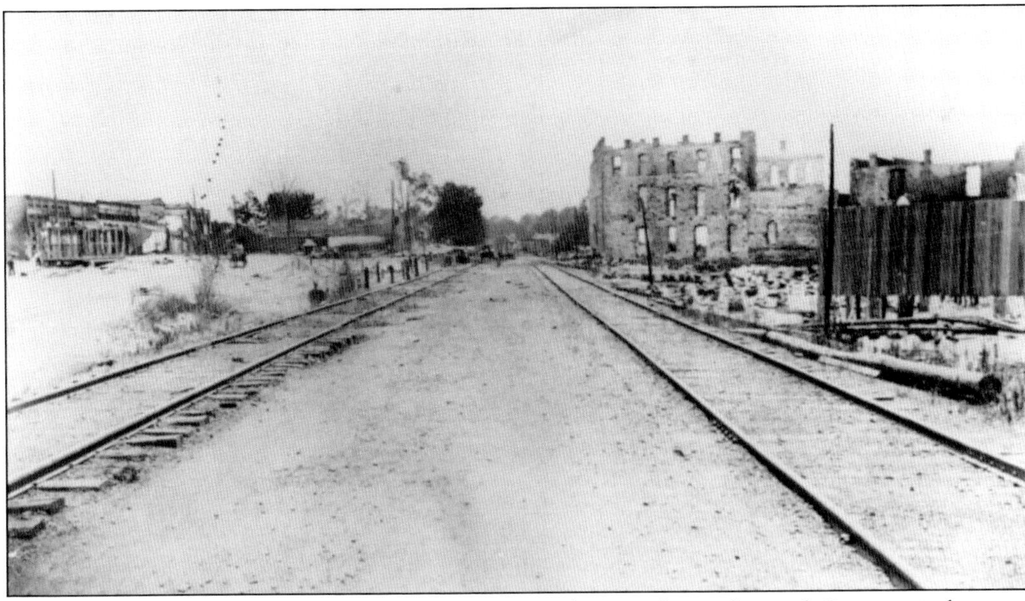

June 13, 1902, the entire town of Alexander City and 13 residences burned. Strong winds spread the flames of a small fire behind Robinson's Machine Shop on Main Street, burning buildings and then roaring down Alabama, Broad, Green, Adams, and Jefferson Streets. There were 28 structures destroyed by the fire: Robinson's shop, J.H. Fuller's store, Adams Hotel, Alexander City Bank, Citizen's Bank, the post office, the depot, boxcars, train tracks, wooden sidewalks, and livery stables with animals inside. (Courtesy of Robert Martin.)

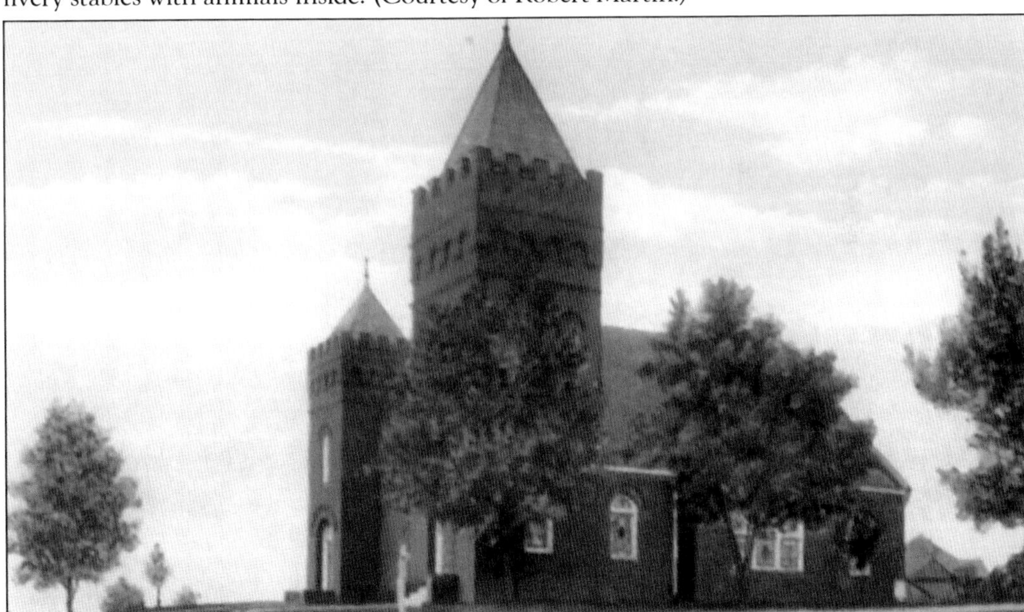

In 1872, the interdenominational meetings of a small group led by Rev. William T. Patillo were held under a bush arbor. The Methodist church was a recently completed brick structure that replaced the wooden building constructed in the 1870s. The rocks used in the foundation were from the farm of Jim Young, who hauled them with a two-mule wagon. The cornerstone was laid in 1903. The Romanesque-style church held its first service in 1906. (Courtesy of Sandra Wilson.)

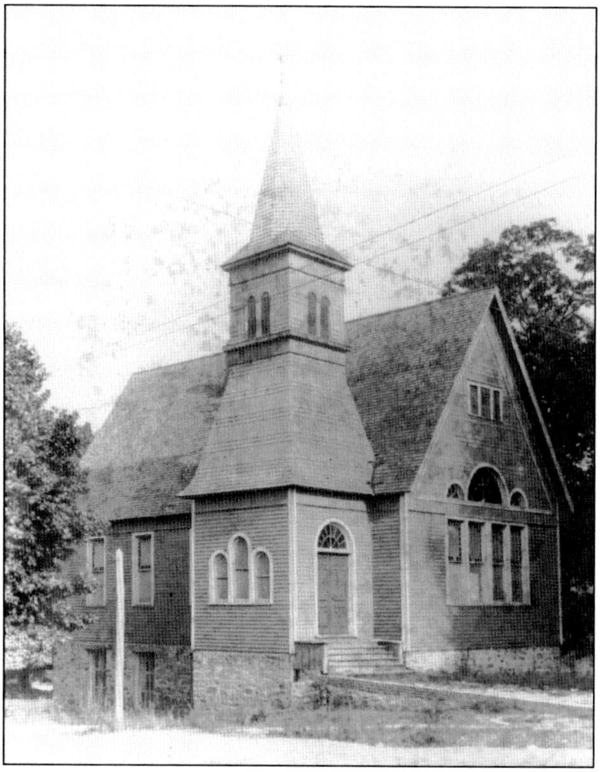

The First Presbyterian Church was the only building in the business district to survive the fire of 1902. The postmaster set up his office in the church basement. The First Presbyterian Church, with 17 members, originated March 2, 1893, at the home of Robert Clinton Sandlin, first ruling elder. Located on South Main and Tallapoosa Streets, the building was constructed in 1895 and renovated by the law firm of Morris, Haynes, and Hornsby in the mid-1900s. (Both, courtesy of Sandra Wilson.)

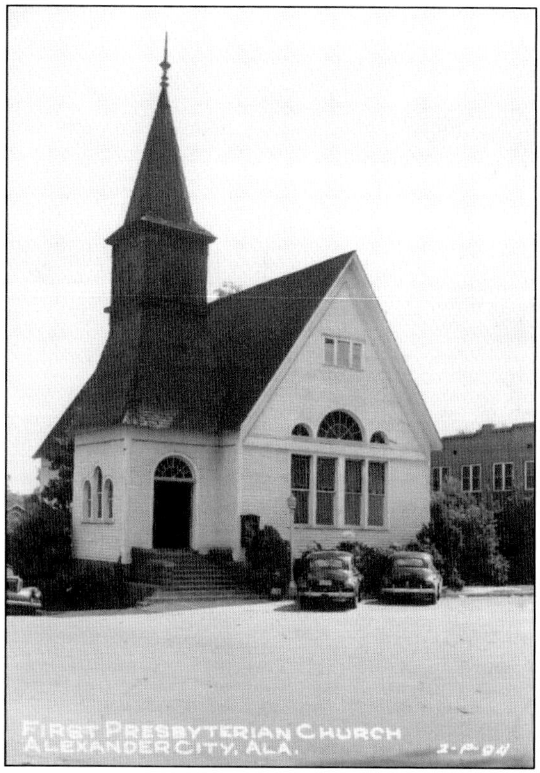

In 1872, the small group of Methodists and Baptists began plans for more permanent meeting places. Organization of the Youngsville Baptist Church was led by Rev. A.K. Tribble. Early officers were deacons J.T.P Christian and B.B. Reams. When the town's name was changed, the church name also was changed to the Alexander City Baptist Church. Services were held once a month. The church was built in 1877 and valued at $1,000. (Courtesy of Robert Martin; photograph by Robert Graves.)

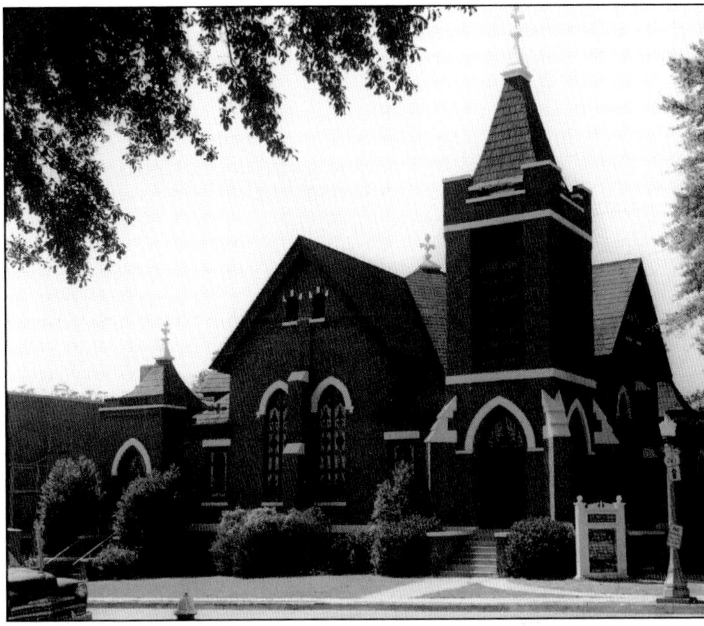

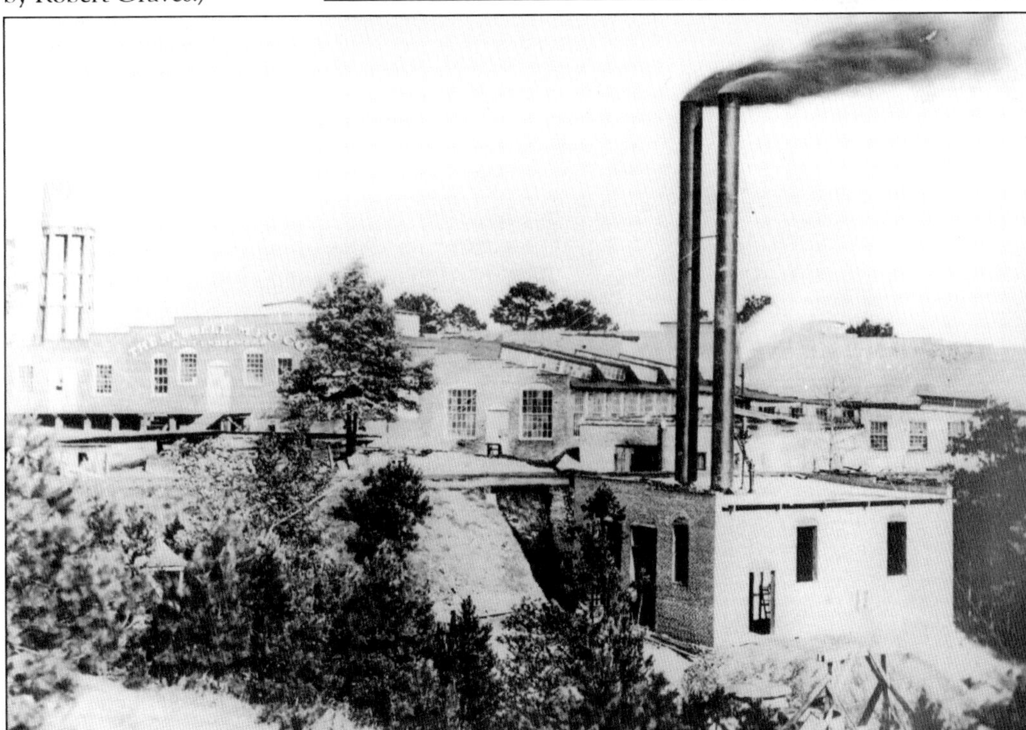

In 1902, twenty-six-year-old Ben Russell purchased a small knitting mill in Georgia with the financial backing of his wife, Roberta Robb. The 50-foot-by-100-foot mill building was placed on 320 acres of land. The first garments were ladies' and children's underwear. There were six knitting machines and 10 sewing machines. By 1908, the mill had expanded to operations in spinning and to "woven cloth in 1931 and athletic apparel in 1931 or 1932," according to the Alabama historical marker. (Courtesy of Robert Martin; photograph by Robert Graves.)

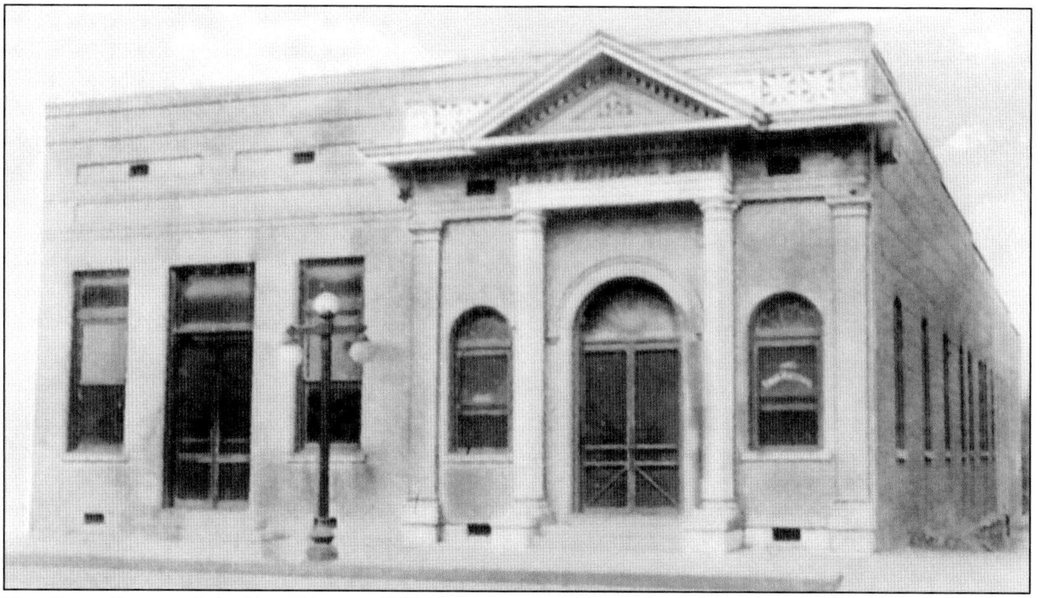

Ben Russell started the First National Bank, along with a textile mill, a mill village, church, school, foundry, hotel, dairy, bakery, laundry, wholesale grocery, and numerous other enterprises. Later, the bank was operated by John Russell Thomas under the name Aliant Bank. Russell became involved in land development in Tallapoosa and Coosa Counties and in Florida. He started the first Alexander City Chamber of Commerce. (Courtesy of Russell Lands.)

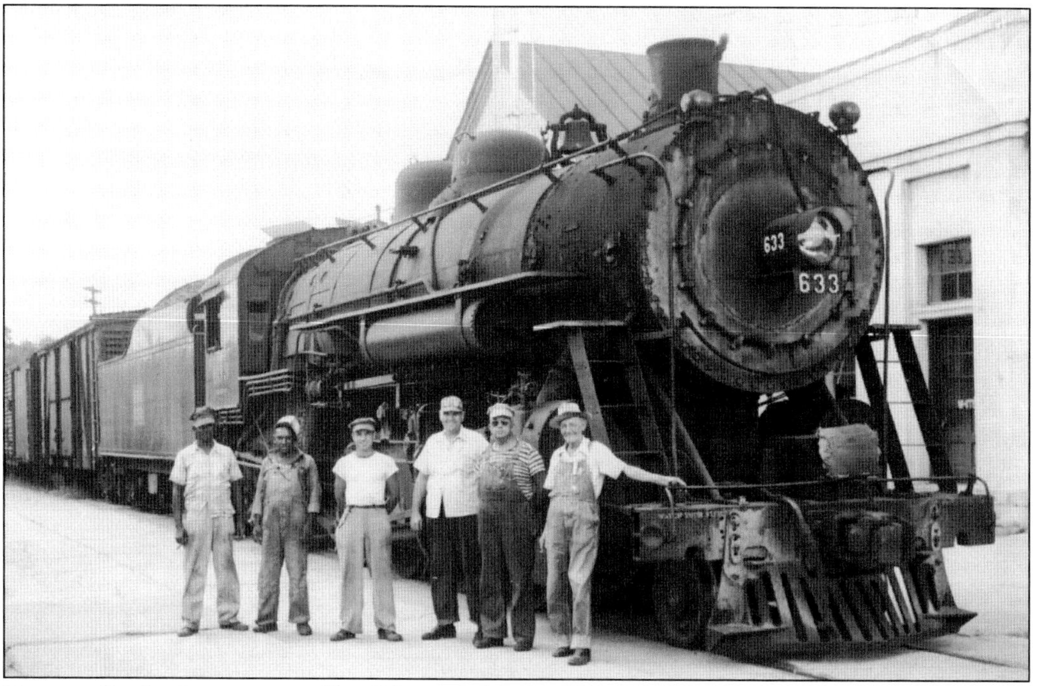

On one of its final runs, engine No. 633 stopped at the Alexander City Depot. The steam locomotive was invented in 1830 and rode the rail for 123 years until Southern Railroad dieselized all of its trains in 1953, ending the steam engine era and ushering in a new future for the railroad industry. (Courtesy of MainStreet Organization.)

Two

Gold Mines and Cotton Mills

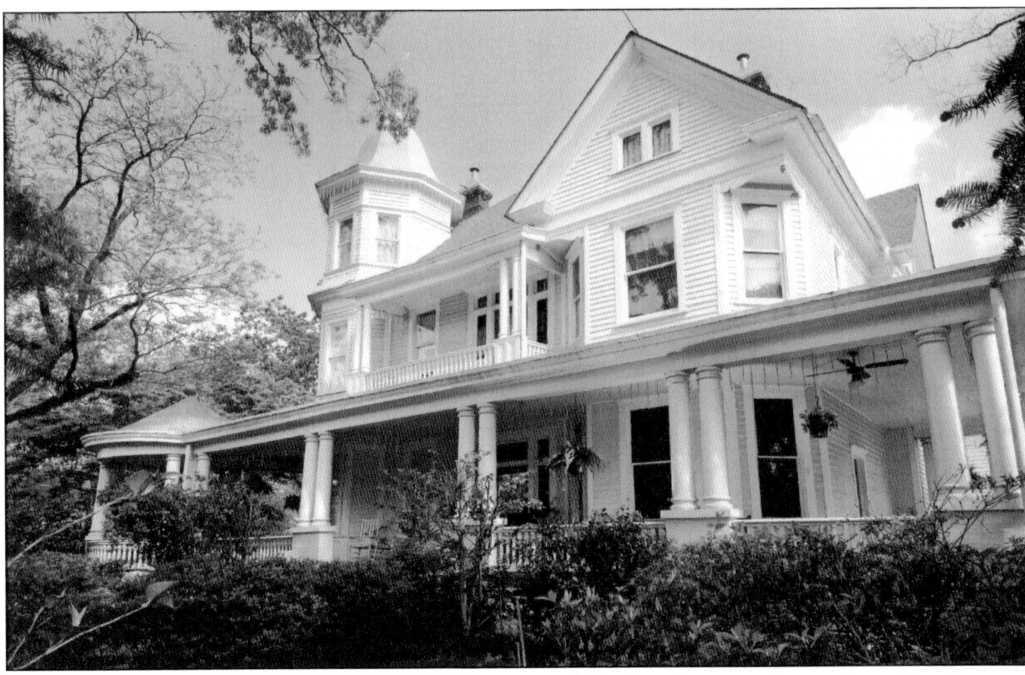

The Herzfeld home was the location of the original bush arbor meetings where Baptists and Methodists met together until they built their respective churches. Reuben Herzfeld was a German emigrant who came to Alexander City in 1875. He opened a store and built the Alexander City Bank, the oldest business in the city. The restored home now serves the public as the Mistletoe Bough Bed and Breakfast Inn. (Courtesy of JoAnn Frazier.)

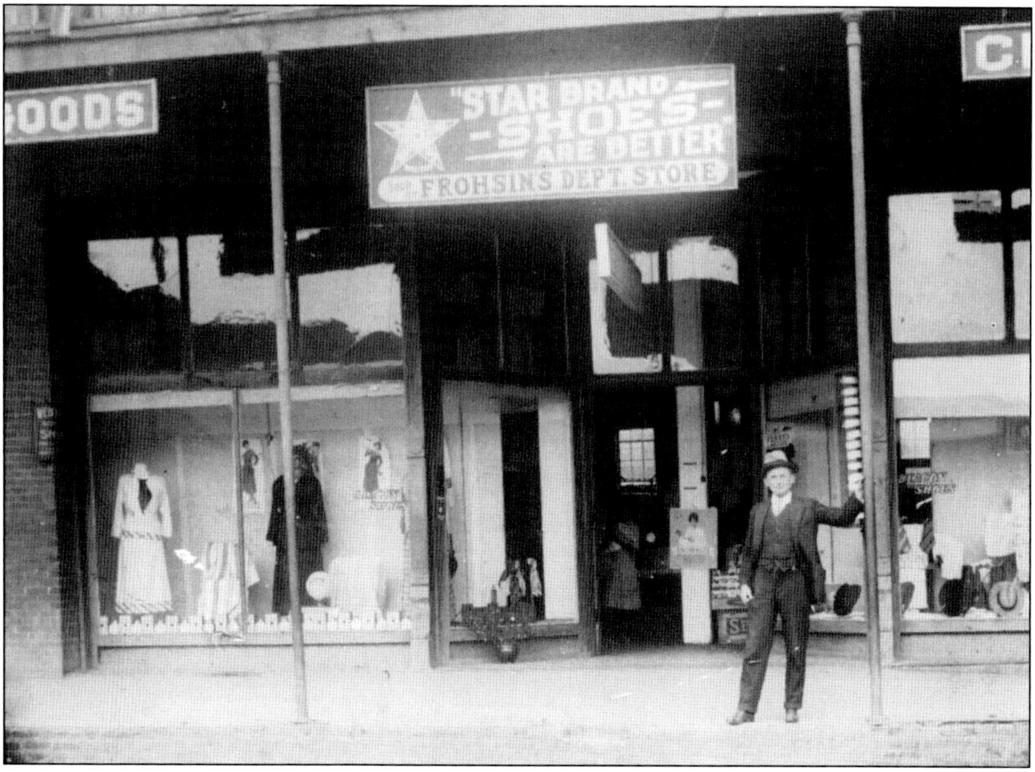

Isaac Frohsin bought the Herzfeld Brothers business and founded Frohsin's Department Store in 1891. The general merchandise business was known as I. Frohsins. He sold hats, work boots, button shoes, corsets, underwear, household linens, and furniture. His children—Ralph, Leon, Lewis, and Clara—worked as partners in operating the store after their father's death. (Courtesy of MainStreet Organization.)

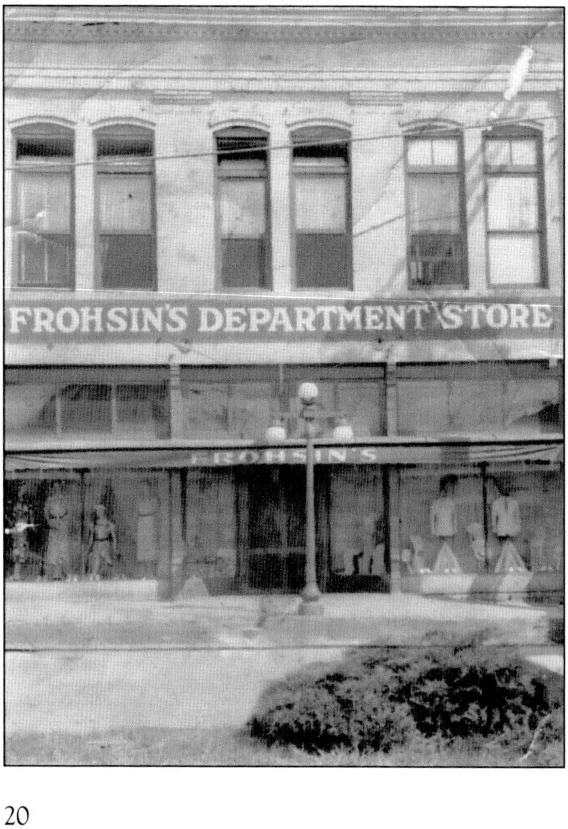

Reuben Herzfeld operated a bank in the Herzfeld Brothers store until it outgrew the space and was moved down the street. When Isaac Frohsin bought one-half interest in the store for $5,000, it became Herzfeld and Frohsin. After harvest time, sharecroppers, small farmers, and their families could camp overnight in an area reserved for their wagons and livestock to deposit or spend the money they earned for their crops. (Courtesy of MainStreet Organization.)

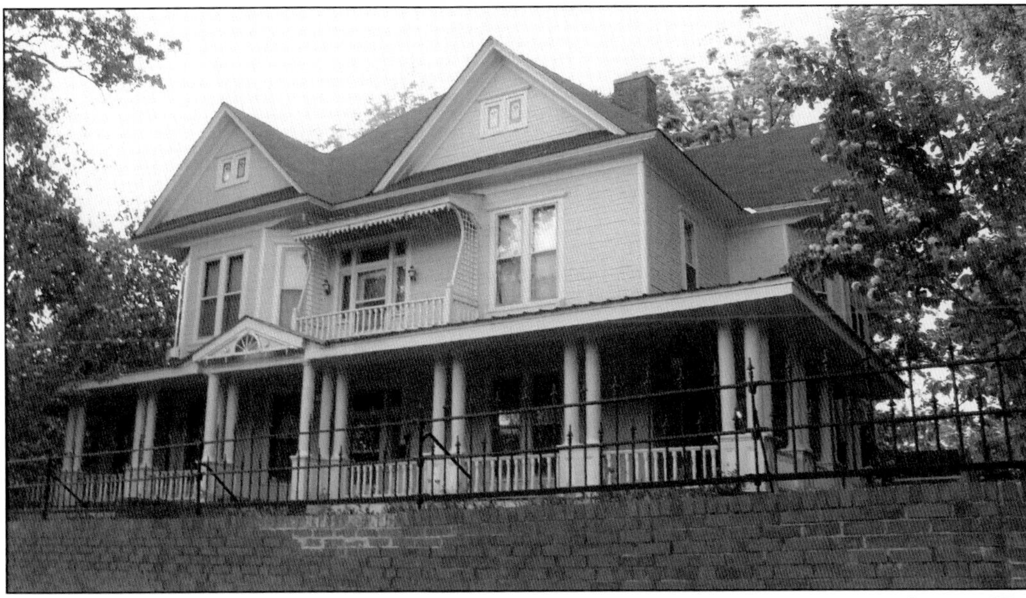

Listed on the historical register, the Joiner-Coley house served as the private residence of Dr. Andrew Jackson Coley. He was a doctor, half-owner of a livery stable, mayor of Alexander City (1902–1903), and chairman of the Industrial Fire Relief Committee in charge of receiving monetary help for the town after the 1902 fire. A renowned physician, Dr. J.A. Goggans opened an infirmary in the house, which also served as his office and residence. (Courtesy of Peggy Walls; photograph by Tammy East.)

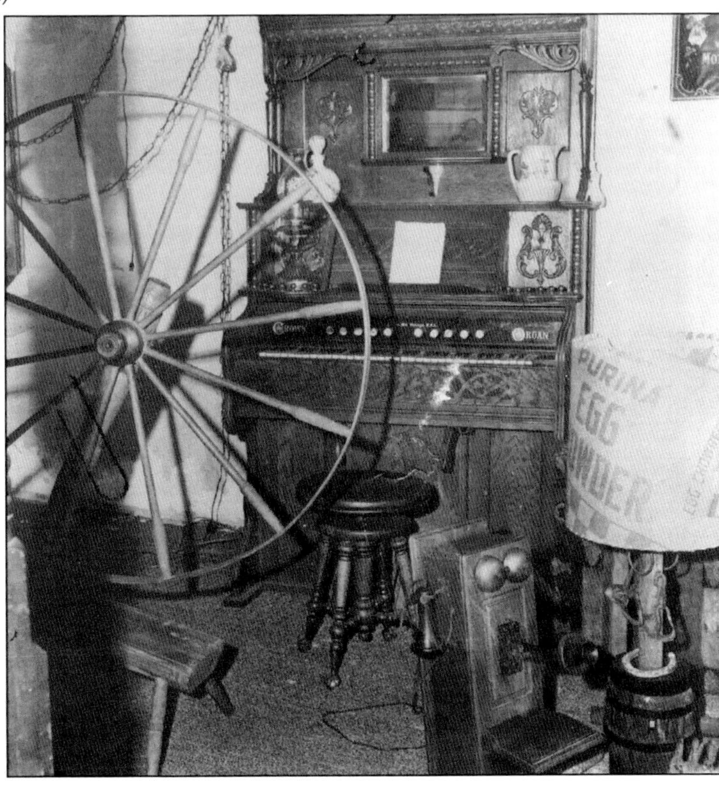

The Radney Furniture Store was one of the tallest buildings in old Alexander City. Early goods included spinning wheels, crank telephones, pump organs, photograph templates, and porcelain pitchers. The Radney family served the community in commerce, legal, and political careers. W.L. Radney Jr. was mayor of Alexander City from 1960 to 1972. (Courtesy of MainStreet Organization.)

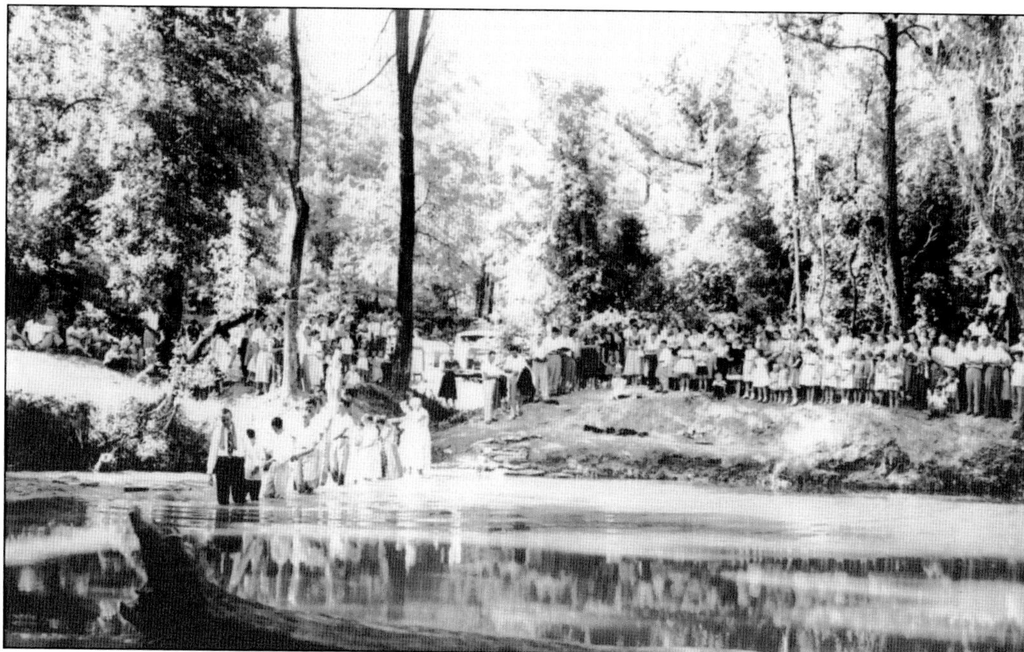

Spring traditions included river baptisms and cemetery cleanings. People who joined a church during the winter months waited to be baptized in the spring. Gathering on the bank to observe the ceremony are family members, the church flock, and a politician or two eager to shake hands with the crowd. (Courtesy of Fletcher Adamson; photograph by Roy Jones.)

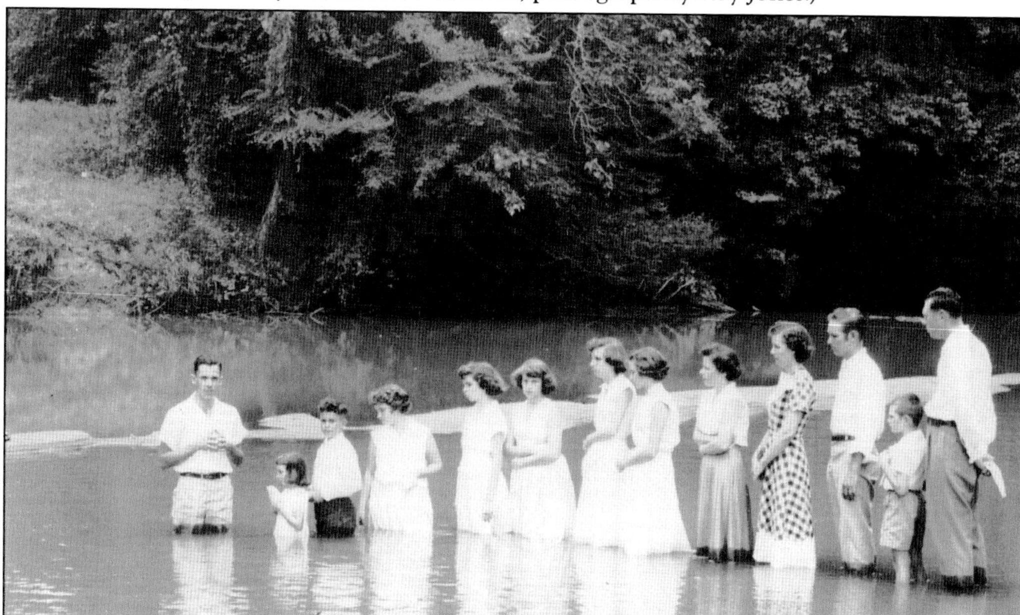

Following the religious practice of baptism by immersion, new members line up and prepare to be lowered into the water and baptized. Shown from left to right are Rev. Earl Tharp, G.W. Hodge, P.M. Wedgeworth, Harold Blythe, Haley Jackson, Mollie Burnette, Alice Foshee, Hazel Massey, Richard Patterson, and Mrs. J.A. Gordon. (Courtesy of Fletcher Adamson; photograph by Roy Jones.)

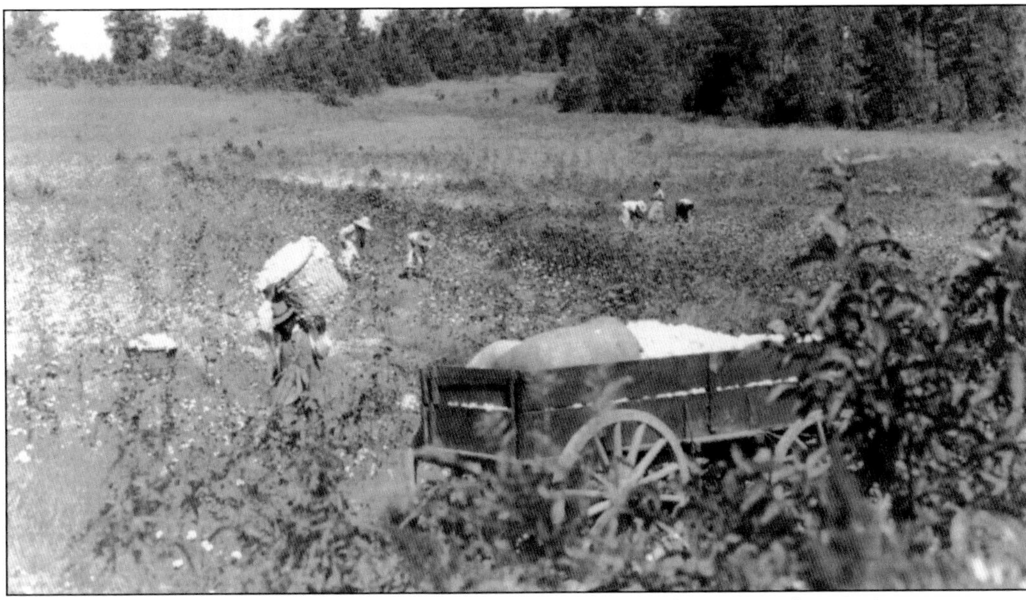

In the early 1900s, cotton was king in Alabama, elevating or depressing the state's economy and personal fortunes of the sharecropper and small farmer. Alabama was known as "The Cotton State" because of its central location in the Cotton Belt. Cotton picking was a backbreaking job and one that paid according to fluctuating market rates. With widespread cotton crop failures in the early 1900s, farm families suffered, although they worked very hard. (Courtesy of Robert Martin; photograph by Robert Graves.)

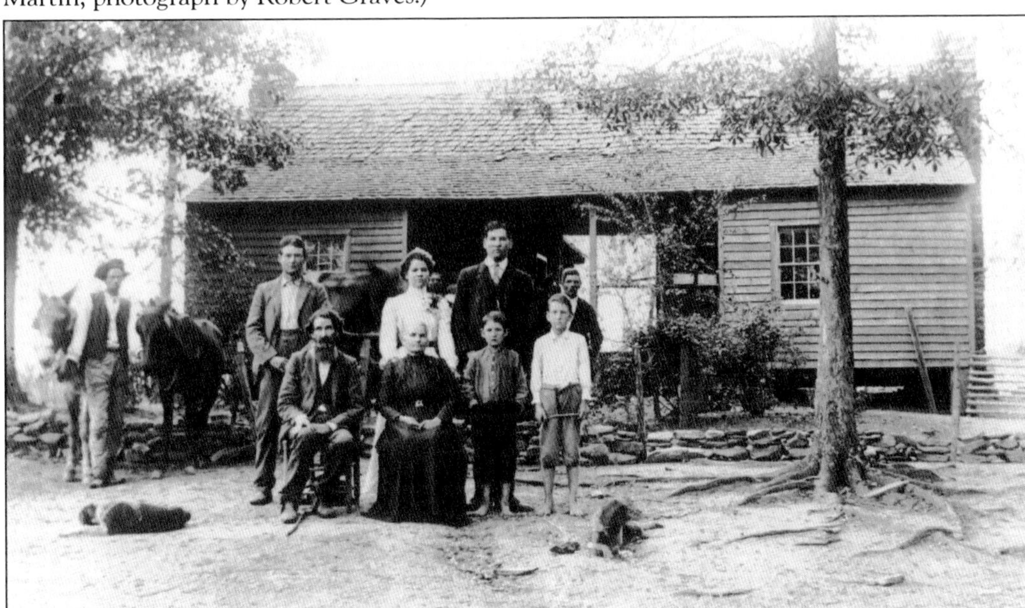

The family picture made at the old Scott home on Scott Road includes the future principal of the old Russell School. Pictured from left to right are (first row) George W. Scott, Sara Ann Mexico Scott, Joseph Price Scott, and future Russell School principal Reuben Young Scott; (second row) William James Columbus Scott, Ethel Scott Turner, and Elisha Winfield Scott. A worker stands on the left side, holding the mules. Hunting dogs rest in the dirt yard. (Courtesy of Scotty Foshee.)

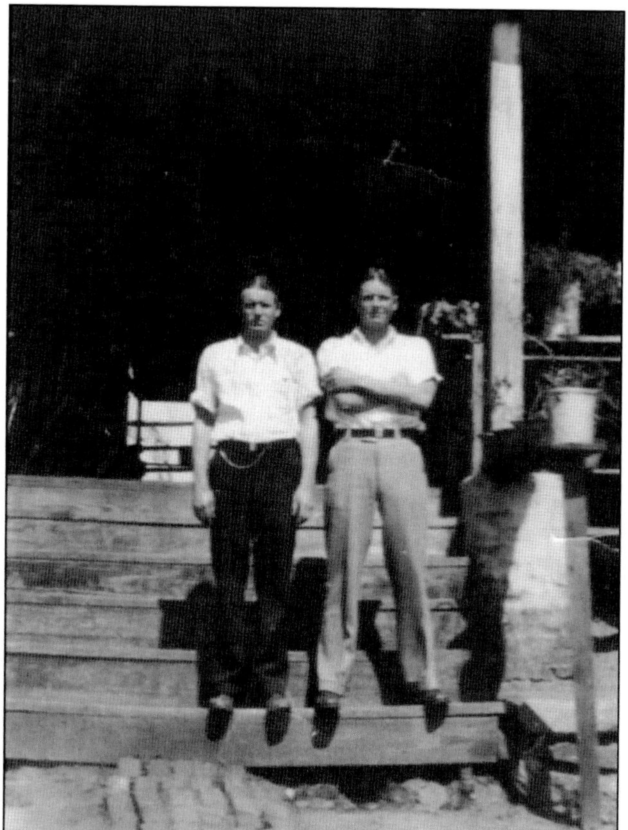

Beginning in the 1880s, the Tallapoosa Mining Company operated until World War I, when lack of supplies and manpower resulted in the mine's closing in 1916. Standing on the steps are mucker Talmadge Jackson (left) and timberman Kermit Jackson, both of whom worked at the mine during the 1930s operation. Below, James Orland "Cowboy" Osborn worked in the mine prior to its closing in 1916. (Both, courtesy of Peggy Walls.)

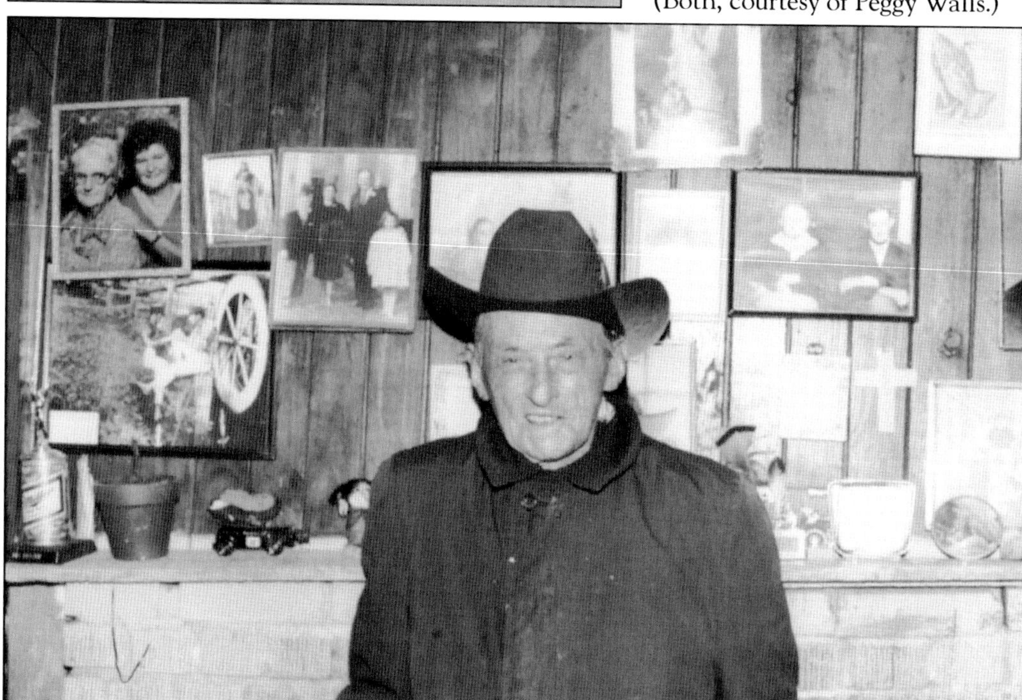

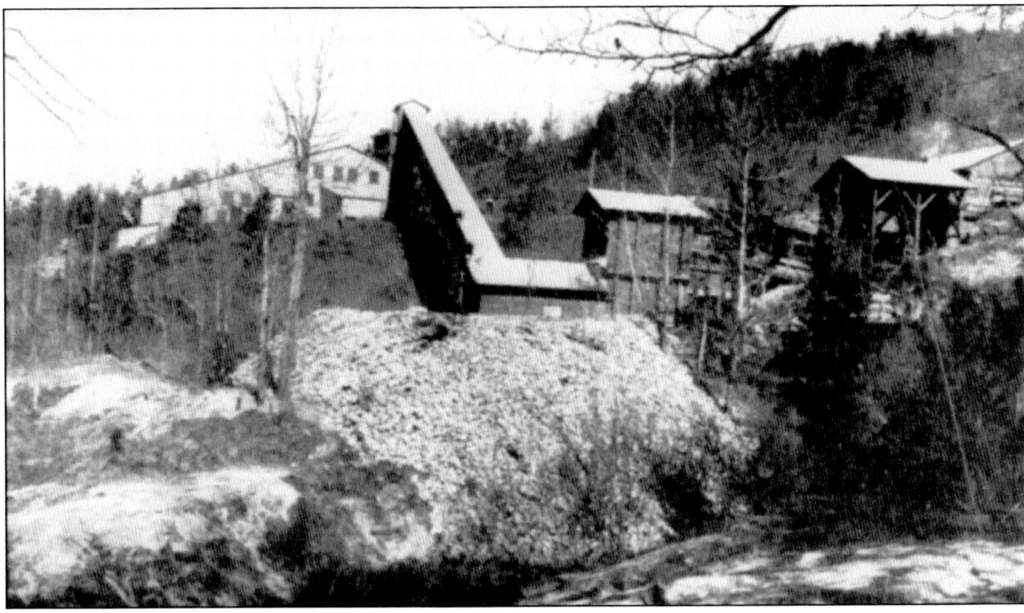

In 1933, the Hog Mountain Mining and Milling Company reopened the mine. In 1936, the production of gold at Hog Mountain caused Alabama to be recognized as the top gold-producing state in the Appalachian Mountains. The mine closed a year later due to increased costs in operation. (Courtesy of Peggy Walls.)

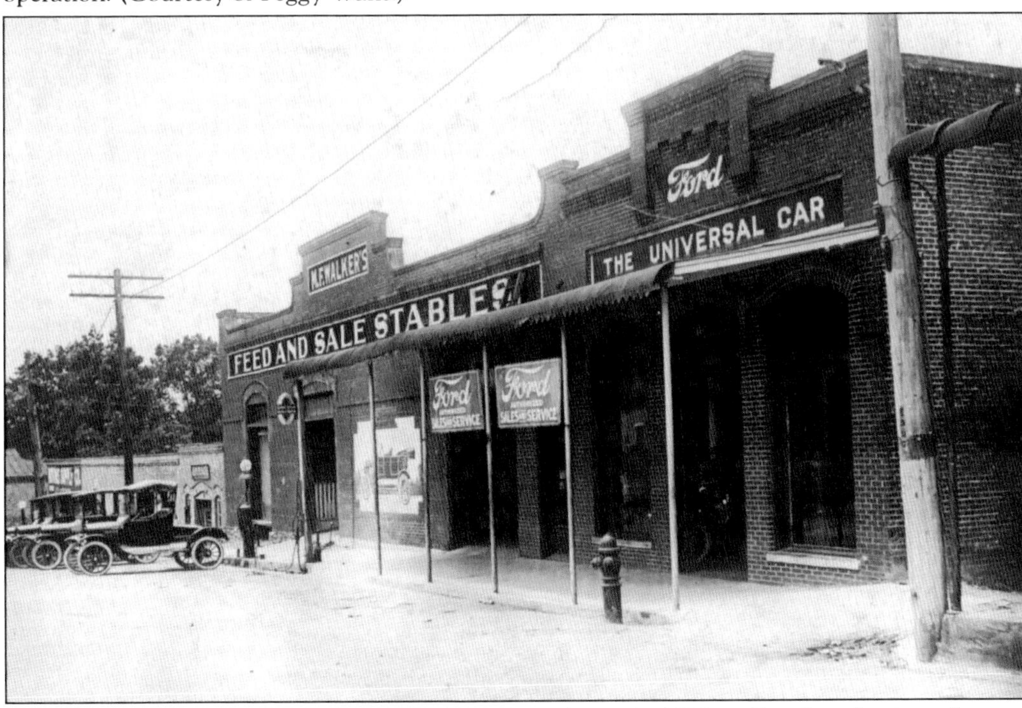

Walker Ford Company, located on Broad Street in the early 1900s, offered a selection of cars to Alexander City residents who wanted to be among the first to own one of the new horseless carriages. The arrival of the Model T Ford attracted people who were curious to see the car. The loud sound of the engine and horn sent farm animals scurrying for cover. (Courtesy of MainStreet Organization.)

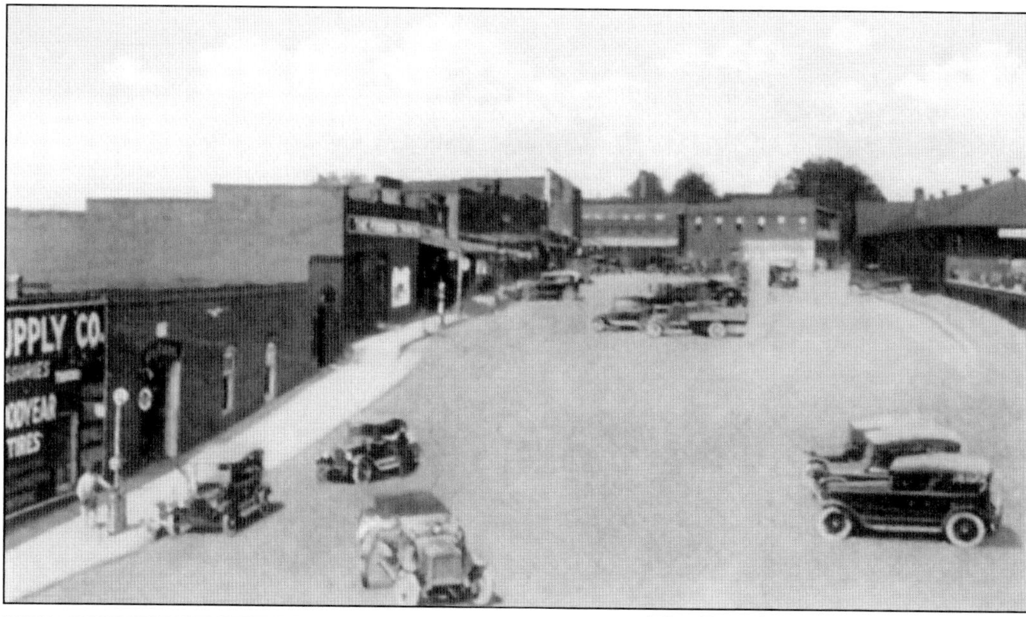

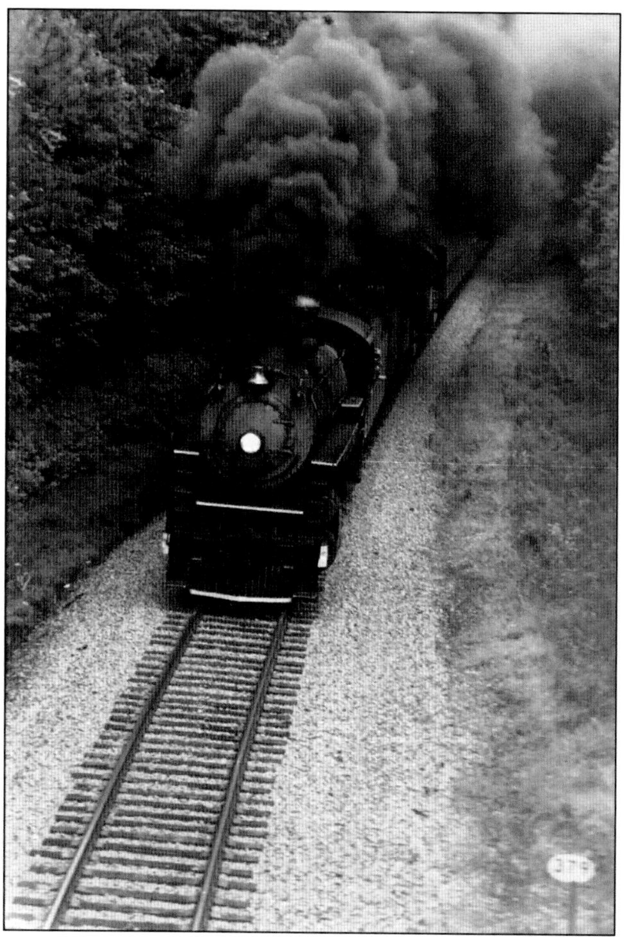

The Broad Street postcard shows the old train depot on the right. Model T Fords line the streets unevenly, and in front of the supply company, a gas tank stands ready to service customers. A large ad on the building features Goodyear tires. Though businesses have changed, the layout of Broad Street has remained the same well into the 20th and 21st centuries. (Courtesy of MainStreet Organization.)

The Model T Ford offered a convenient conveyance for local traveling. The train delivered goods for the general merchandise stores, introduced new products, visitors, and opportunities for travel. New ideas stimulated the local populace and growth in commerce. (Courtesy of Hazel Baker.)

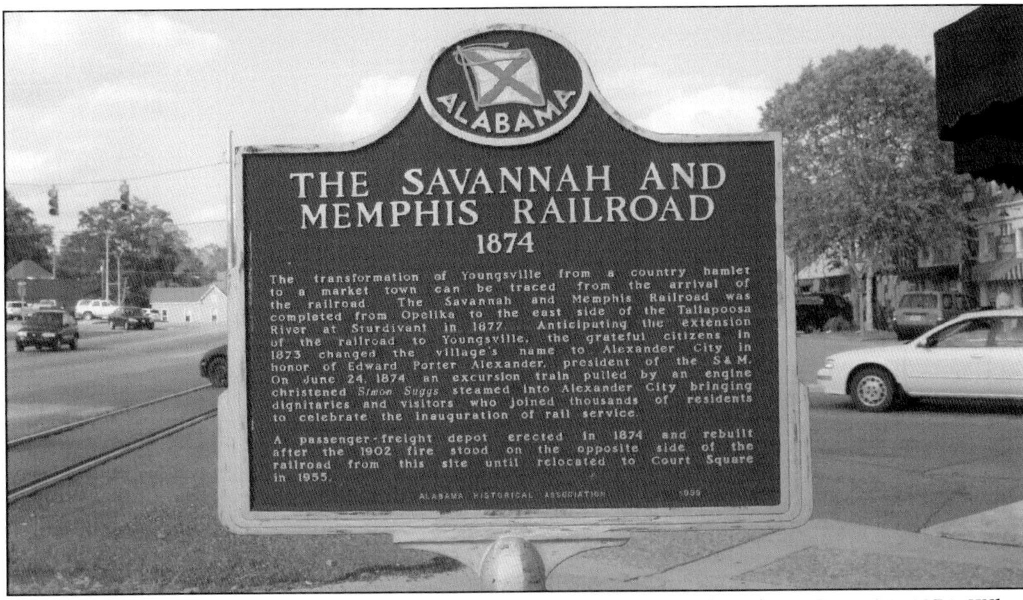

The grand opening celebration of the Savannah & Memphis Railroad was June 24, 1874. When the railroad representatives arrived in town, they found the name Youngsville had been changed to Alexander City to honor railroad president Edward Porter Alexander. The train stopped at a new passenger freight depot that was constructed to replace the one destroyed in the 1902 fire. An excited citizenry welcomed the railroad people and *Simon Suggs* the engine. (Courtesy of Peggy Walls; photograph by Tammy East.)

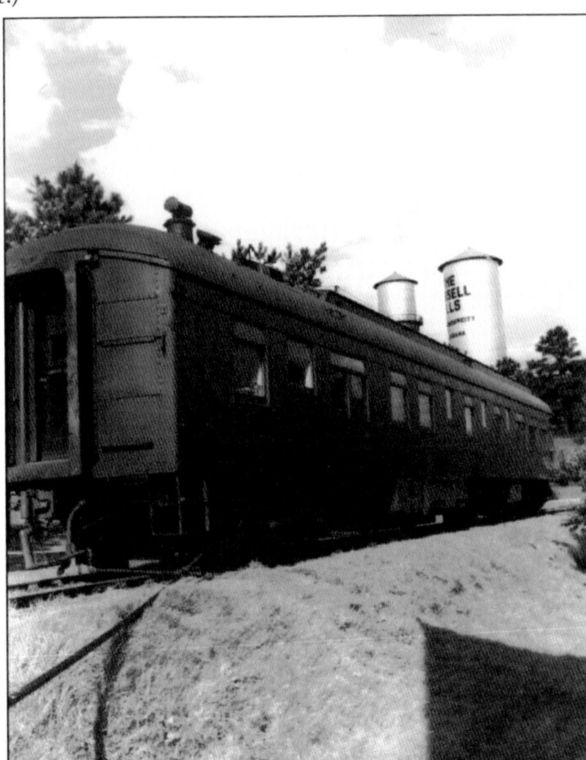

Local businesses benefited from having the railroad run through the middle of town. In the early 1900s, the Alexander City Cotton Mill and the Russell Manufacturing Company expanded production and sales with the convenient access to shipping their products that the railroad brought. (Courtesy of Robert Martin; photograph by Robert Graves.)

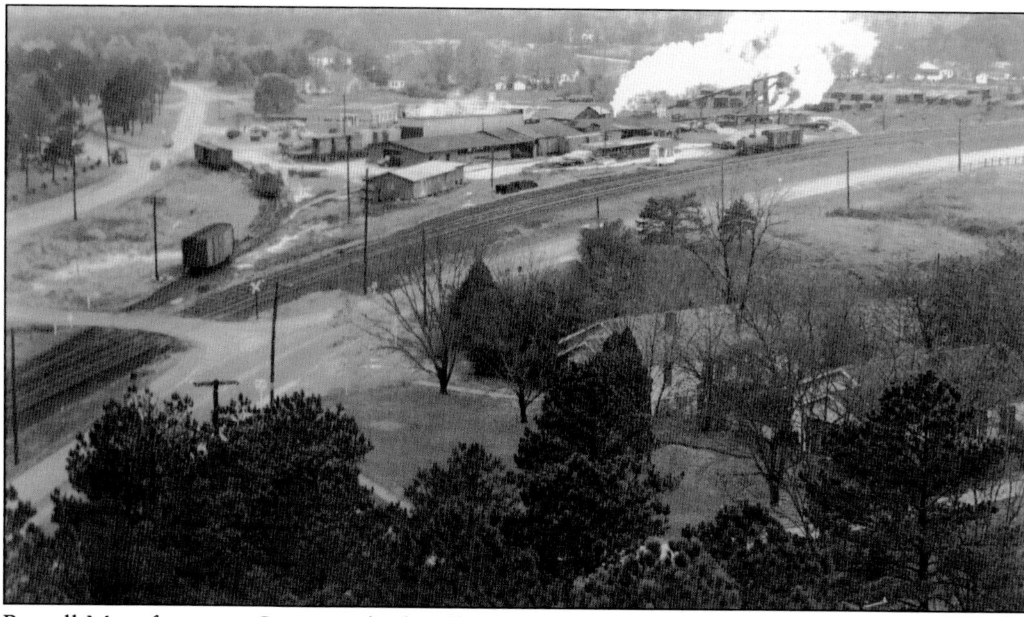

Russell Manufacturing Company built village homes to accommodate workers near their jobs. Russell School and other businesses sprang up around the company. Supervisors' homes can be seen on the right of the railroad. The town expanded with the company, as businesses grew to meet the needs of plant workers and officials. (Courtesy of Robert Martin; photograph by Robert Graves.)

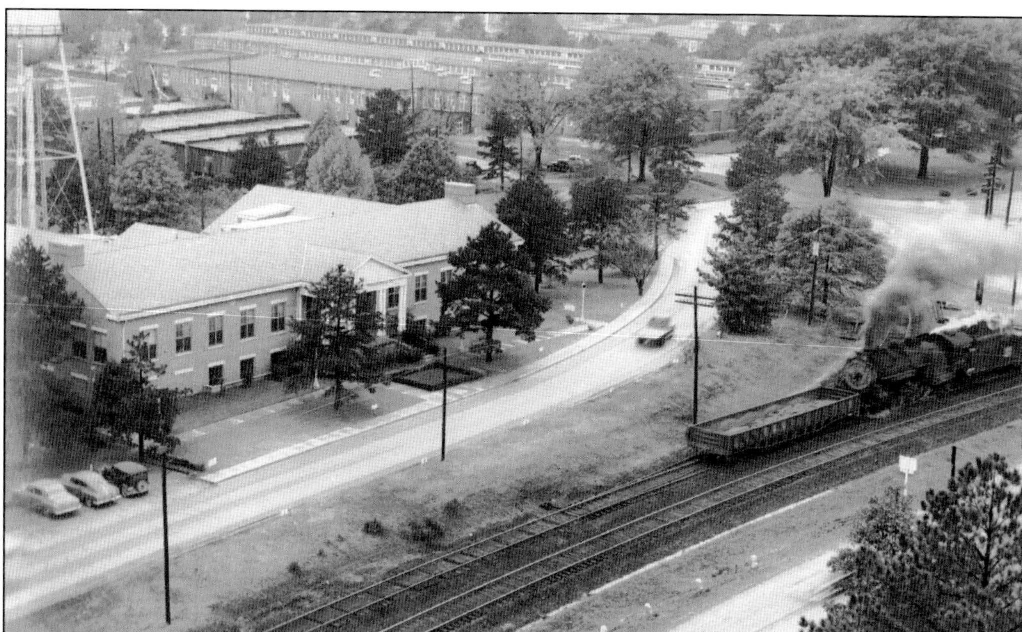

The local mills provided employment in cutting, sewing, equipment maintenance, supervising, and shipping. Staff in the personnel office processed employment applications daily for Russell Mills. The growth of textile mills and villages peaked in the 1940s, though their presence continued to stimulate growth of businesses, churches, and organizations through much of the 20th century. (Courtesy of Robert Martin; photograph by Robert Graves.)

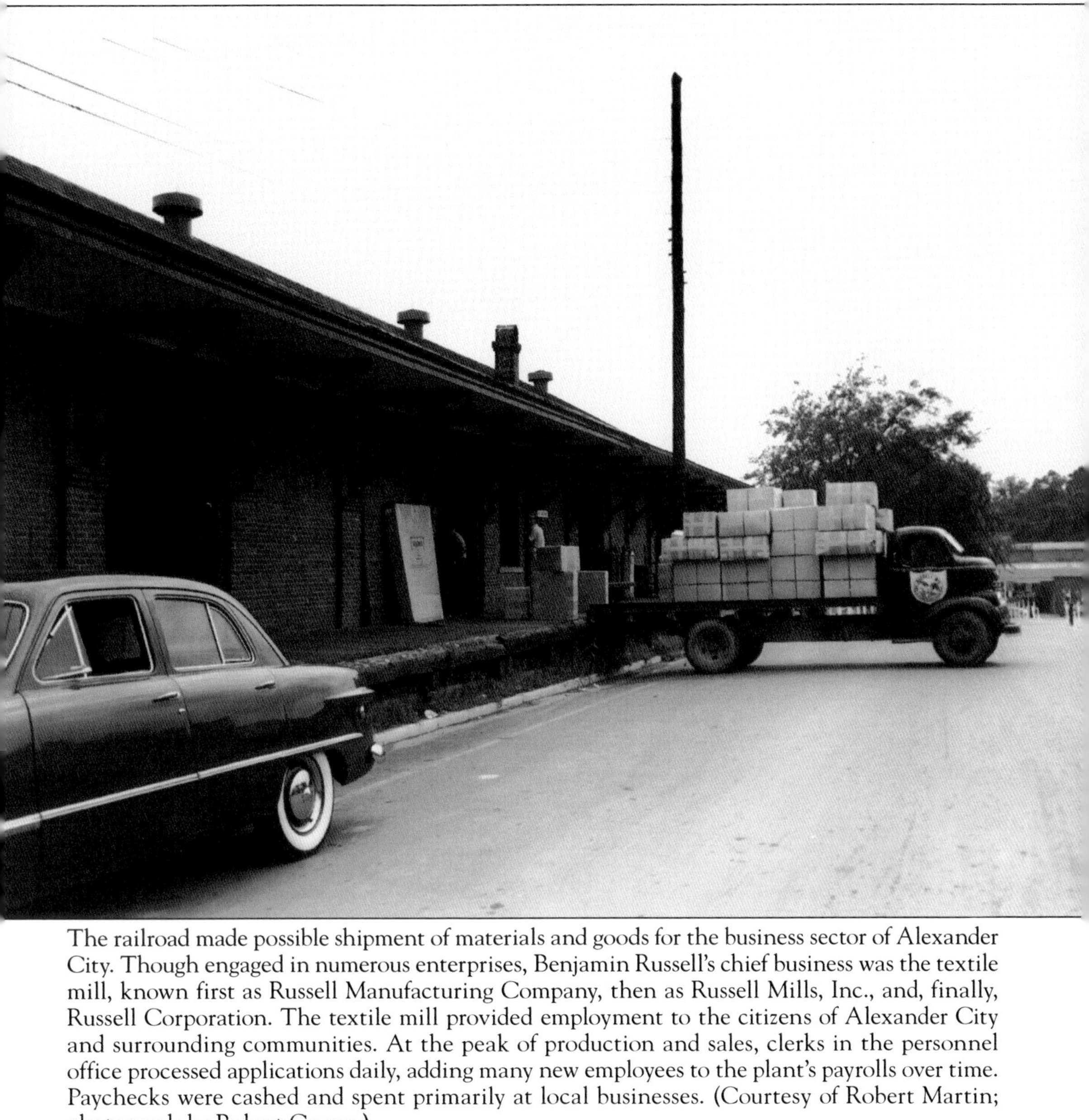

The railroad made possible shipment of materials and goods for the business sector of Alexander City. Though engaged in numerous enterprises, Benjamin Russell's chief business was the textile mill, known first as Russell Manufacturing Company, then as Russell Mills, Inc., and, finally, Russell Corporation. The textile mill provided employment to the citizens of Alexander City and surrounding communities. At the peak of production and sales, clerks in the personnel office processed applications daily, adding many new employees to the plant's payrolls over time. Paychecks were cashed and spent primarily at local businesses. (Courtesy of Robert Martin; photograph by Robert Graves.)

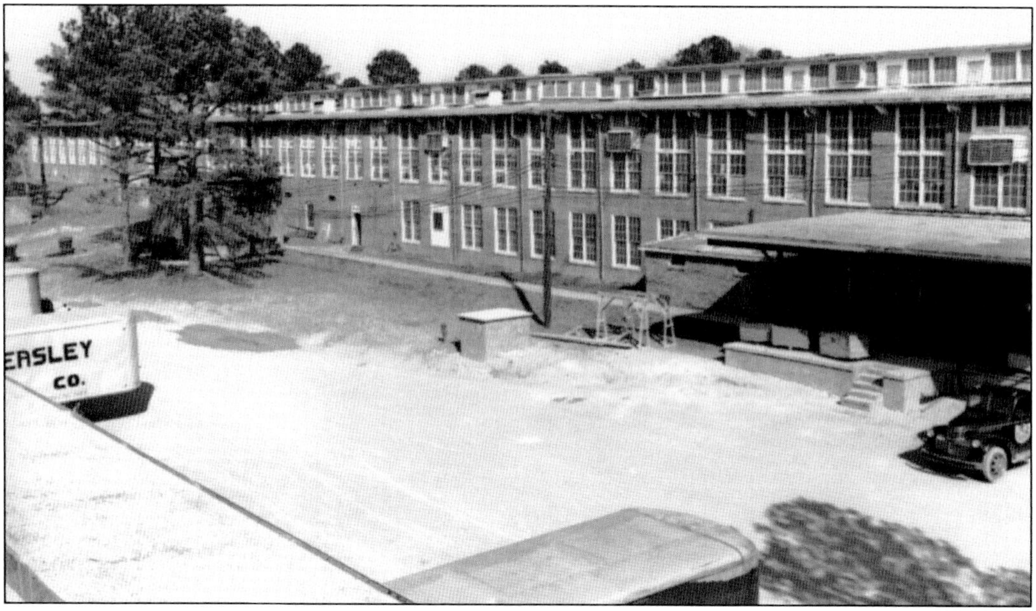

The cross-section of the back of Russell Mills shows a platform used for unloading goods from the railroad or other divisions of the mill. In the early years of textile production, air-conditioning was not available, and mill hands worked in the heat inside, as well as on loading docks. (Courtesy of Robert Martin; photograph by Robert Graves.)

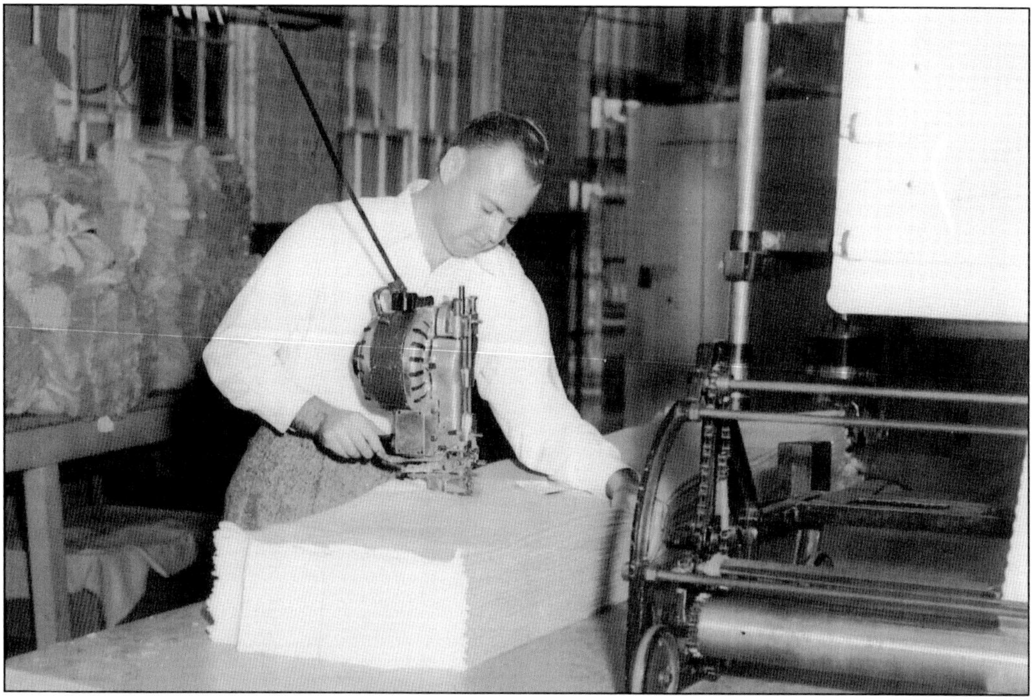

Each plant had designated jobs, and workers were trained to perform the tasks in an efficient manner. This cutter demonstrates his skill by cutting through the stacks of cloth, completing one step of production. Workers were paid according to output as an incentive to greater productivity. (Courtesy of Robert Martin; photograph by Robert Graves.)

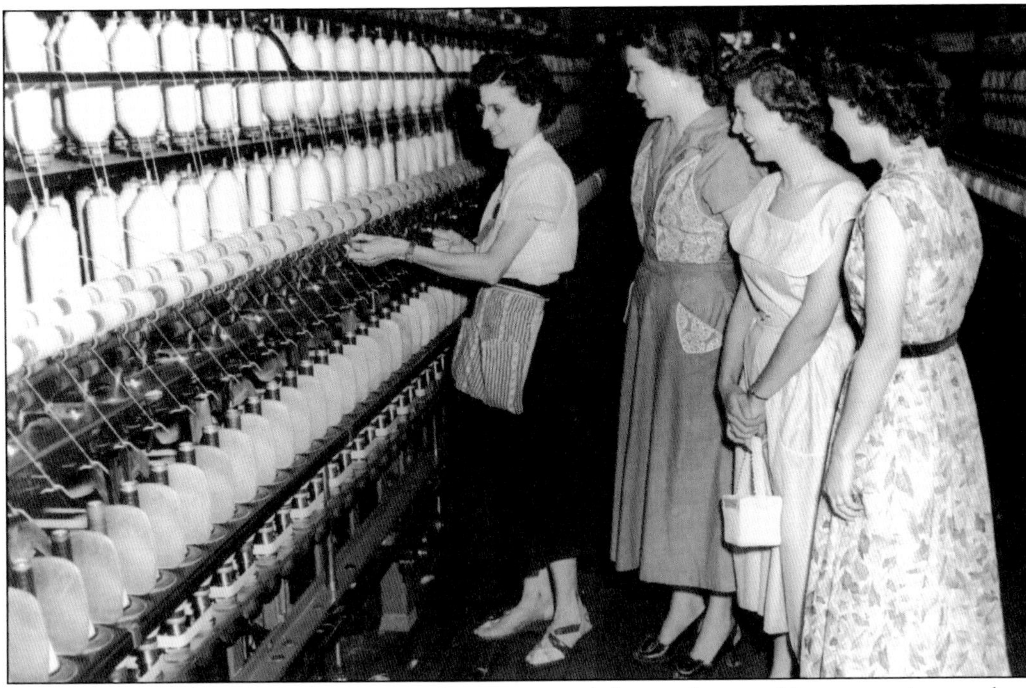

Inspectors visited regularly, examining the process and the product, making suggestions on how to improve the rate of production and to lessen any defects in the final product. Women often filled the roles of supervisors and inspectors, giving them a position that was not widely available to women in the early 1900s. (Courtesy of Robert Martin; photograph by Robert Graves.)

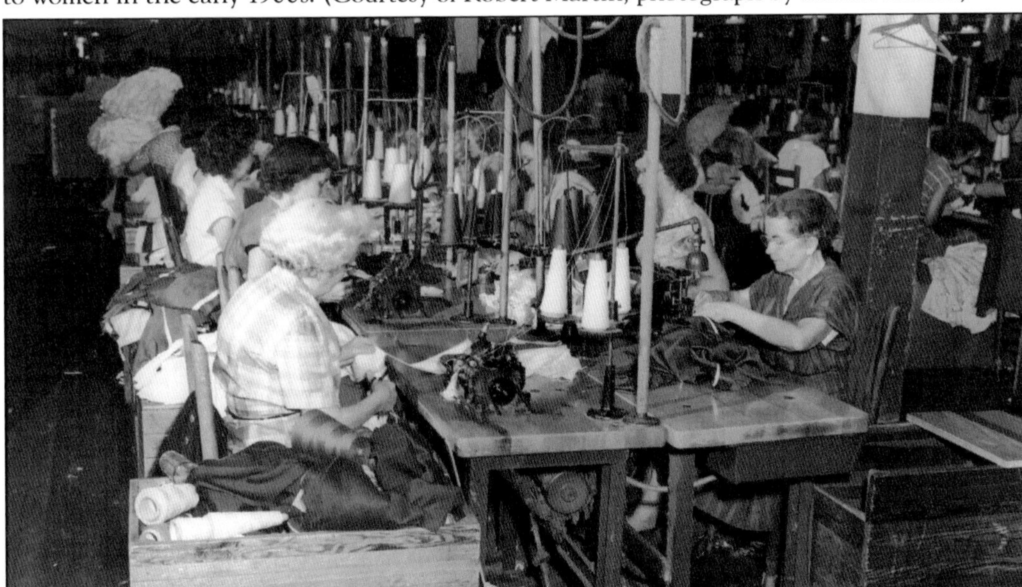

Sewing was hard work, but the job offered a chance to earn money for basic necessities. During the early 20th century, the mill jobs often were the first opportunity that women had to work away from home and farm. After finishing their shift at the mill, workers went home to domestic chores, gardening, and other farming tasks. (Courtesy of Robert Martin; photograph by Robert Graves.)

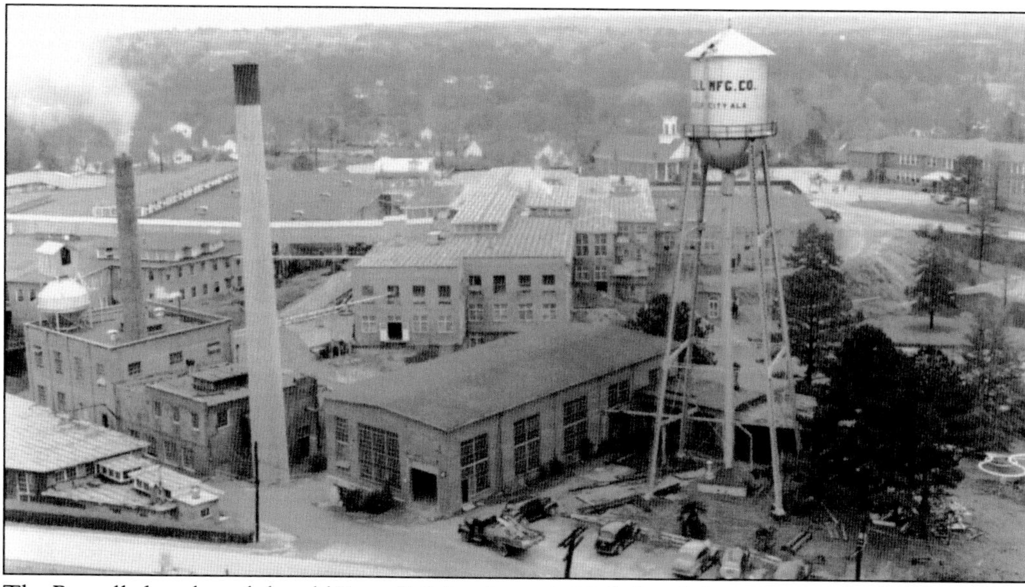

The Russell church and the old Russell School are visible behind the mill complex. From the first schools in the city that began in 1887, with only 75 to 80 students attending in private residences, educational facilities progressed with the mills. The schools were combined into the Alexander City High School and the Benjamin Russell High School. The church in the photograph was used as a kindergarten for many years. (Courtesy of Robert Martin; photograph by Robert Graves.)

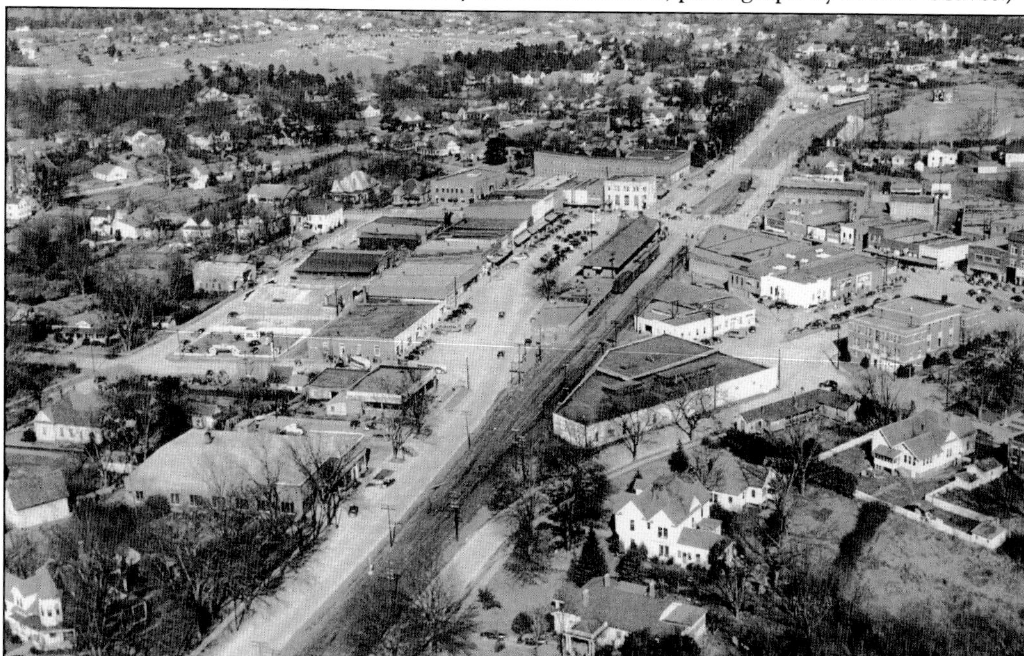

This aerial view of Alexander City shows how the town sprang up on both sides of the track. On the right, the courthouse, Masonic building, Radney Furniture, a municipal building, and assorted businesses are visible. On the left, cars are parked along the curb and center of Broad Street, with the depot on the right. The Alexander City Bank and Russell Hotel mark the end of the business buildings. Hamp Lyon Stadium is on the right. (Courtesy of Hazel Baker.)

Three

Two Textile Mills

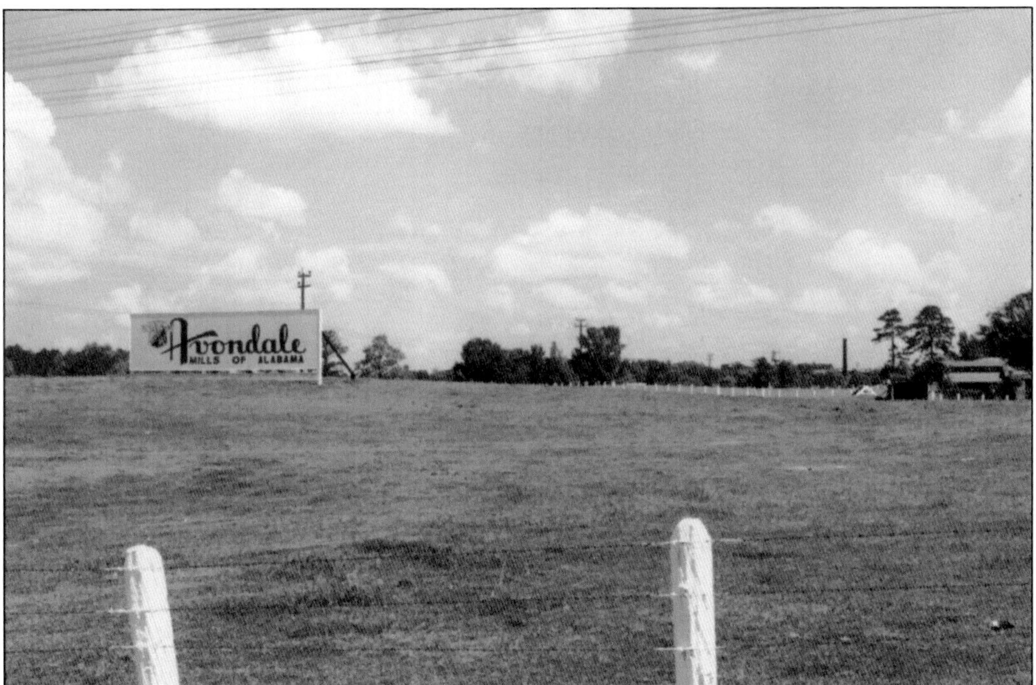

In 1919, Avondale Mills bought the Alexander City Mill and changed the name to Bevelle in honor of one of Gov. Braxton Bragg Comer's daughters. B.B. Comer's son J. Fletcher served as chief administrator of the plant, which started as a gray goods producer. The company provided workers with the convenience of living close to their jobs, school, church, and medical and dental care. When the plant turned to manufacturing mattress ticking, the Avondale name became world famous. (Courtesy of Laura Oliver.)

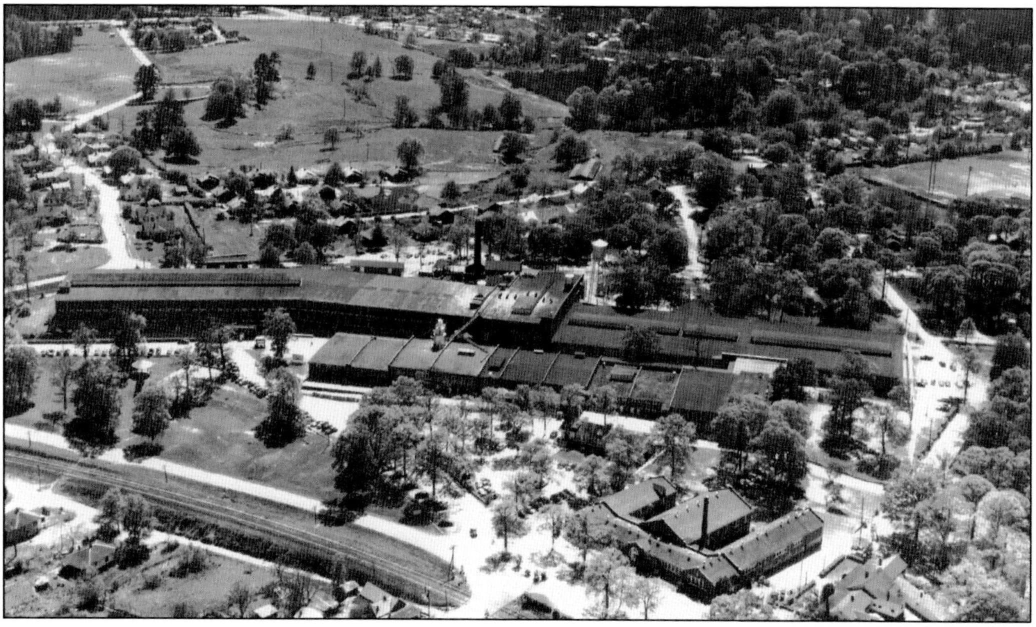

This 1947 aerial view shows Bevelle Mills with the school and recreation buildings in the foreground. Avondale Mills is the world's largest producer of ticking materials. Avondale ticking remained popular throughout the 1950s with mattress companies, such as the Spring Air Company. In *McCall's* January 1959 issue, Spring Air advertised Avondale ticking in their "Once a Year Spring Air 'Turn Back the Clock' Mattress sale." (Courtesy of Laura Oliver.)

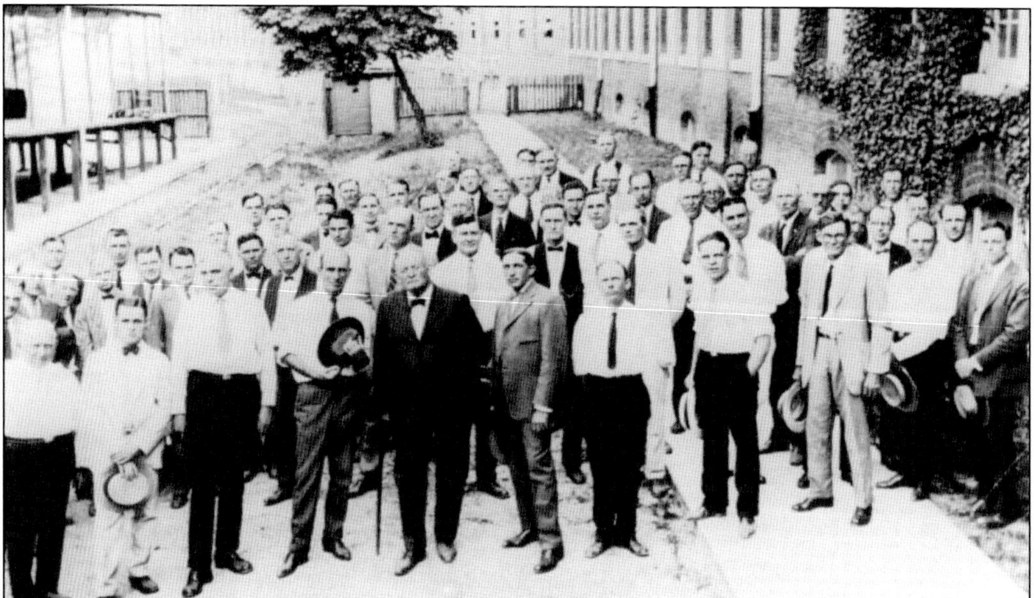

Alexander City residents tour the Avondale Mills Bevelle plant. Those identified are (from left to right in the first row only) E.A. Jackson, Rev. H.L. Laws, W.D. Graves, J. Fletcher Comer, J.C. Maxwell, Mayor T.C. Russell, Mr. Mitchum, R.P. Little, Rev. Nelson, M.E. Rawls, and Carey Harlan. J. Fletcher Comer was credited with the early successes of the Bevelle plant and the establishment of Bevelle village around the mid-1920s. (Courtesy of Don Holley.)

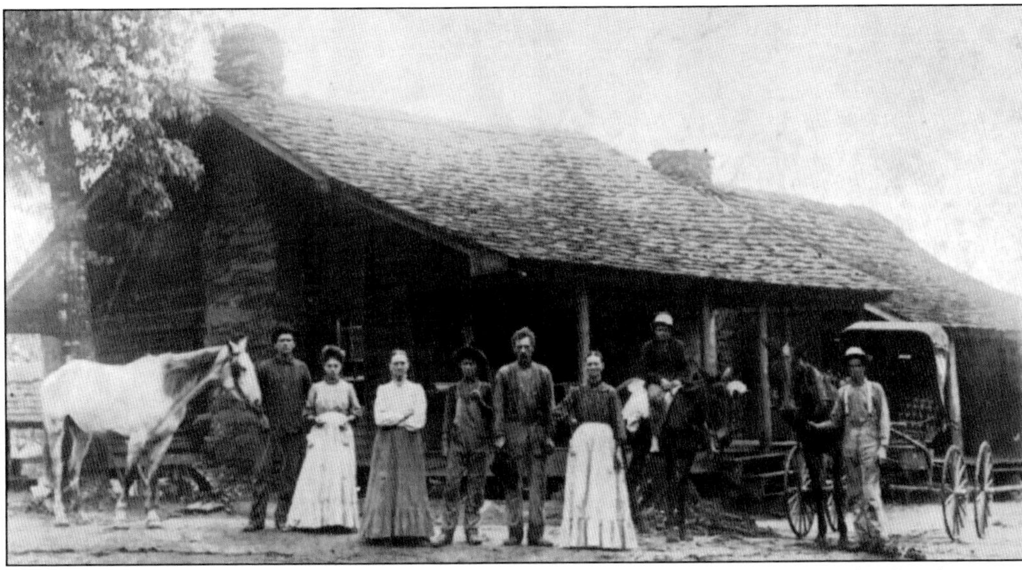

This 1908 image of the Holley family was made on a farm near New Site. The family moved to Alexander City in the early 1920s to work in the Bevelle plant. From left to right are family members J.A. and Gertrude H. Holley; Batty, Leslie, Buddy, and Josephine Nolen; and Shirley and Alonza Hutcherson. They were typical of many workers who moved into the mill village for employment and improved living conditions. (Courtesy of Don Holley.)

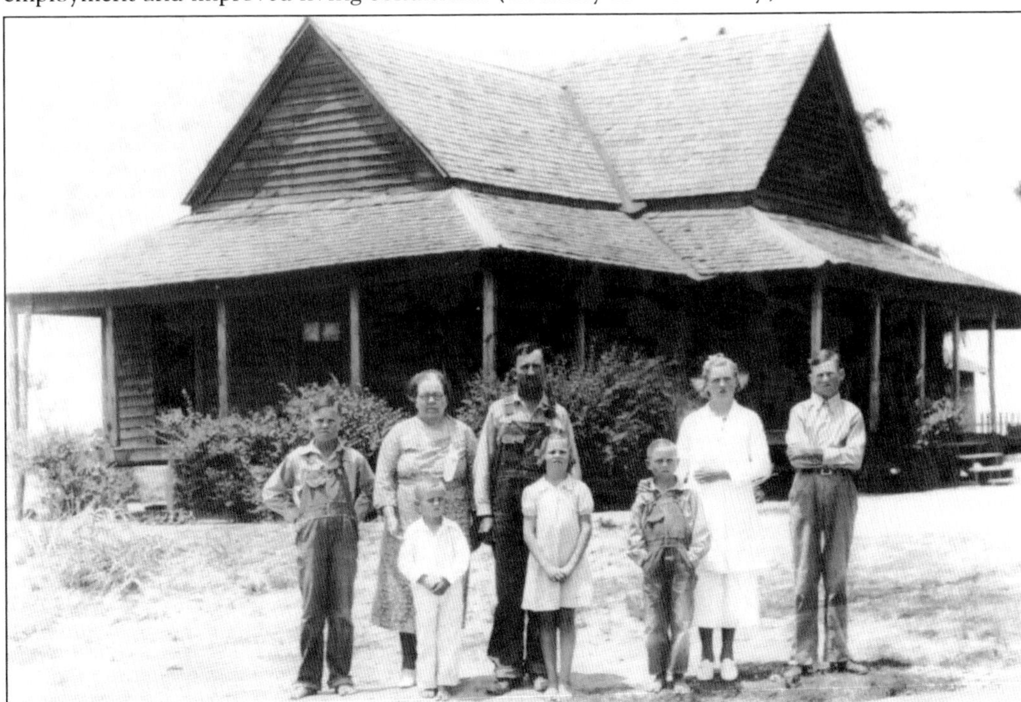

In the early 1900s, families, such as the Gosses (pictured here), moved from the New Site area to become some of the first workers and supervisors in the Alexander City cotton mills. They abandoned the farm and the backbreaking work of planting, weeding, and harvesting crops for the steady income that mill work brought. (Courtesy of Linda Meadows.)

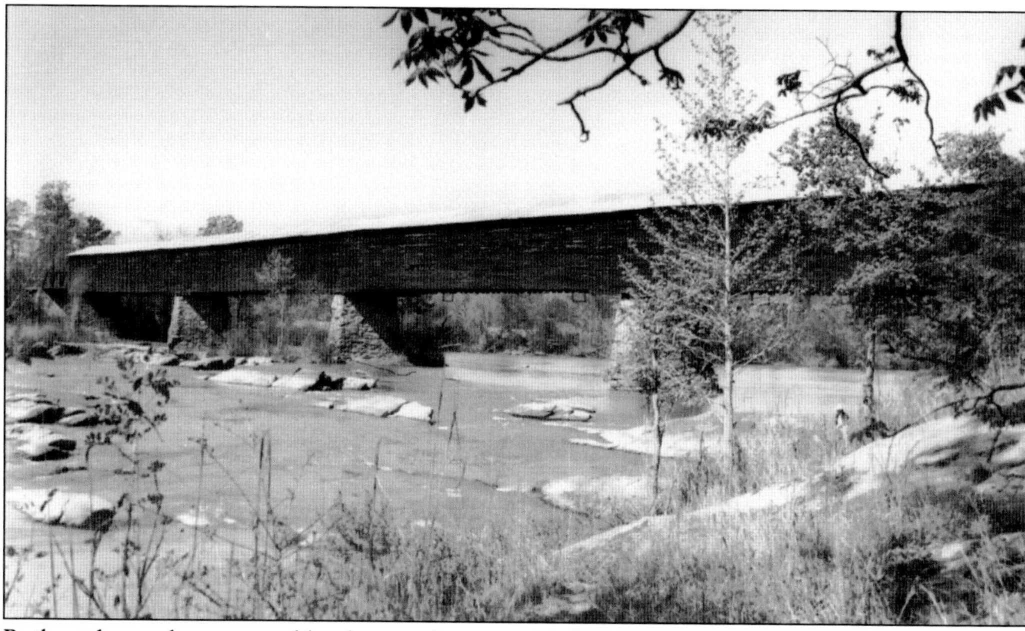

Built with wooden pegs and lumber cut from nearby forests, the Horseshoe Bend covered bridge spanned the Tallapoosa River near Horseshoe Bend Park. In the mid-1990s, winds damaged the aging bridge severely. A new bridge was built parallel to the Horseshoe Bend bridge before it was burned to prevent anyone from being harmed by entering the dilapidated structure. (Courtesy of Robert Martin; photograph by Robert Graves.)

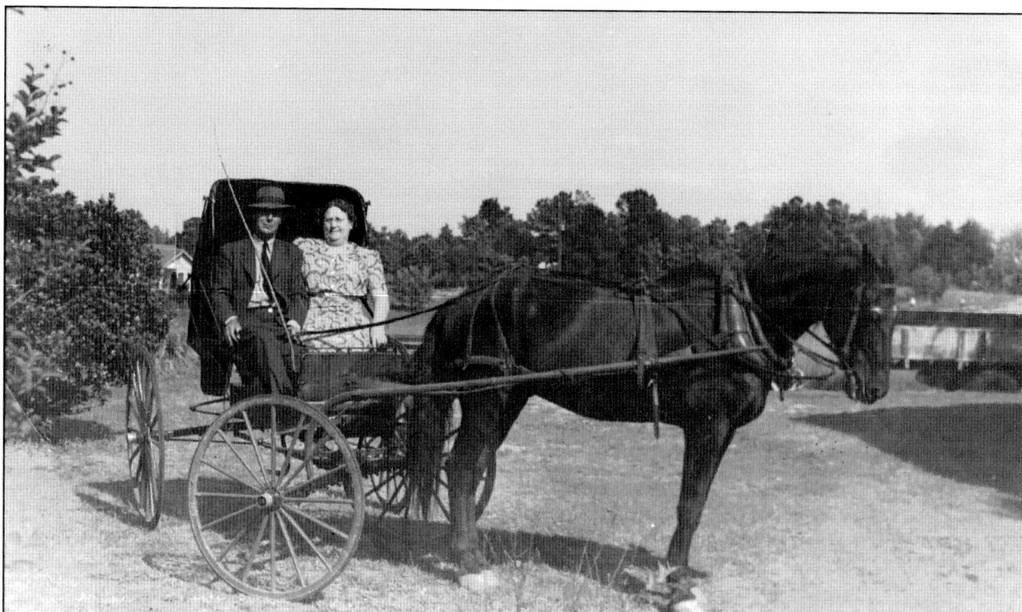

Visiting coworkers and neighbors in Bevelle, Andy and Lala Adcock paused to have their picture taken for the *Avondale Sun*, the company newspaper, in which they were recognized for their "No-Lost-Work Time" and good safety records. Like a number of other early hires, they moved with their family from a rural community near Alexander City. The Adcocks came from New Site with daughters Elizabeth, Robbie Jean, and Edna Earl. (Courtesy of Jane McLeod.)

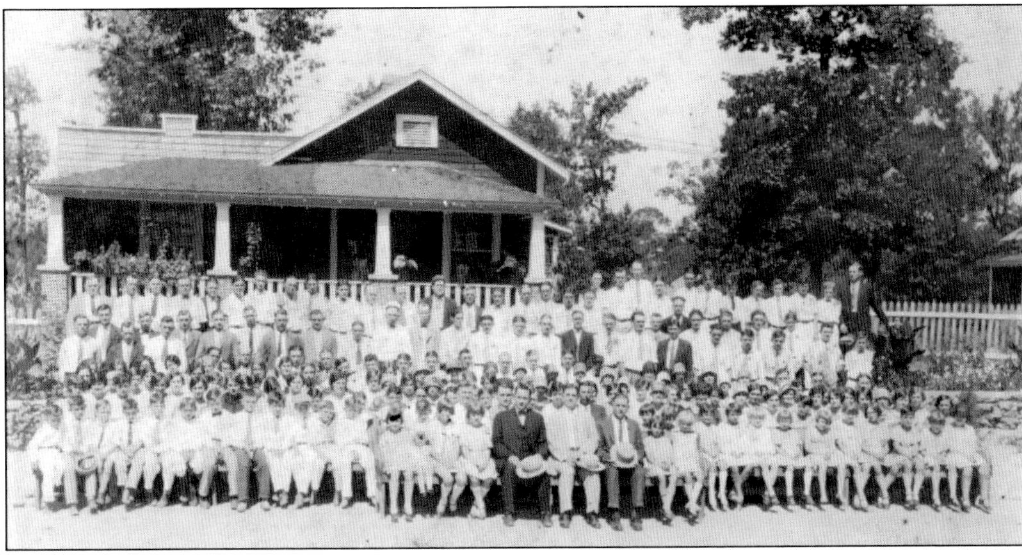

Bevelle mill houses can be seen in this c. 1922 picture behind the small organizational group comprised of Baptists and Methodists, who alternated in leading the combined worship services. (Courtesy of Laura Oliver.)

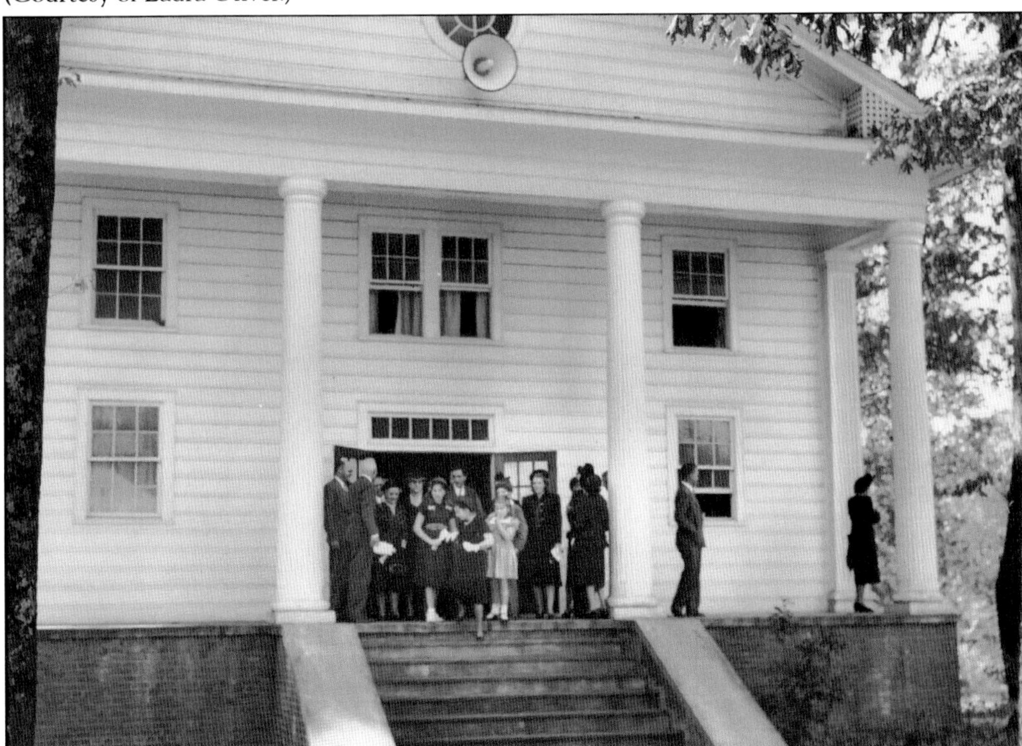

The Comer Memorial Baptist Church was erected by the Comer family in 1934. The church was dedicated to the memory of B.B. Comer, a farmer, merchant, manufacturer, and statesman. A bronze plaque hangs in the vestibule of the church, which was constructed near the complex of Bevelle plant buildings. The site of revivals, all-day singing, and dinners on the ground, the church served as a social center and a place of worship. (Courtesy of Laura Oliver.)

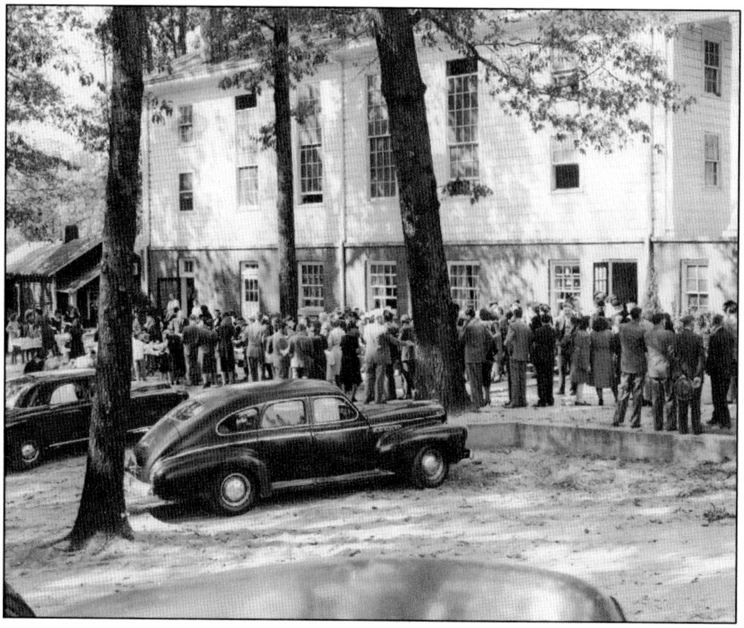

The Comer Memorial Baptist Church and the Comer Methodist Church were built side by side and were so well attended that a village house in the back of the churches was designated for the overflow of attendees. The event pictured is the dedication of the church organ donated by the Comer family. Three of Gov. Braxton Bragg Comer's children were in attendance. (Courtesy of Laura Oliver.)

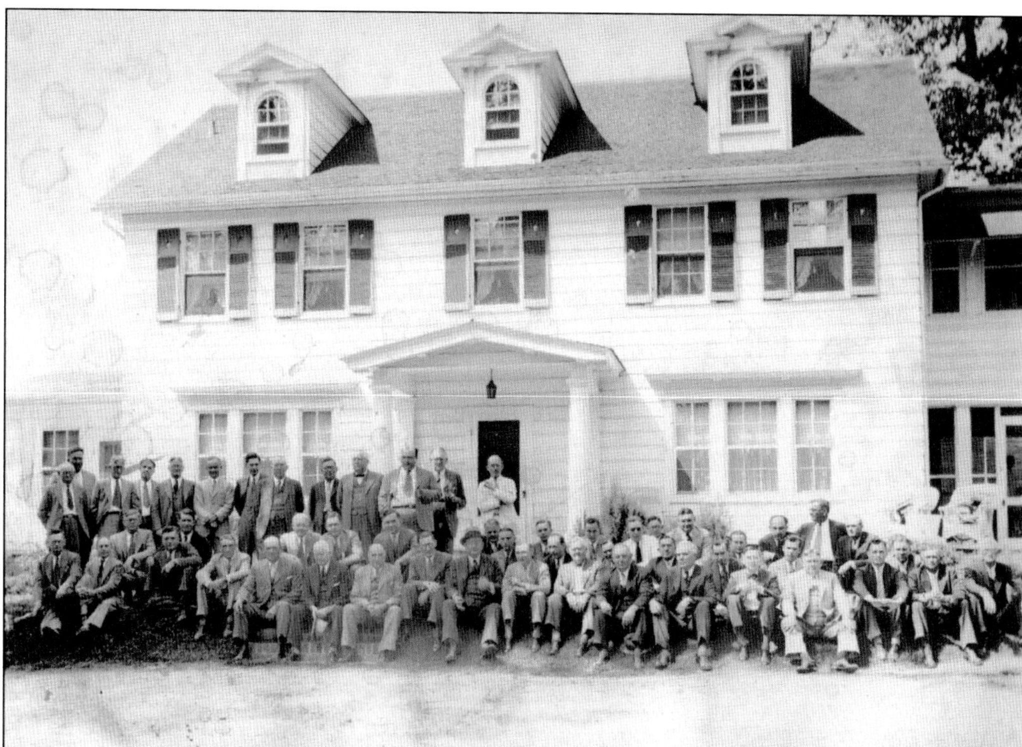

Following a Bevelle plant inspection around 1925, a group of local businessmen and visiting dignitaries gathered at the home of manager J. Fletcher and Helen Comer. The group participated in the all-day events that included a company-sponsored barbecue, entertainment by the Bevelle band, and an operetta by Mary Holbrook's students. (Courtesy of Jacob Henderson.)

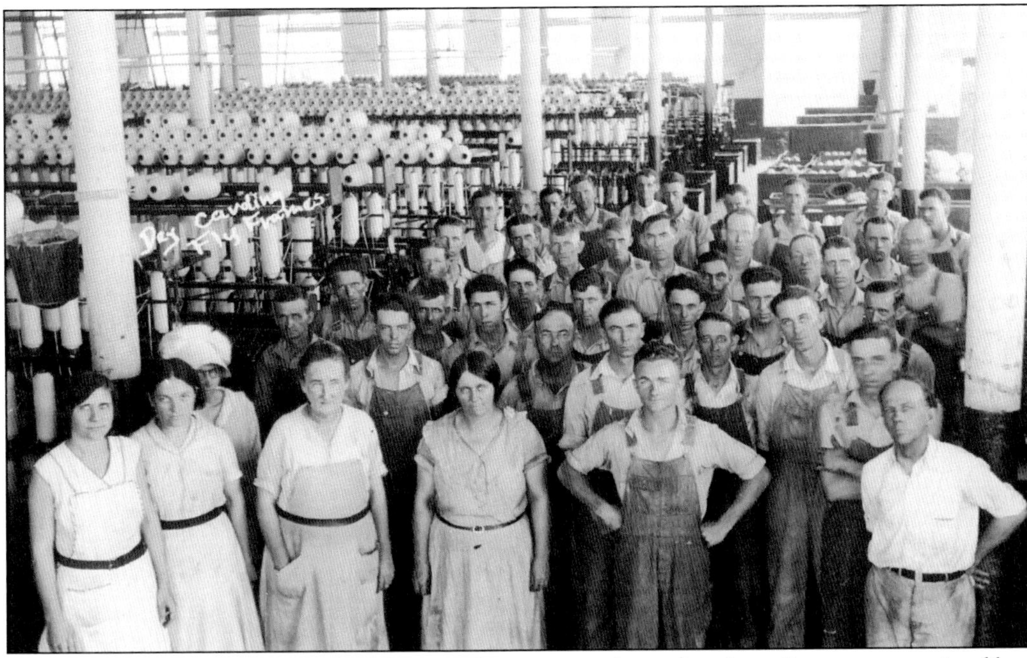

By 1931, the Great Depression had deepened among rural people, whose lives were sustained by a limited income from farming, sawmilling, and handyman jobs, such as carpentry. The attraction of a regular paycheck and benefits and amenities, such as churches and schools, brought many farm families to the mills and mill villages. (Courtesy of Laura Oliver.)

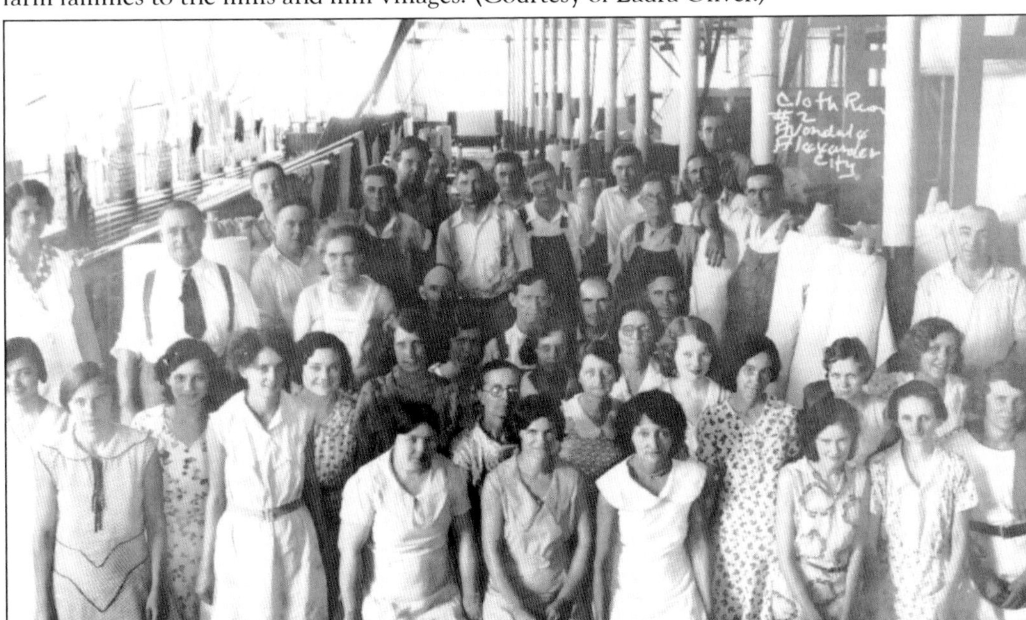

Bevelle workers in cloth room No. 2 pose for an *Avondale Sun* photograph around 1931. The ladies are dressed in cool, cotton dresses and men in denim overalls. In a white shirt, tie, and suspenders, the supervisor has his sleeves rolled up to work alongside the mill hands. According to the *Avondale Sun*, the bolts of "Selected Cotton," grown and harvested in Alabama cotton fields and seen here, are ready for processing into textile products. (Courtesy of Laura Oliver.)

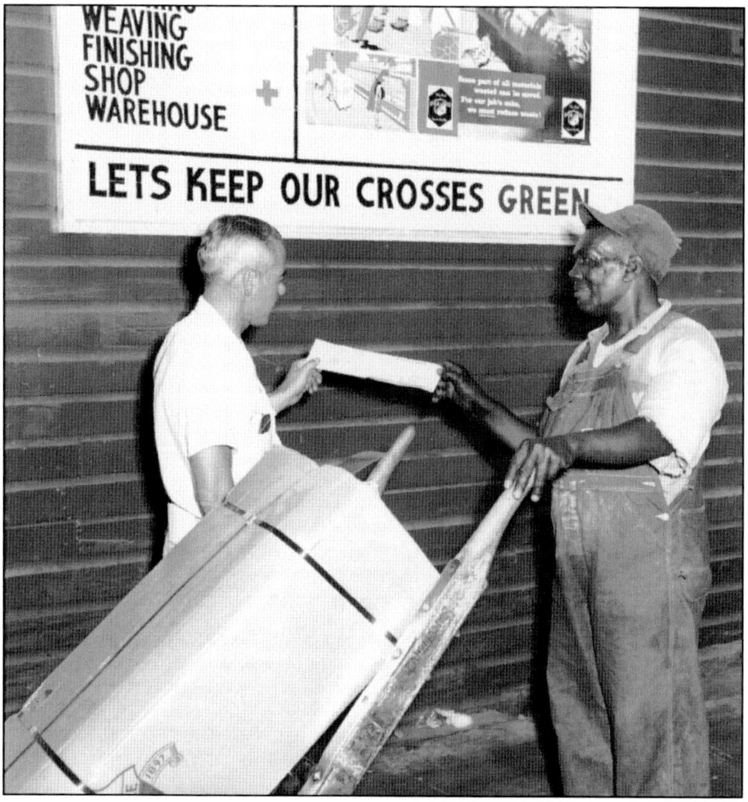

Avondale mill workers received an annual vacation bonus each Fourth of July. In the picture, Bevelle supervisor Jack Bice presents Maso Grubbs with his vacation bonus. Grubbs worked for the Comer family throughout his lifetime, moving with J. Fletcher and Helen Comer from their farm in Eufaula to the Sylacauga textile plant and to Alexander City with the opening of the Bevelle plant. Grubbs worked as a butler and chauffeur and as a mill employee until his retirement. (Courtesy of Laura Oliver.)

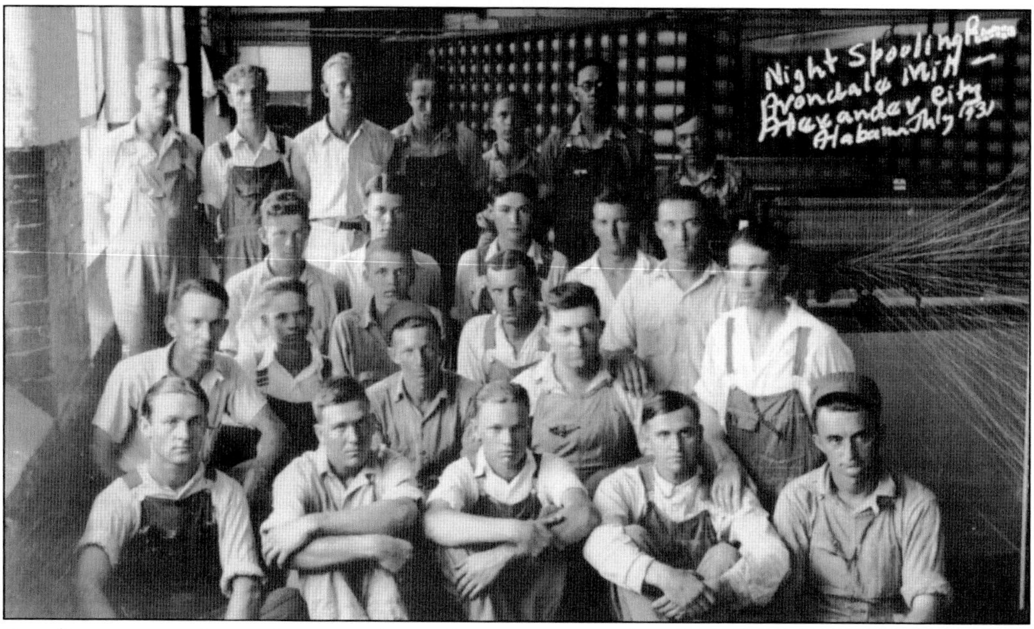

Spooling room night employees gather to have a picture taken during the day in July 1931. With large spools of thread filed neatly in pigeonholes and webs of thread spread in filtered sunlight, the scene does not portray the normal activity of workers and noise of the machinery during a typical work shift. (Courtesy of Laura Oliver.)

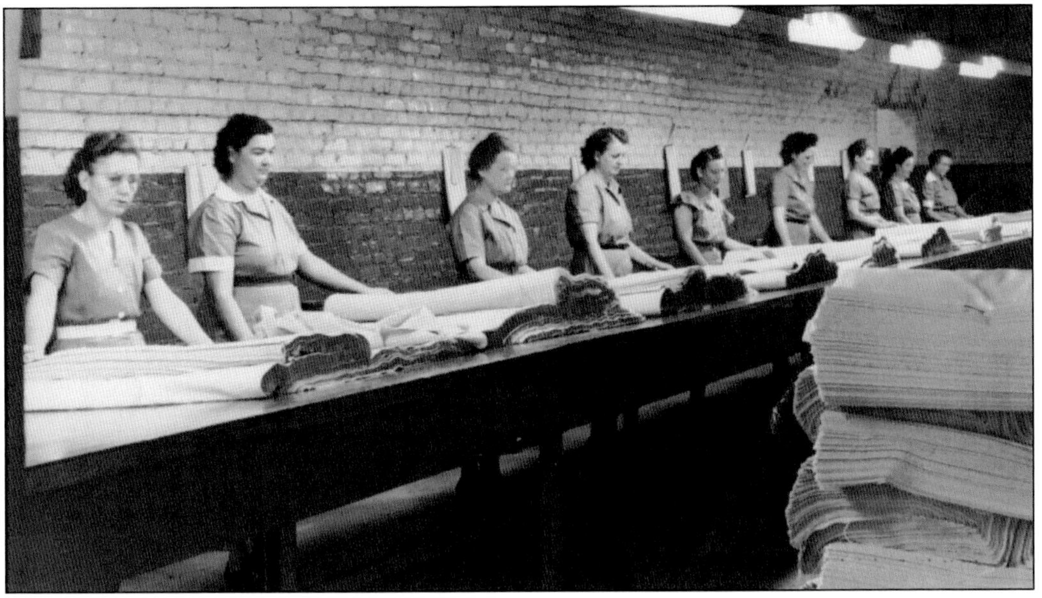

Ladies wore plain cotton dresses that absorbed perspiration before a cooling system was installed. Performing their jobs side by side, the workers had opportunity to interact daily and to develop many close and lasting friendships. Workers were identified by their jobs as spinners, slashers, weavers, folders, and inspectors. (Courtesy of Laura Oliver.)

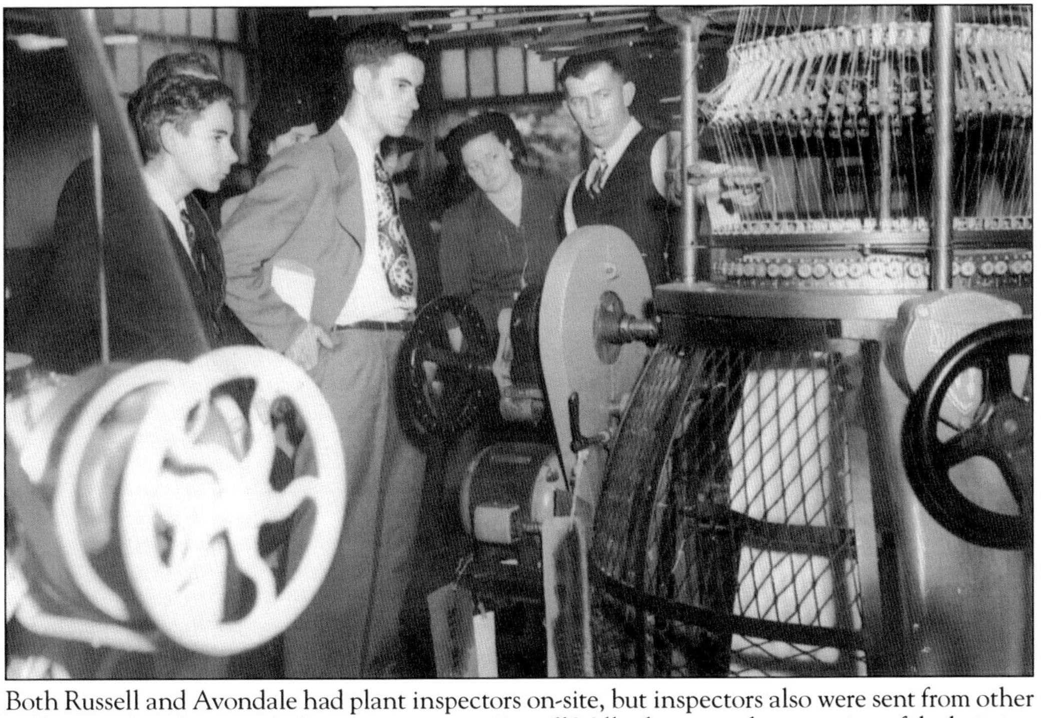

Both Russell and Avondale had plant inspectors on-site, but inspectors also were sent from other mill sites. This photograph shows inspectors at Russell Mills observing the operation of the knitting machine. The annual inspections of both mills were the highlight of the year, celebrated with barbeques, bands, and other entertainment. The work environment was spotless, and so were the mill grounds. (Courtesy Main Street Organization; photograph by Robert Graves)

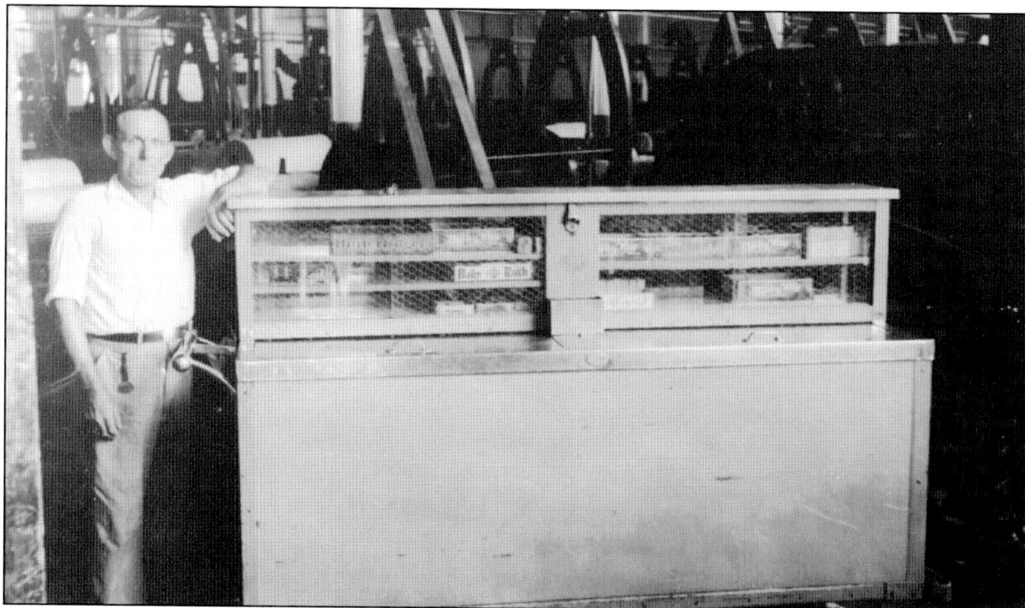

Raymond Weddle pushed the dope wagon (a rolling concession stand named for the Coca-Cola, or dope, for sale) around the mill for workers to have an opportunity to buy refreshments. Other dope wagon workers were Bill Tapley and Shorty Brown. Favorite treats were sandwiches, chips, and Baby Ruth and Butterfinger candy bars. In the 1930s, Cokes could be purchased for a nickel or bought with a googaloo—company-issued coins that were recognized as cash within the mill businesses. (Courtesy of Jacob Henderson.)

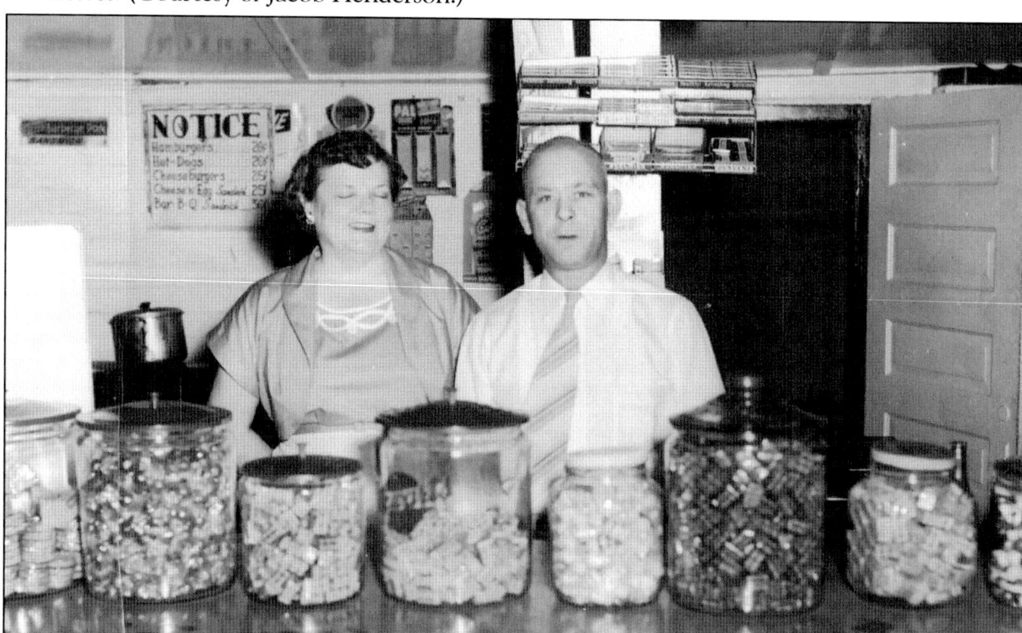

Marie Waldrop and Elmer Shorty Brown stand ready at the clubhouse to serve hot or cold sandwiches to Bevelle residents or customers from within the larger Alexander City and outlying areas. Affordable prices, listed behind Waldrop, advertise hamburgers at 25¢, with cheese burgers only a few cents more. (Courtesy of Laura Oliver.)

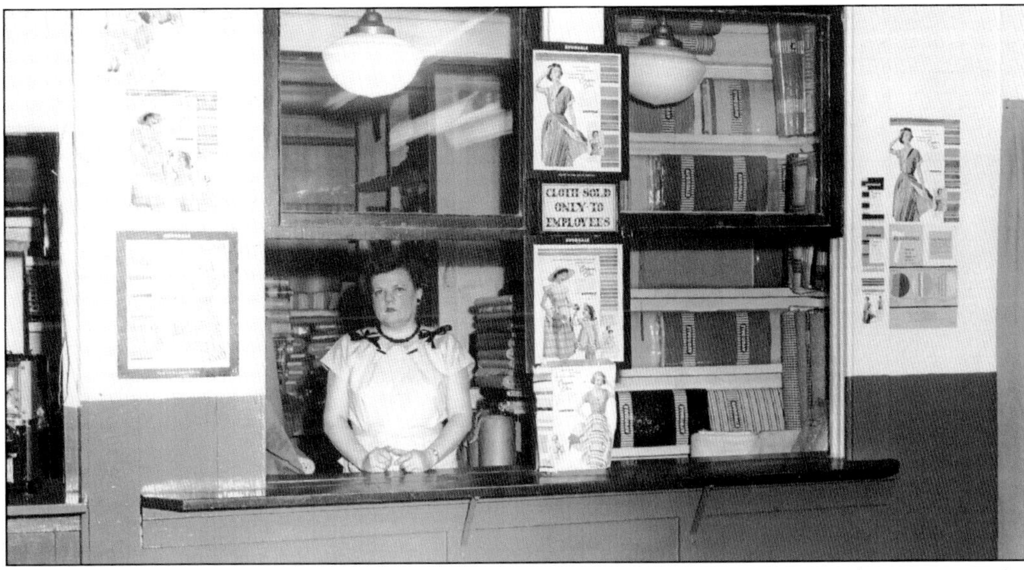

Marie Waldrop tends the Avondale cloth store. During the 1940s, favorite materials were seersucker for suits, dresses, and children's play clothes; twill for coats; and ticking for mattresses. Other materials included wide sateen, chambray, yarns, and threads in small spools or wrapped on large cones. Cloth in the store was available for sale to employees and their families only. Increases in sales resulted in the expansion of the cloth store to one-third of the space in the clubhouse. Posters and magazine advertisements promoting Avondale fabric, fashions, and mattress ticking were regularly featured in national magazines, such as the *Saturday Evening Post*. (Above, courtesy of Laura Oliver; below, courtesy of Jane McLeod.)

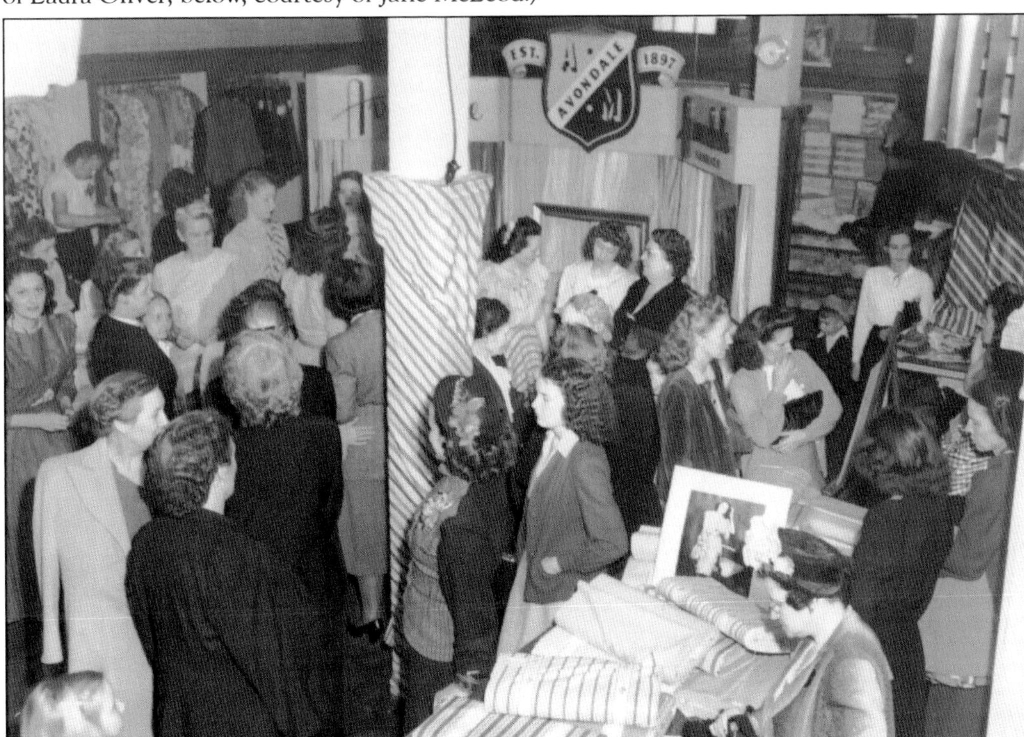

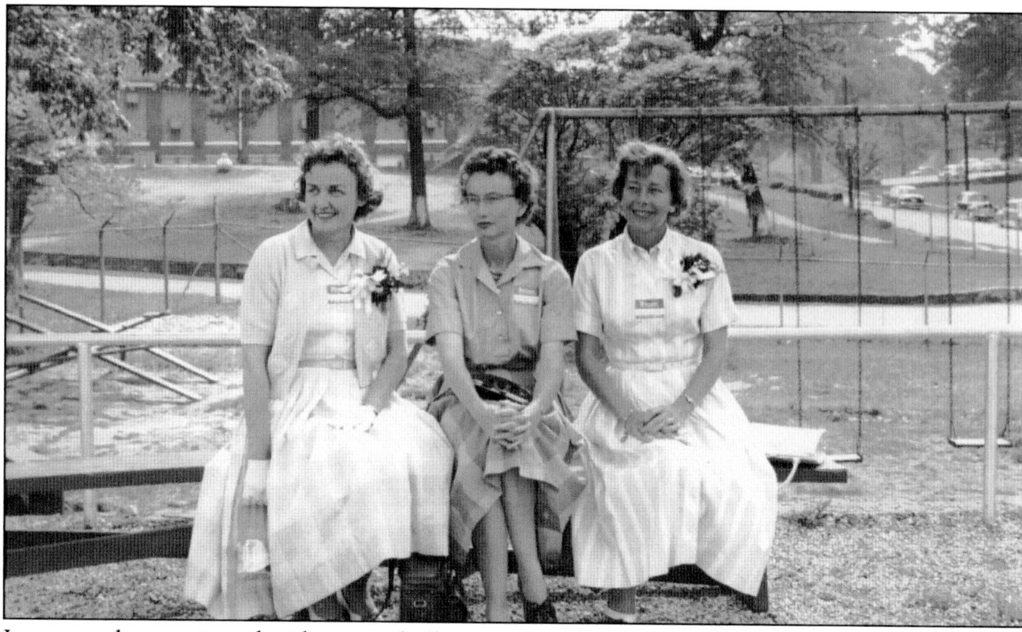

In cotton dresses pinned with cotton ball corsages and name tags, these three ladies take a break from inspection duties to pose for an *Avondale Sun* picture. The visiting inspectors sit on the Bevelle School playground equipment, with the Bevelle plant in the background. (Courtesy of Laura Oliver.)

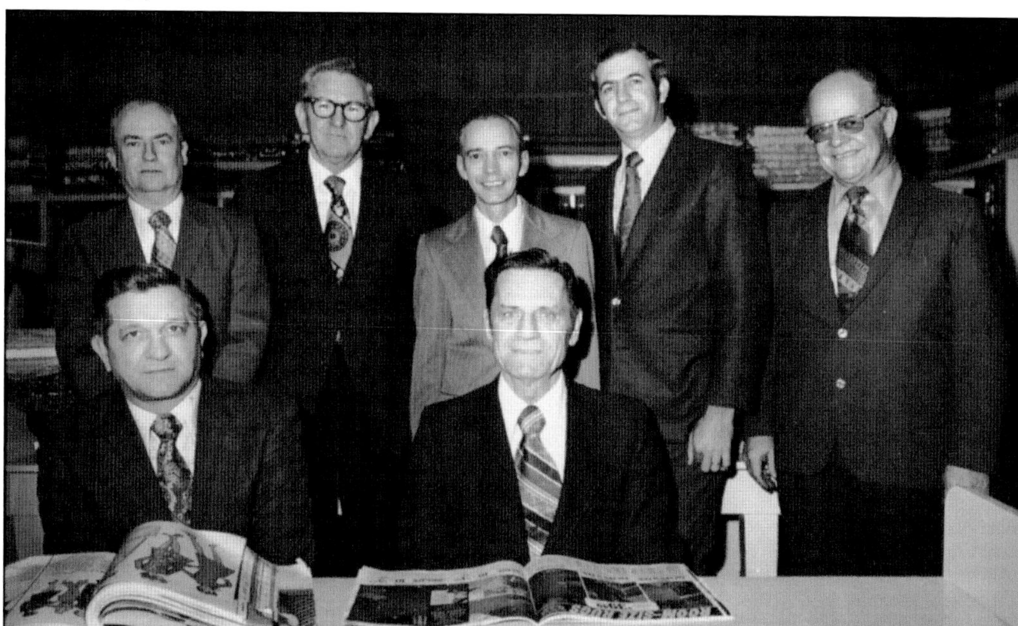

Bevelle supervisors plan advertising and sales campaigns. Seated are Clareston Oliver (left) and Troy Holley, looking at advertisements of Avondale products. Standing behind them, from left to right, are Frank Speaks, Marlin Mann, Cecil Roberts, Harold Bierley, and Hobson Kennedy. The magazine advertisements include Butterick Patterns, featuring dress styles for Avondale chambrays. (Courtesy of Laura Oliver.)

Four

Celebrating Progress

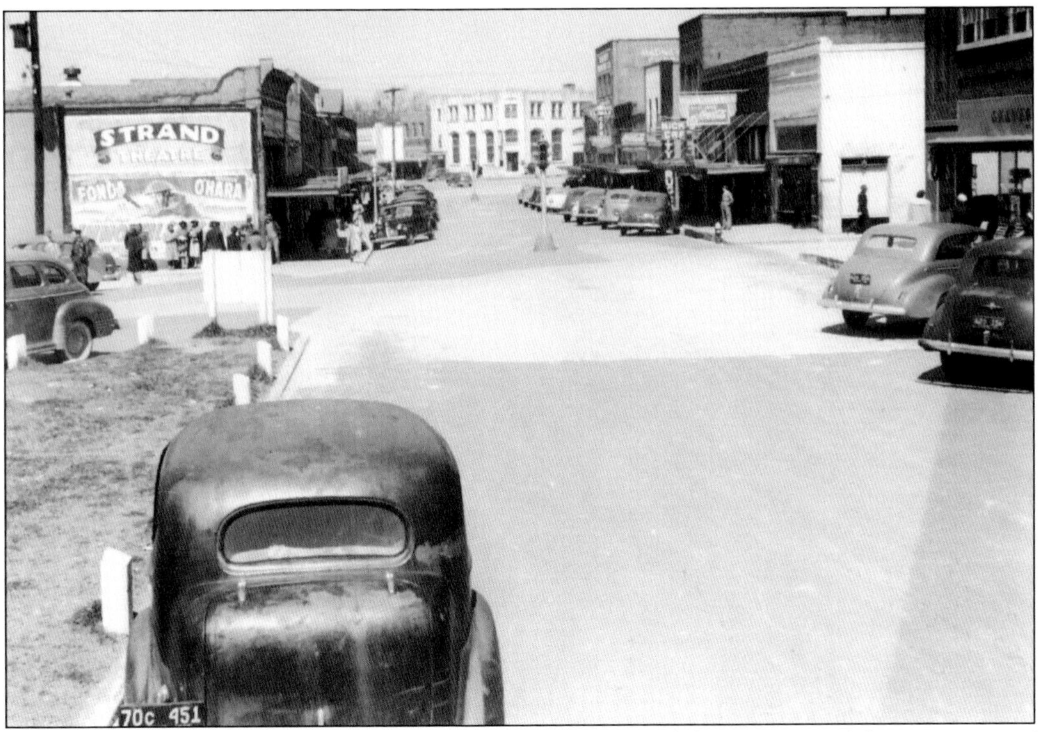

Mack Jackson owned and operated the Strand Theatre on Alabama Street. Advertisements of movies were displayed in large, color prints on the side of Buzbee's Feed and Seed Store. Admission to a Saturday morning matinee at the Strand on Alabama Street or at the Bama Theatre on Tallapoosa Street cost 15¢. The Bama Theatre granted free admission to children who brought a Holsum Bread wrapper on Saturday mornings. Going to the picture show was a treat for people of all ages. (Courtesy of Robert Martin; photograph by Robert Graves.)

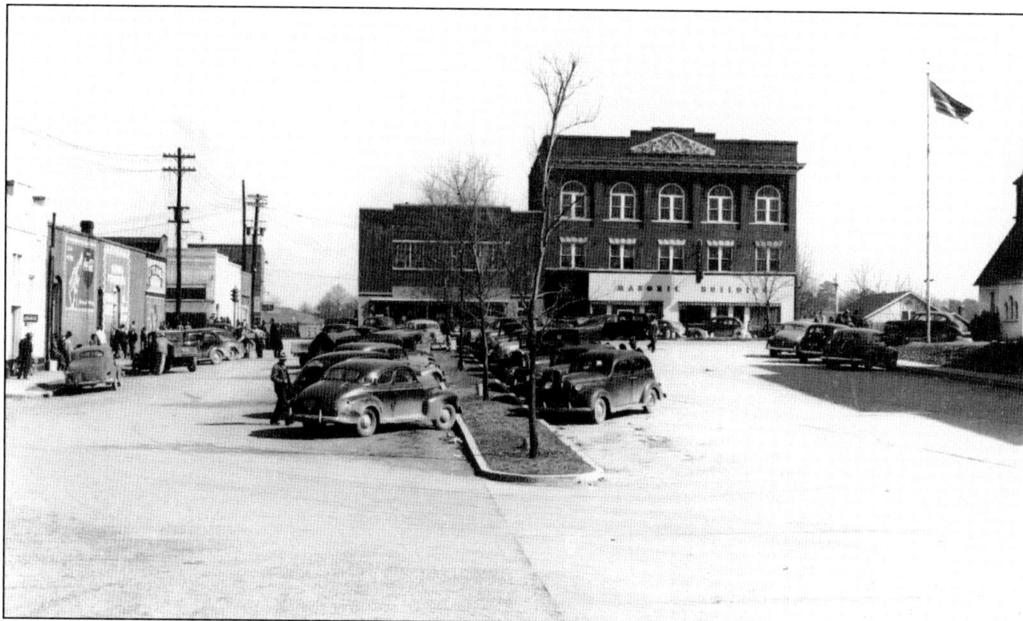

The Masonic building on Main Street is a landmark for visitors and a historical site. The first Masonic lodge in the Youngsville's area was No. 138 in the Bradford community. In 1866, Youngsville received permission from the Grand Lodge of Free and Accepted Masons of Alabama to form a Masonic chapter. The present Masonic Lodge No. 435 was built in 1910 with three floors and maintained by the Mason members. (Courtesy of Robert Martin; photograph by Robert Graves).

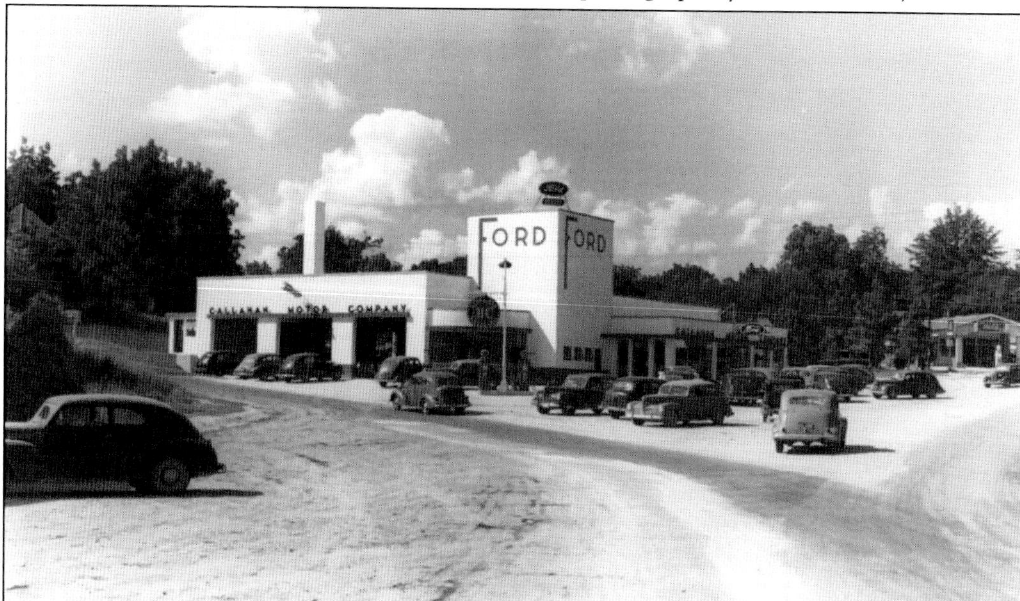

Callahan Ford Motor Company was located in the fork of South Central Avenue, Church Street, and Cherokee Road. Owner Jim Callahan offered a full line of service, with front-end work by specialist Aubrey Moncrief. In the right corner of this 1940s image is A.J. McClellan's mom-and-pop store with gas tanks. On the left is Dr. Jesse H. Miller's Coca-Cola plant. (Courtesy of Robert Martin; photograph by Robert Graves.)

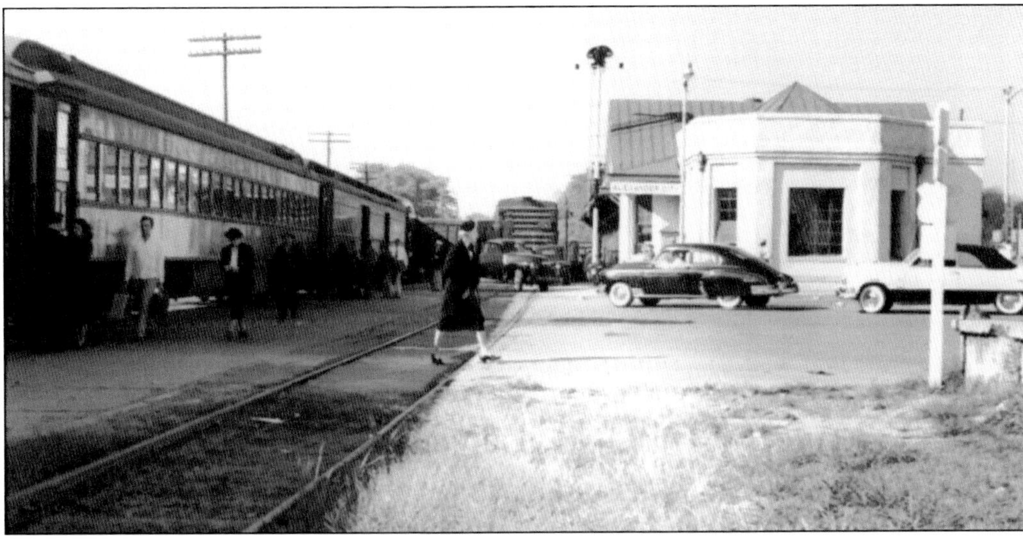

The Central of Georgia Railway traveled from Birmingham through Alexander City on its way to Opelika and Columbus, Georgia, carrying freight and passengers. City residents regularly went to meet the train to observe people arriving or passing through the city. Wooden benches were available for waiting near the tracks. The ticket booth and a place for luggage were located inside the depot. (Courtesy of Robert Martin; photograph by Robert Graves.)

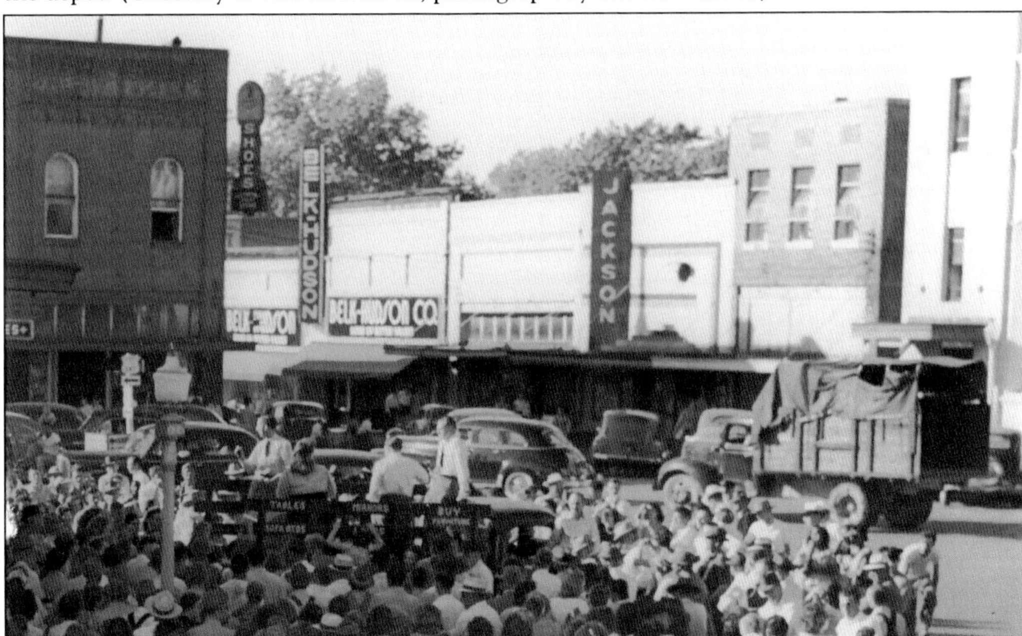

The temporary platform and seating were constructed in preparation for the Thomas Martin Day ceremonies. Thomas Martin was honored for his contribution to writing laws that govern building and operating Alabama dams. Martin was recognized for his leadership in constructing Martin Dam, which made electricity available to people in Alexander City and surrounding areas. A crowd of locals gathers to take part in the celebration. In the background are Jackson's Theatre and Belk Hudson's store, with the Red Goose Shoe Store sign at the end of the line of businesses. (Courtesy of MainStreet Organization; photograph by Robert Graves.)

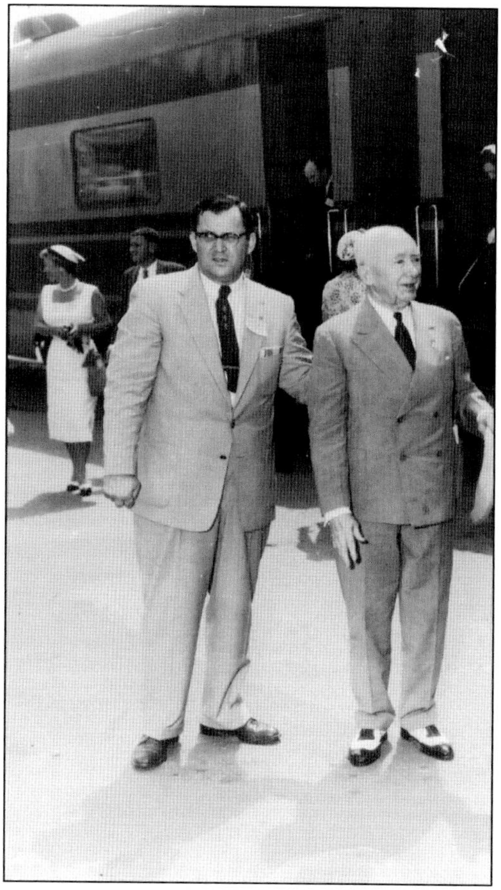

Simeon Wilbanks, vice president of the railroad and key organizer of the Thomas Martin Day event, met Martin (right) at the train station and escorted him to the platform. Building on the groundwork of earlier Alabama Power presidents William P. Lay and James Mitchell, Martin wrote Alabama legislation that brought about construction of the 40,000-acre lake and dam that bear his name. (Courtesy of MainStreet Organization; photograph by Robert Graves.)

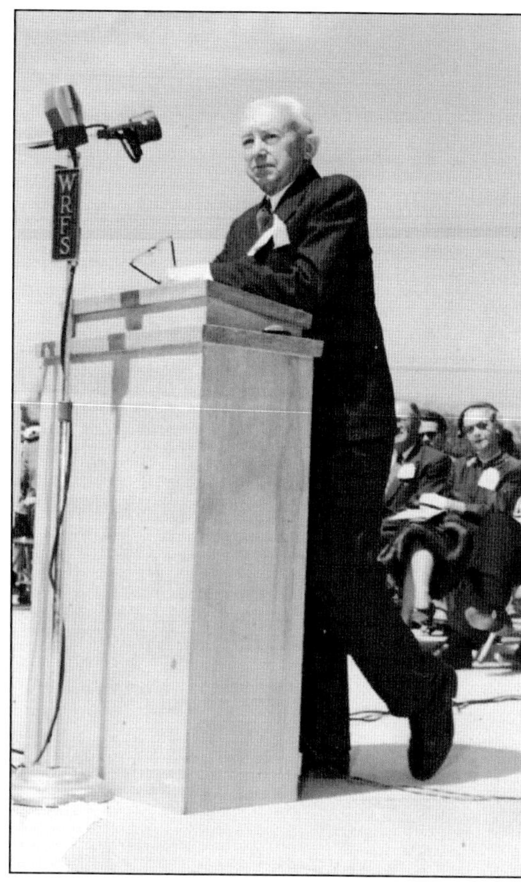

Thomas Martin spoke at local events promoting the progress of lake developments. Although the creation of the dam displaced families that lived in the lake communities, people were able to enjoy the benefits of electricity and recreation that the dam generated. (Courtesy of MainStreet Organization; photograph by Robert Graves.)

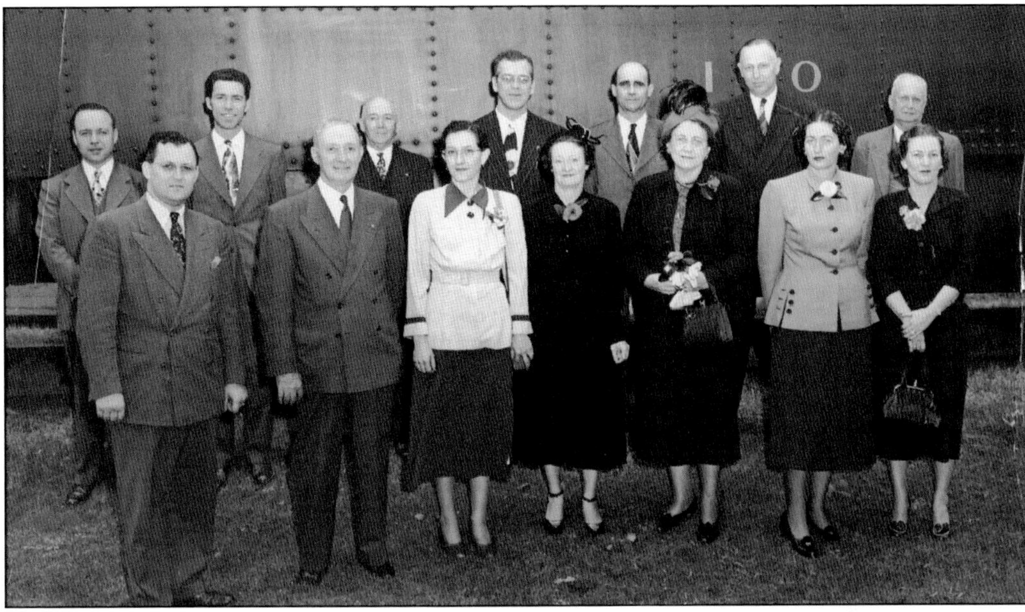

In the first row, from left to right, are Simeon Wilbanks, Thomas Martin, and Elizabeth Wilbanks. Business community representatives, in no specific order, are Zeke Fox, Helen Duncan, Joe Robinson, Obie Thomas, Frances Frohsin, and Edith Russell. Businesses, as well as individual residences, benefitted from the creation of a recreational lake area that attracted visitors and prospective businesses. (Courtesy of MainStreet Organization; photograph by Robert Graves.)

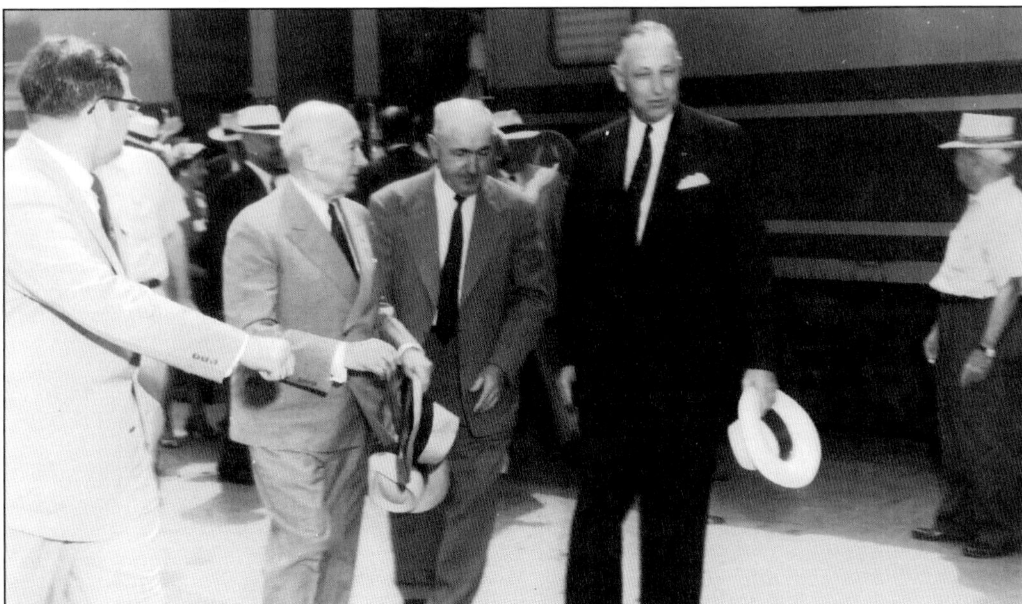

Thomas Martin arrived by a special train accompanied by Central of Georgia president W.F. Dillard. The gentlemen were guests of a special recognition program held on town square. They had lunch at Lake Hill and rode in a flotilla down the Tallapoosa River to Kowaliga and Martin Dam. From left to right are Simeon Wilbanks, Thomas Martin, unidentified, and W.F. Dillard. (Courtesy of MainStreet Organization.)

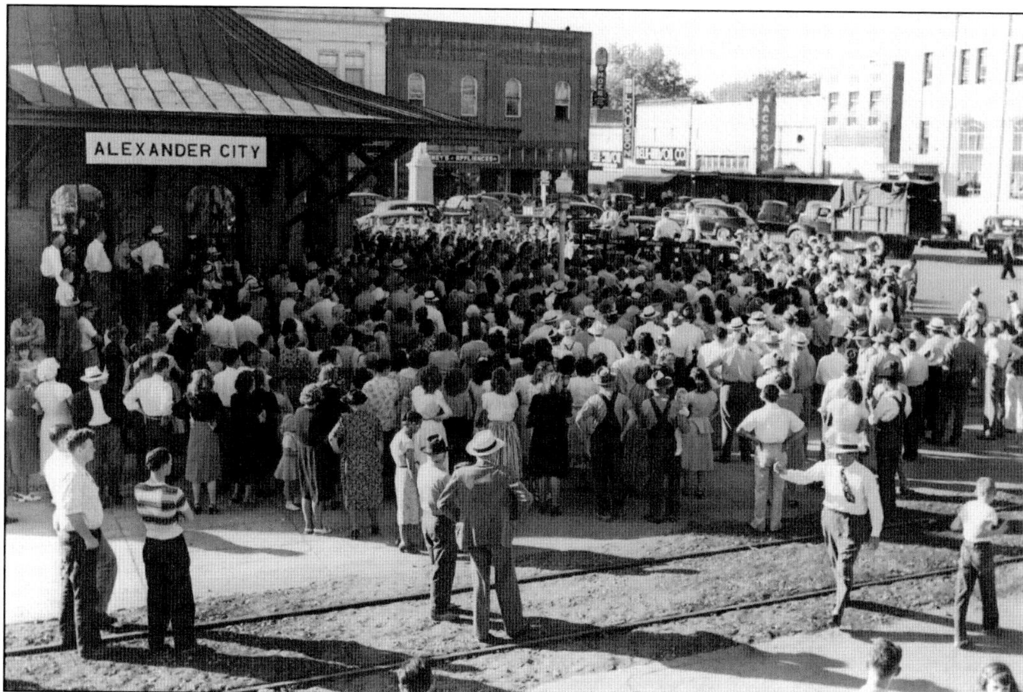

The large crowd attending the Thomas Martin Day ceremonies thronged down Broad and Main Streets beyond the Alexander City depot to welcome and honor Thomas Martin, president of Alabama Power, and W.F. Dillard, president of the Central of Georgia Railway. Speakers praised Martin and Alabama Power for making electricity available, which enhanced the quality of people's lives and accelerated the town's growth. (Courtesy of MainStreet Organization; photograph by Robert Graves.)

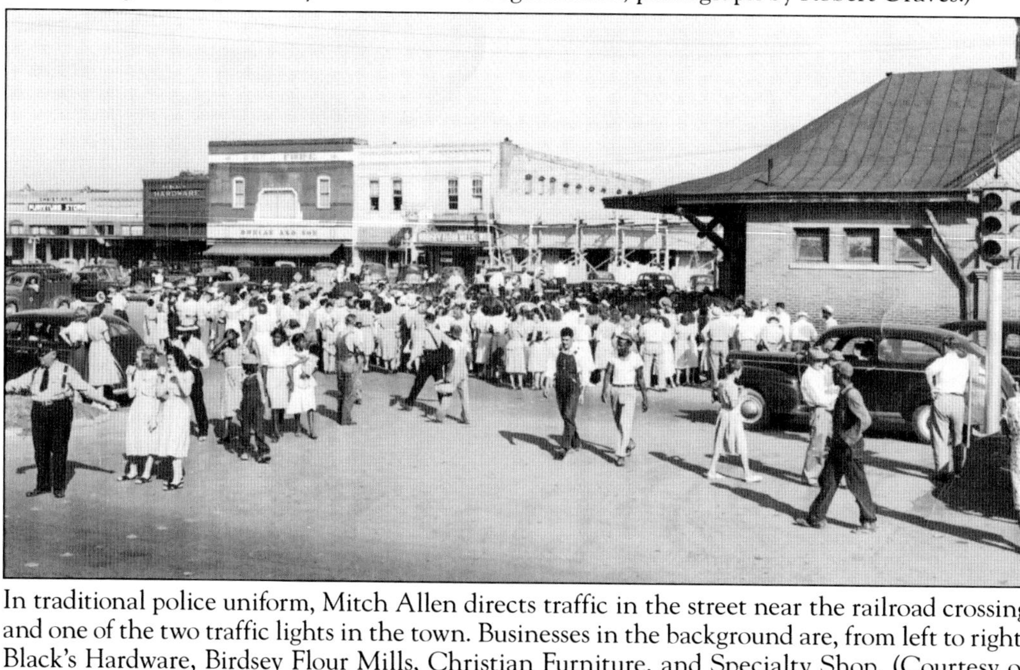

In traditional police uniform, Mitch Allen directs traffic in the street near the railroad crossing and one of the two traffic lights in the town. Businesses in the background are, from left to right, Black's Hardware, Birdsey Flour Mills, Christian Furniture, and Specialty Shop. (Courtesy of MainStreet Organization; photograph by Robert Graves.)

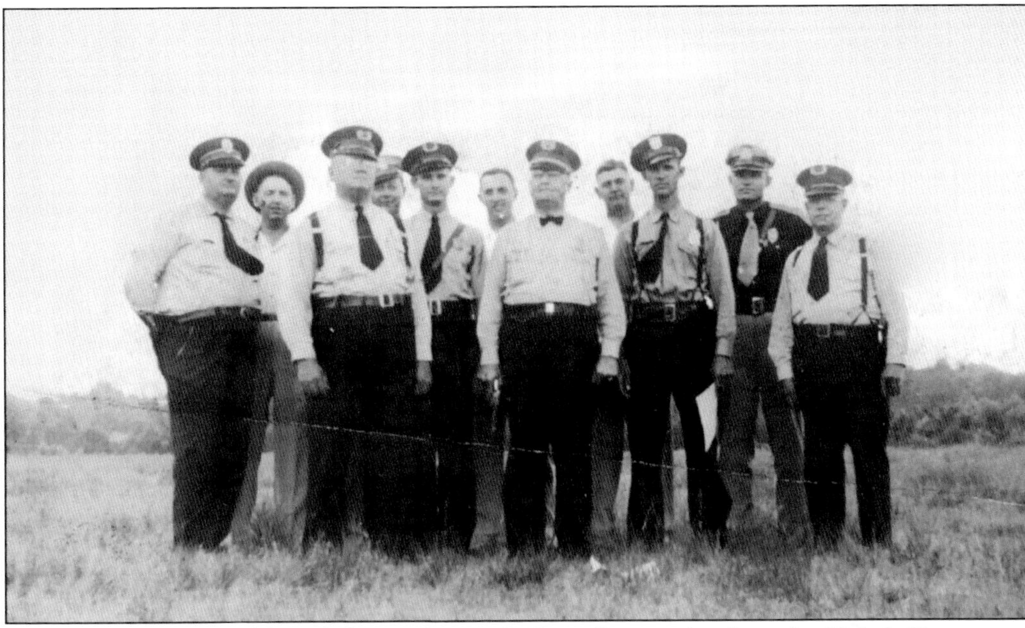

Town officials pictured from left to right in 1946 are (first row) police chief Mack Horton and Mitch Allen; (second row) A.J. Price Sr., Bob Benton, Winfred Patterson, Earl Towns, and Howell Stowe; (third row) an unidentified highway patrolman, Dr. James Cameron, Onis Alford, and an unidentified man. (Courtesy of Lynn Royal.)

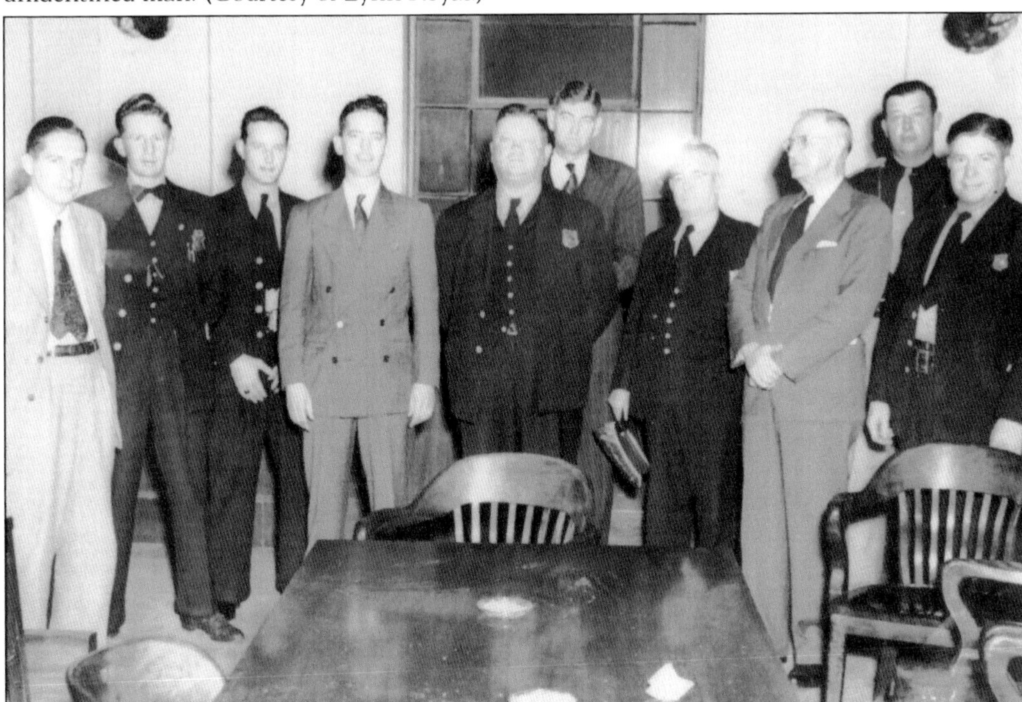

Police chief Mack Horton and his officers stand ready to protect the citizens of Alexander City. This picture was taken in city hall in the 1940s and submitted by retired police chief Lynn Royal. (Courtesy of Lynn Royal.)

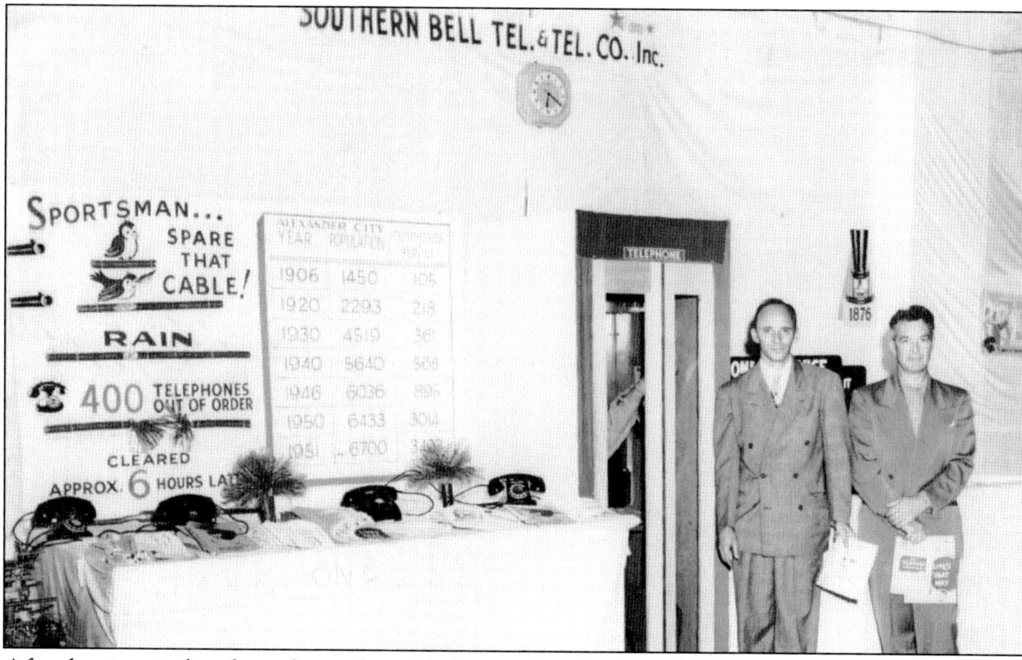

After buying timber for poles and establishing a line from Dadeville to Sylacauga, Ben Russell created the first telephone company in Alexander City in 1901. The switchboard was set up in the back of the Citizens Bank building. In 1904, Russell sold the franchise at a substantial profit to Southern Bell Company. (Courtesy of Russell Lands.)

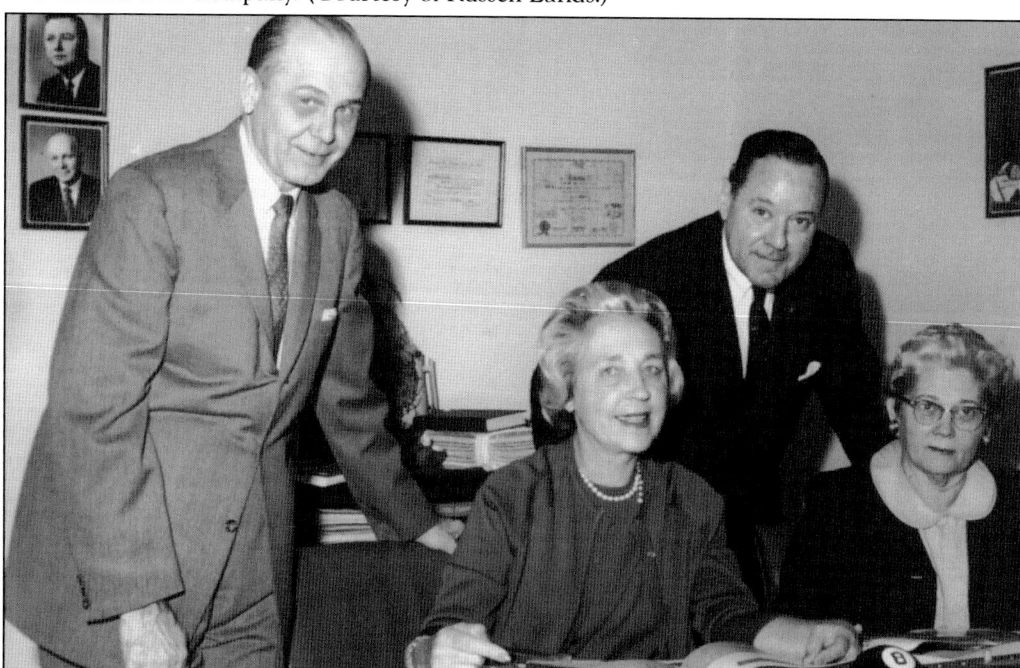

A group meets to discuss future plans for the Adelia M. Russell Library. From left to right are J.C. Henderson (*Alexander City Outlook* publisher), Adelia Russell, James Head (from Birmingham), and Erin Cocke, who became city librarian in 1947. (Courtesy of Jacob Henderson.)

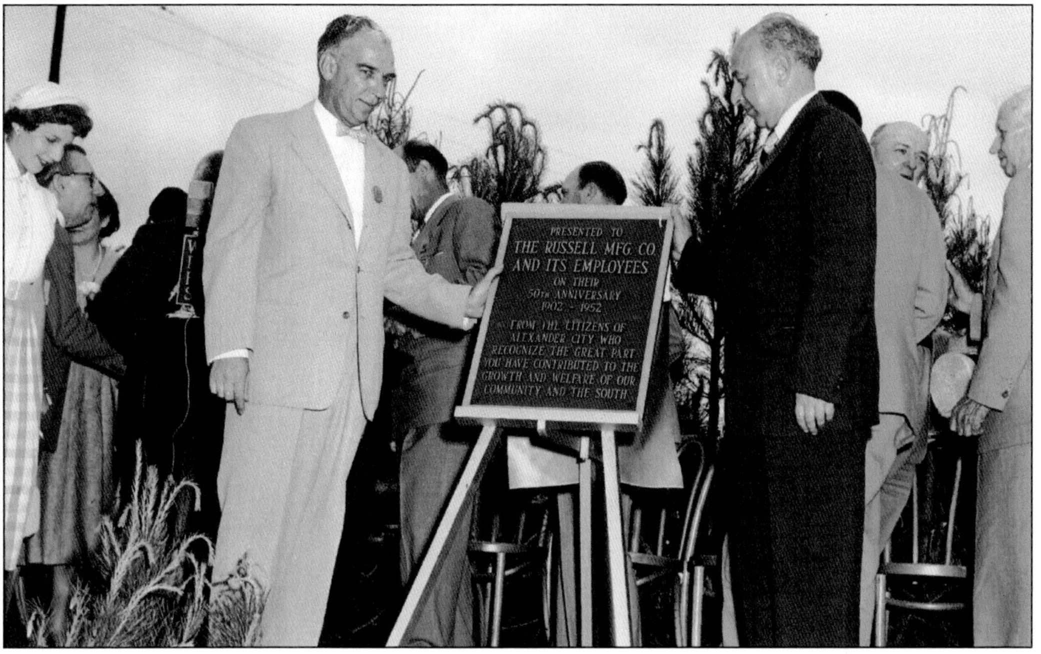

On May 17, 1952, Ralph Frohsin Sr. (right) awards a plaque to Thomas Russell with the following inscription: "Presented to The Russell MFG. Co. and its Employees on their 50th Anniversary 1902–1952—From the citizens of Alexander City who recognize the great part you have contributed to the growth and welfare of our community and the South." (Courtesy of MainStreet Organization.)

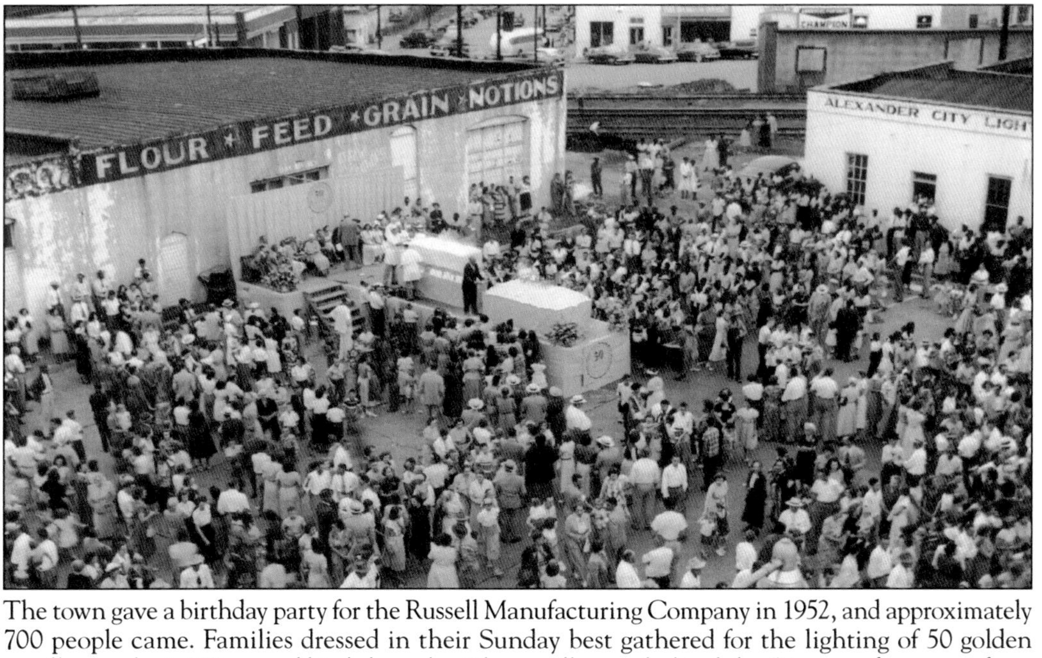

The town gave a birthday party for the Russell Manufacturing Company in 1952, and approximately 700 people came. Families dressed in their Sunday best gathered for the lighting of 50 golden candles on the 1,000-pound birthday cake. The candles symbolized the 50 years of progress, from a small knitting mill to an employer of over 5,000 workers. On an elevated platform, the Russell family and friends were seated beside notable guests, including Florida senator Claude Pepper and Thomas W. Martin. (Courtesy of MainStreet Organization.)

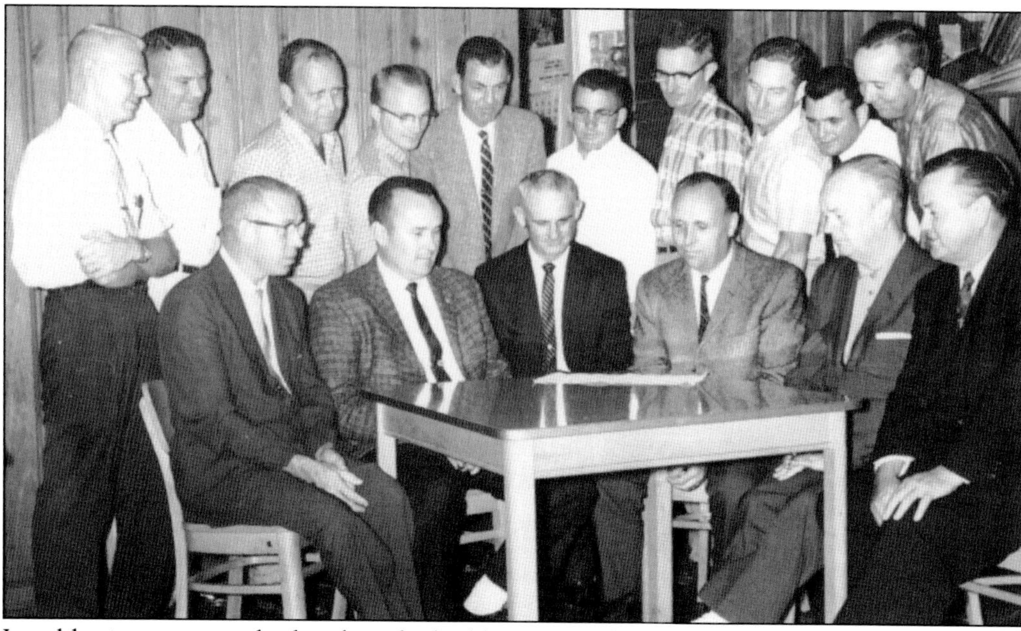

Local businessmen study the plans for building a new fire station to replace the one located at the old train depot. From left to right are (first row) Hugh Thompson, Byron Causey, Col. Winfred Patterson, Phillip Adams, Temple Coley, and L.E. Sellers; (second row) Leon Baker, two unidentified men, Fred Dobbs, Johnny Heard, unidentified, Jessie Cannon, Charles Claybrooks, Marvin Still, and Tommy Jack Cole. (Courtesy of MainStreet Organization.)

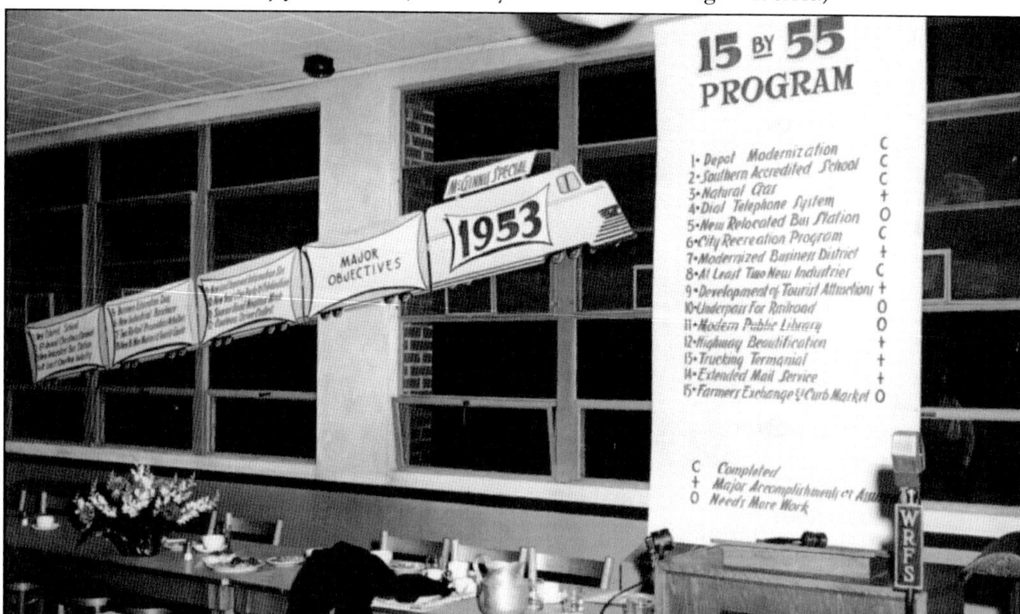

WRFS hosted the "15 by 55" program. Major objectives to accomplish by 1955 included modernizing the train depot, adding a city recreational program, and securing school accreditation. Goals completed were installing a dial telephone system, modernizing the business district, and developing tourist attractions. One key goal needing more work was to establish a modern city library. (Courtesy of MainStreet Organization.)

Benjamin Russell was an industrialist, banker, and entrepreneur. In 1902, after establishing Russell Mills, he constructed the first Alexander City mill village, consisting of 230 homes and a church building. In 1916, he opened Alex City Wholesale Grocery. In 1920, he bought the Nolen Hotel, changing the name to Russco. He built schools, a hospital, a telephone system, a pumping station, pipeline filter plant, and waterworks system. He helped to establish the Alexander City Chamber of Commerce and became its first president. (Courtesy of Russell Lands.)

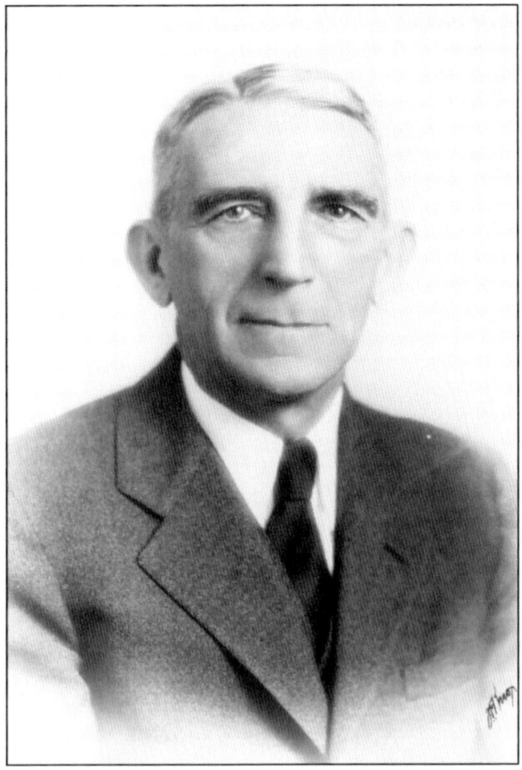

Thomas D. Russell (third from left) and an unidentified man (far right) share a laugh with brothers Braxton (far left) and Miles Comer at the annual spring inspection. The men are standing in front of the Bevelle School with the village in the background. Members of the Russell and Comer textile families represented in the Alexander City area regularly attended or participated in the important civic functions of the town. (Courtesy of Jacob Henderson.)

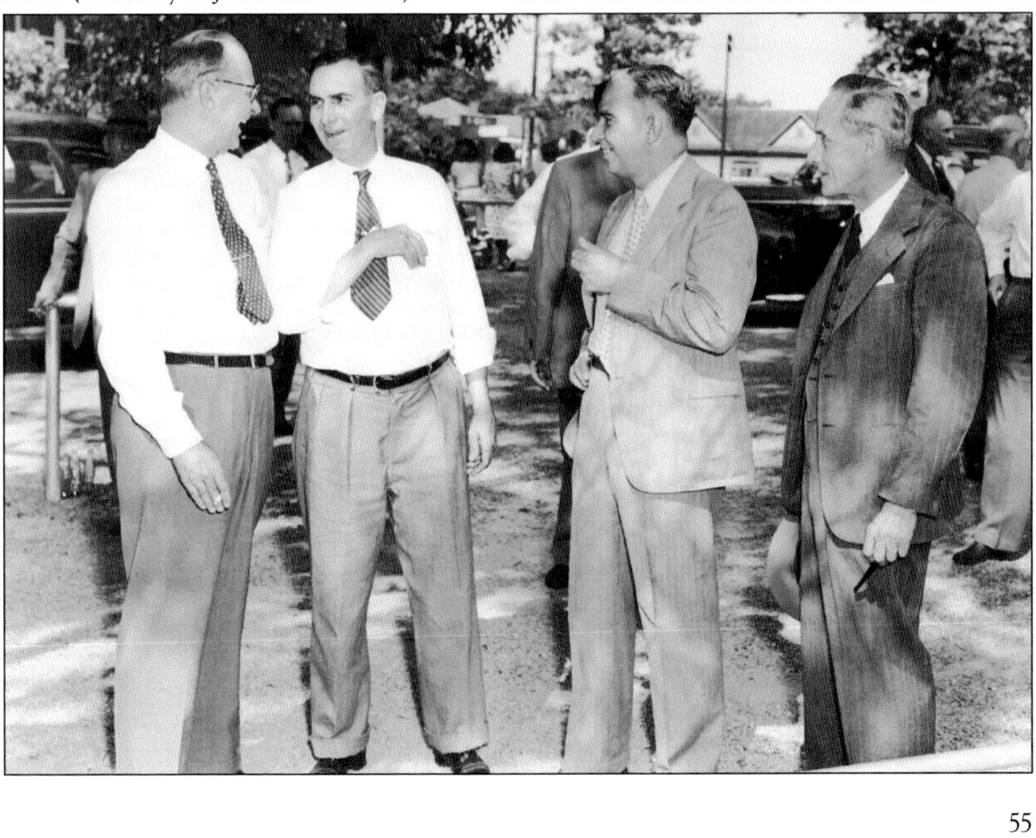

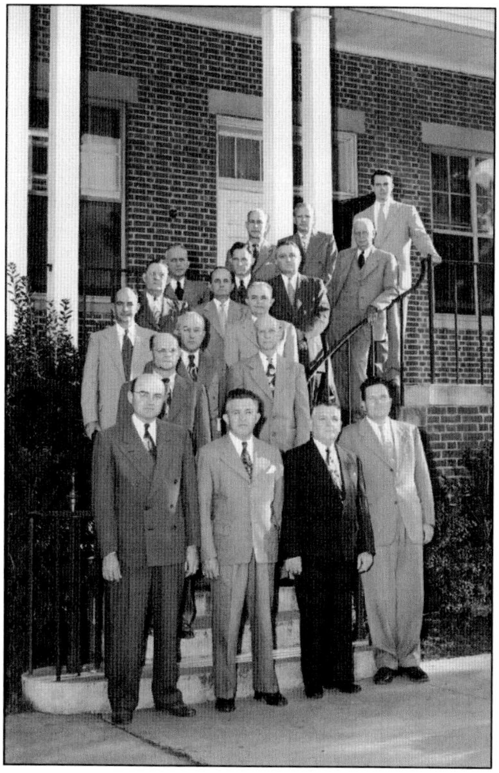

Russell executives lined up on the company's main office steps in the 1950s include, in no particular order, Lewis Askew, Manley Smith, Joe Richardson, Thomas Robinson, Robert Porch, Harlan Blankenship, Russell Thomas, Louis Vernon, Bo Bozeman, Robert Lindsey, L.A. Swanson, Ernest Brooks, Roy Latimer, Sam Bradshaw, Millard Yates, Obie Thomas, and Lemuel Coley. (Courtesy of Russell Lands.)

The Russell Manufacturing Co.'s main office was identified by the eagle crafted by Robinson Iron. A second headquarters was established in Atlanta in 1996. Russell Manufacturing Co. became world famous as a producer and seller of equipment and clothing for professional, collegiate, and high school sports teams. In 1997, the company began downsizing and outsourcing jobs to other countries. In 2006, Russell Manufacturing Co. became a subsidiary of Berkshire Hathaway, with corporate headquarters located in Bowling Green, Kentucky. (Courtesy of Peggy Walls; photograph by Tammy East.)

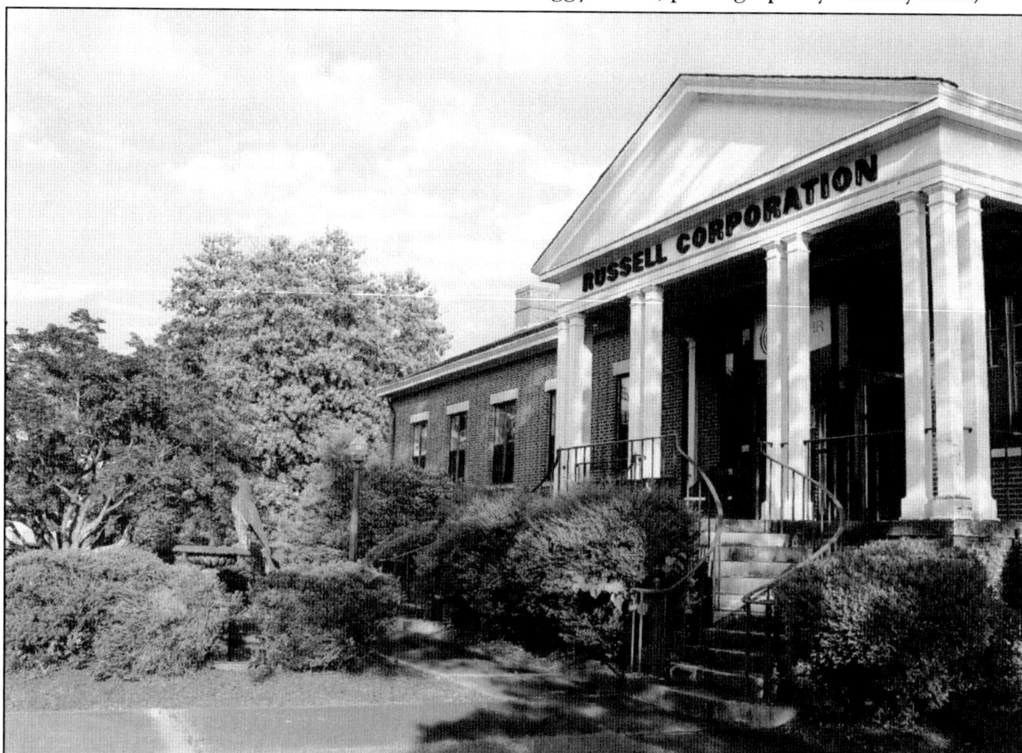

Five

Awards

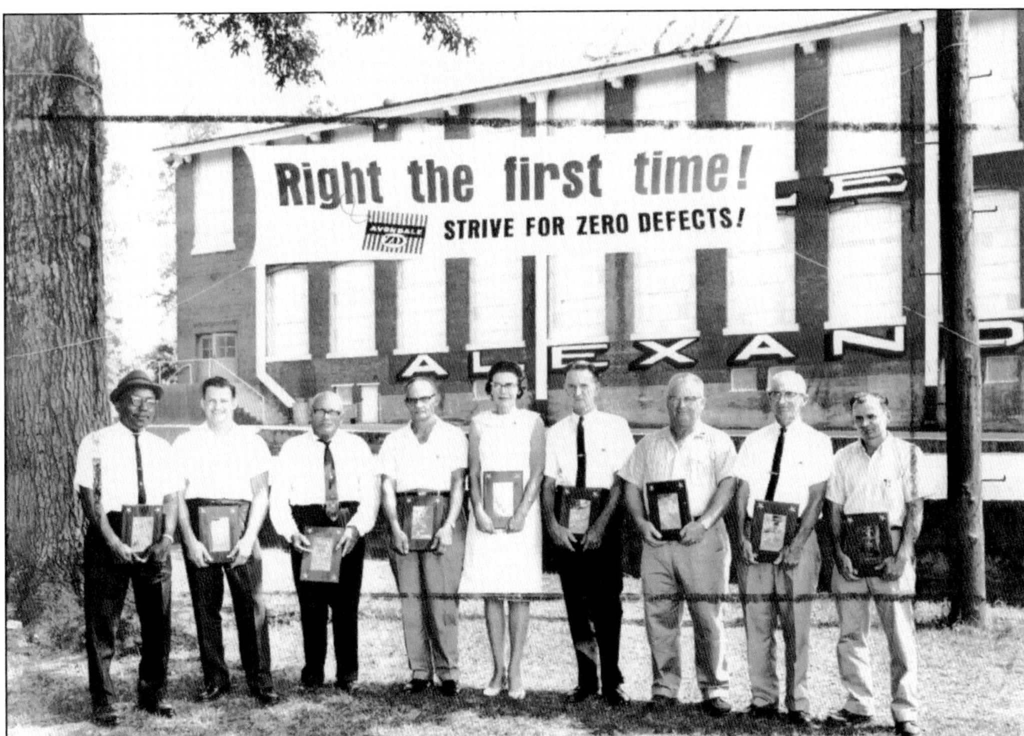

The Zero Defects program championed the need to avoid all errors in production, from the administrative level to the worker. Supervisors and employees who were able to demonstrate an accident-free record of performance were recognized with plaques and featured in *Avondale Sun* articles. Pictured from left to right are Dan Owens, Bobby Traylor, unidentified, Tom Talley, Idell Lankford, Harvey Lankford, John Turner, Brock Smith, and J.C. Tapley. (Courtesy of Laura Oliver.)

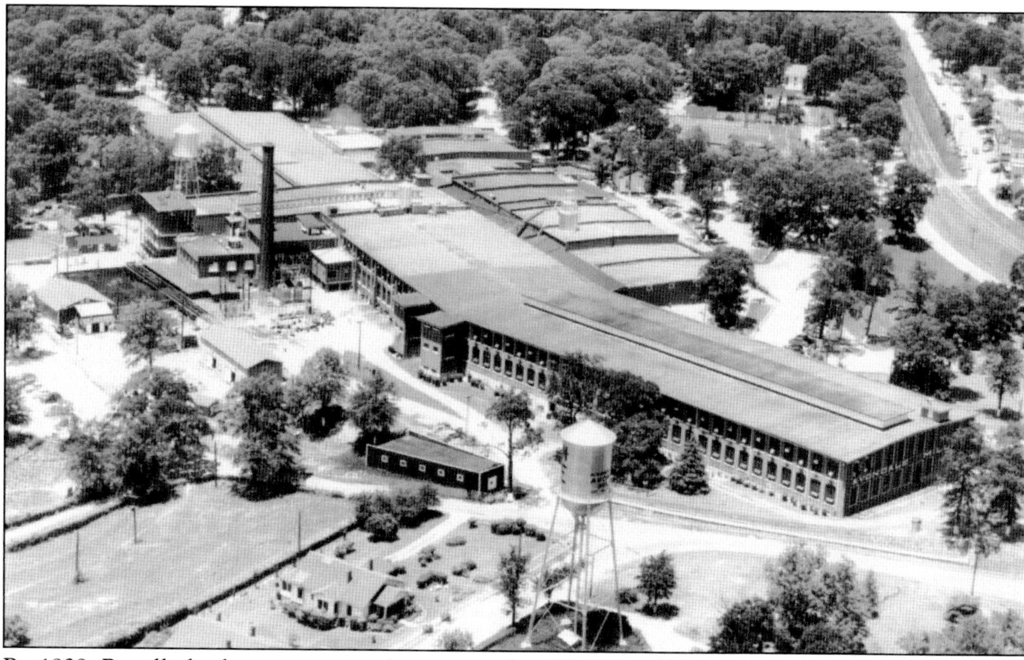

By 1939, Bevelle had two water tanks, one with a 72,000-gallon reservoir filled by springs and one 100,000-gallon tank with a bottom 85 feet above yard level. This aerial view features the Bevelle plant and Maple Street, where the supervisors lived. The Central of Georgia rail line from Birmingham to Columbus runs by the loading side of the plant. (Courtesy of Laura Oliver.)

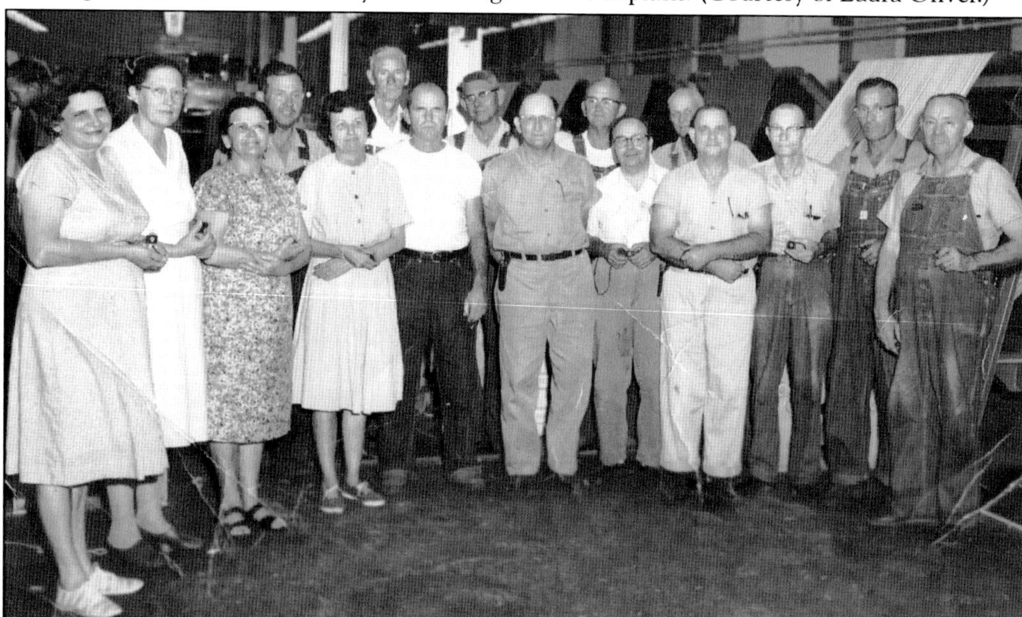

By the 1960s, a second generation of mill workers had displaced the first, who had come from farms determined to make a better life for their children. In the 1920s, plant director J. Fletcher Comer worked to bring a good quality of life to the mill workers. The churches, schools, and athletic and recreational facilities were evidence of Comer's philosophy that it takes an investment in people to make good citizens. (Courtesy of Laura Oliver.)

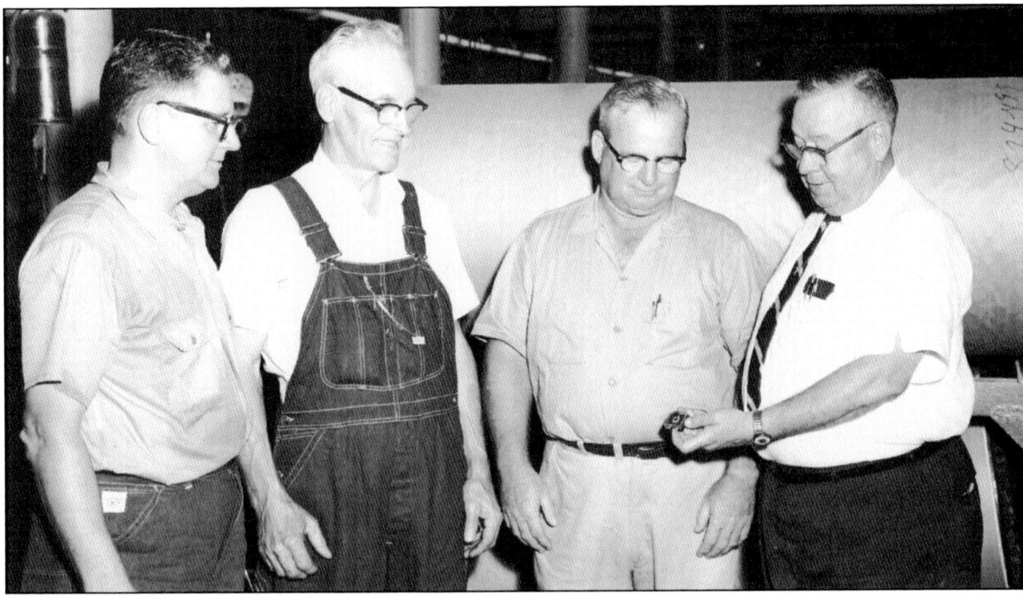

From left to right, Freeman Champion, Ernest R. Dykes, John Turner, and Roy Moore are all smiles as Dykes is awarded a 45-year service pin by Moore. Dykes ran a tying-in machine. As a young boy of 18, he learned of a textile mill in Sylacauga and walked the Central of Georgia rail line from the farm to Sylacauga. There, he found that they were not hiring but learned that Alexander City plant was. He walked the railroad 20 more miles to Bevelle. He was hired and remained with Avondale until his retirement in 1970. (Courtesy of Laura Oliver.)

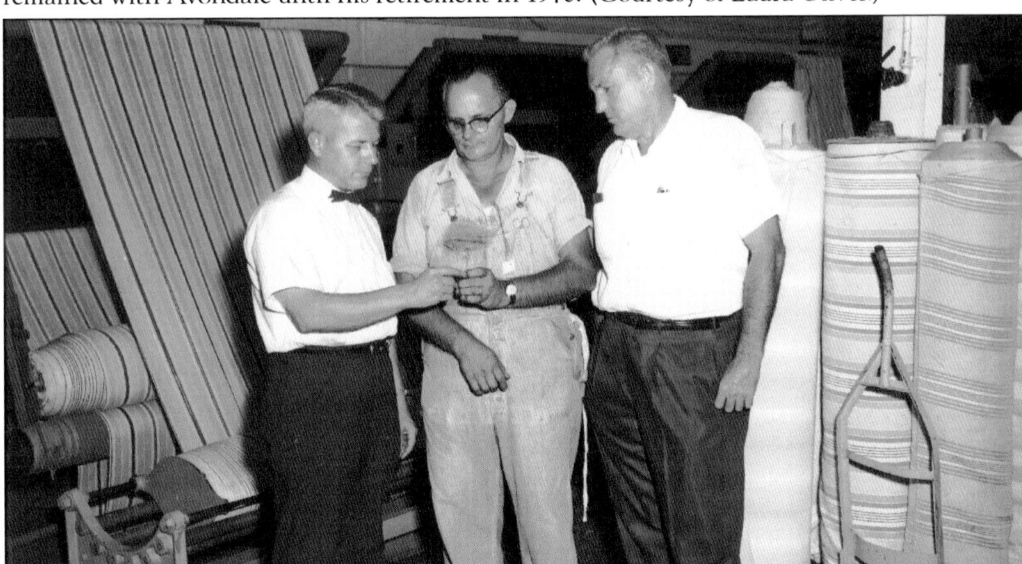

Thomas Tally (center) receives a service pin from department head Lawton Rich (right) and superintendent W.A. Edwards. Bevelle Service awards were given for special recognition, such as safety records, perfect work attendance, number of years of service, and retirement. Coworkers hosted small parties or picnics to honor retiring friends. Village residents retired among neighbors with whom they had worked and whose children had attended school, church, and recreational events together. (Courtesy of Laura Oliver.)

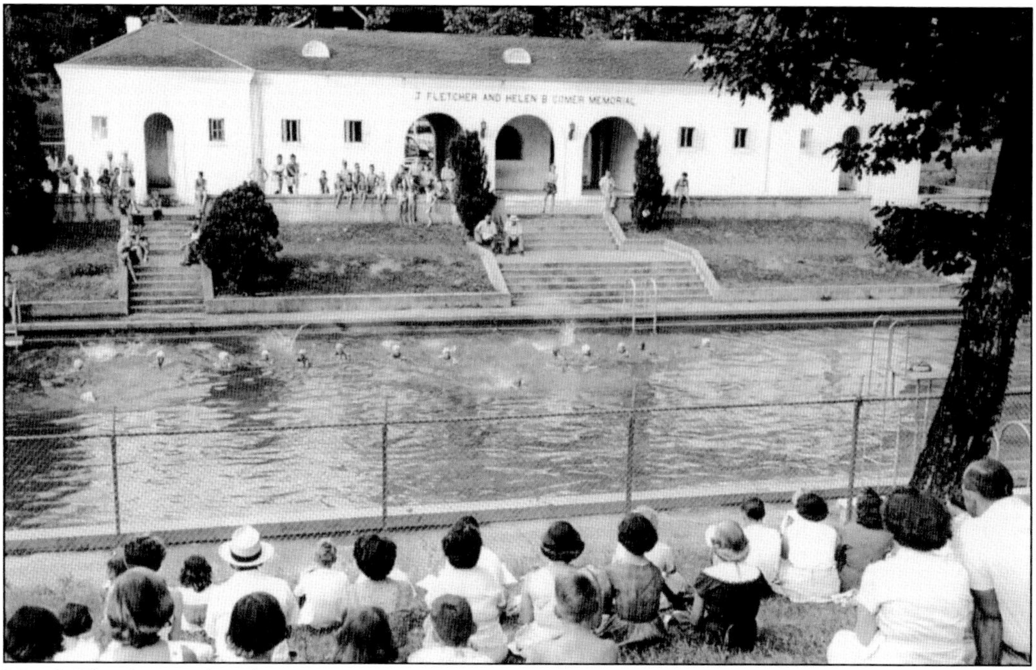

The J. Fletcher and Helen B. Comer Memorial Swimming Pool was built by Bevelle employees and friends and citizens of Alexander City to honor the couple. The pool was open to the Bevelle community but was used primarily by the children in the summer months. Employee families attended the water shows performed by the Bevelle children. (Courtesy of Laura Oliver.)

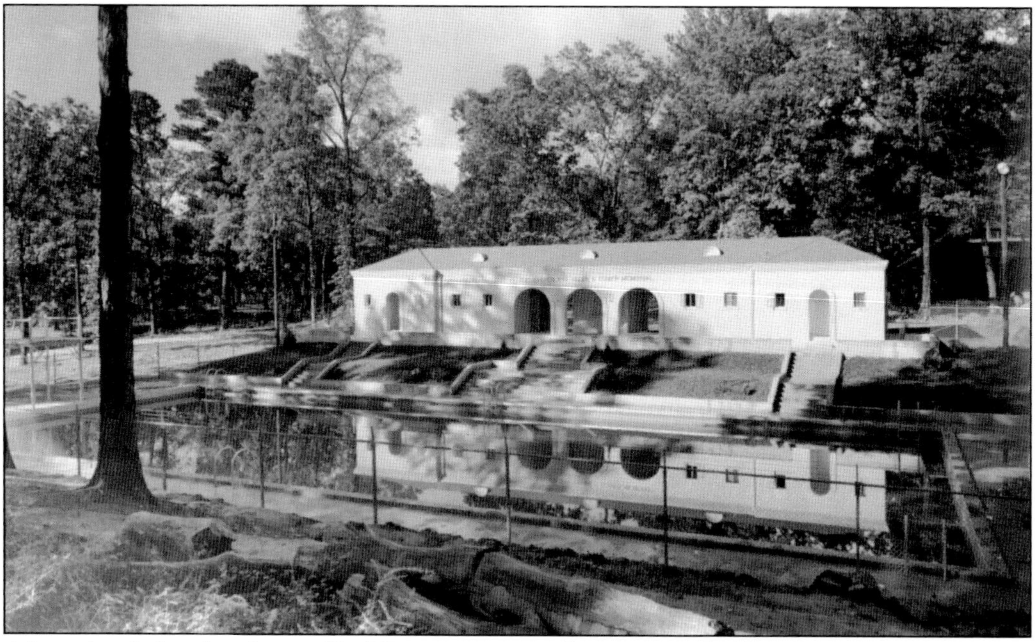

After school closed each year, Red Cross swimming lessons were held in the pool. The summer swimming program culminated in August with the annual water show. The children demonstrated the skills that they had mastered to complete the summer course and be elevated to the next level. (Courtesy of Laura Oliver.)

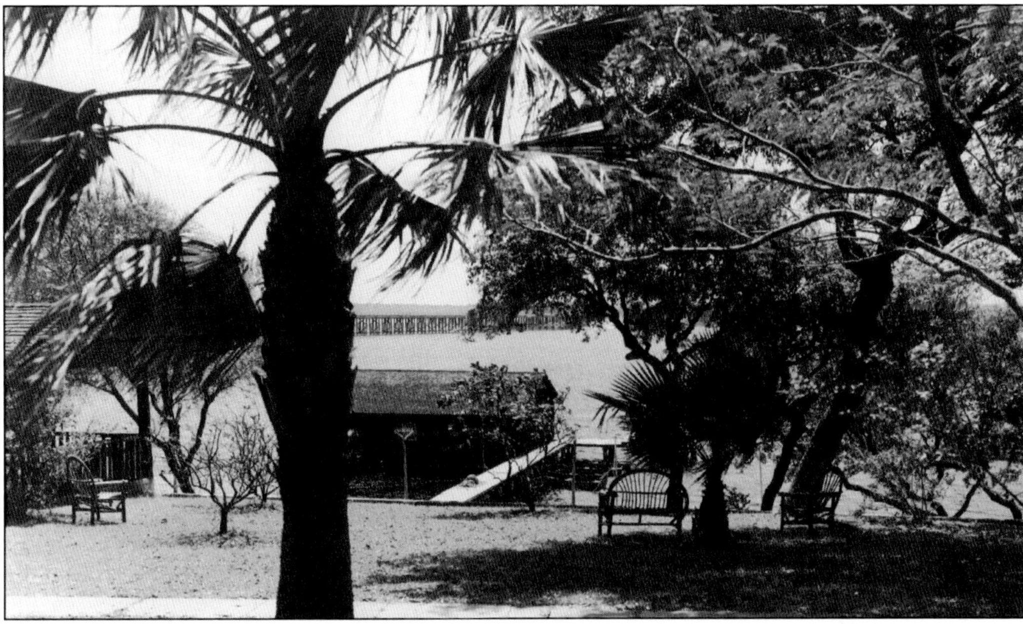

From 1945 to 1987, Camp Helen was a company resort for Avondale Mill employees. By rotating the closing of plants for a week in the summer months, each mill family had an opportunity to enjoy a week's vacation, swimming, beachcombing, and saltwater fishing in a company yacht. Manager Eric Padgett and his family welcomed the mill families and worked with the managers to see that everyone had fun. (Courtesy of Laura Oliver.)

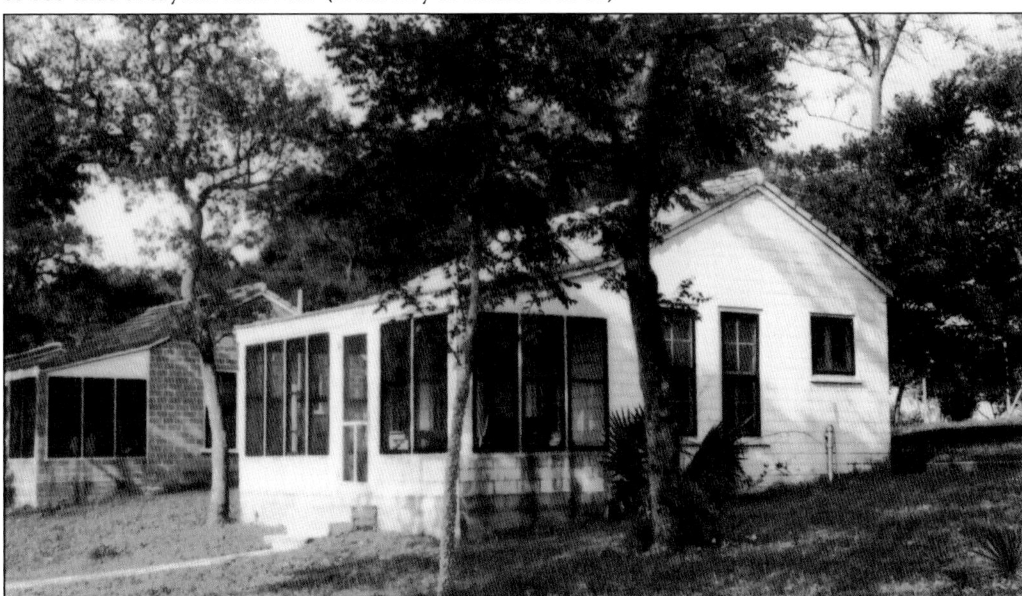

Transportation to Camp Helen was provided by the Avondale Company in a bus driven in the early years by Andy "Punch" Adcock. In 1950, the weekly fee for room in one of the family cabins and three meals a day was $13. Bordered by water on three sides, Camp Helen remains one of the largest coastal dune lakes in Florida and is known as the Camp Helen State Park. (Courtesy of Wayne Forbus.)

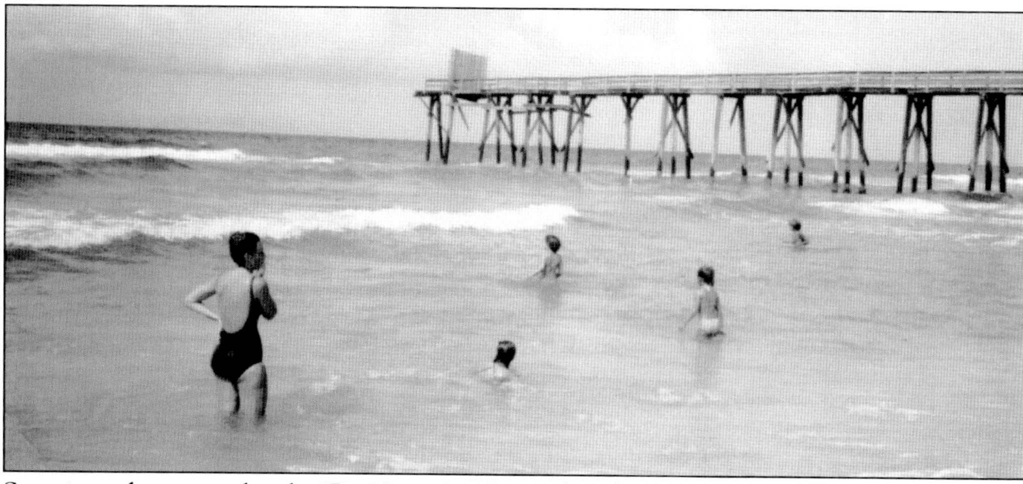

Superintendents stayed at the "Big House" and joined in the camp activities with their workers to ensure that they enjoyed their vacation time. Bevelle children played on the beach and swam in the gulf with lifeguards watching them. They hunted shells, built sand castles, and played croquet in the sand. Each family had the chance to ride on one of the company's yachts to swim and go deep-sea fishing. At the end of the week, the children returned home sunburned, relaxed, and ready for Red Cross swimming lessons. (Courtesy of Bobby Waldrop.)

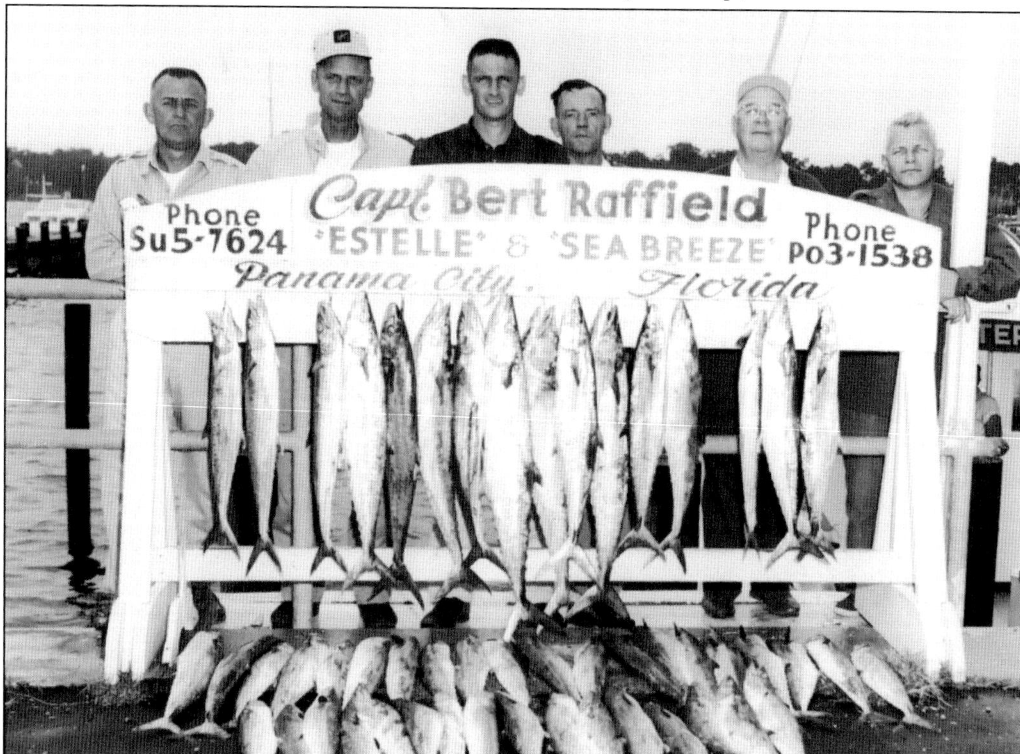

Bevelle plant supervisors load up their fishing rods and go deep-sea fishing in Panama City at the Camp Helen site in the 1950s. They show off their catch at the end of the day. Pictured from left to right are Chal Adamson, Troy Holley, Don Holley, Raymond Weddle, R.P. Moore, and W.A. Edwards. (Courtesy of Don Holley.)

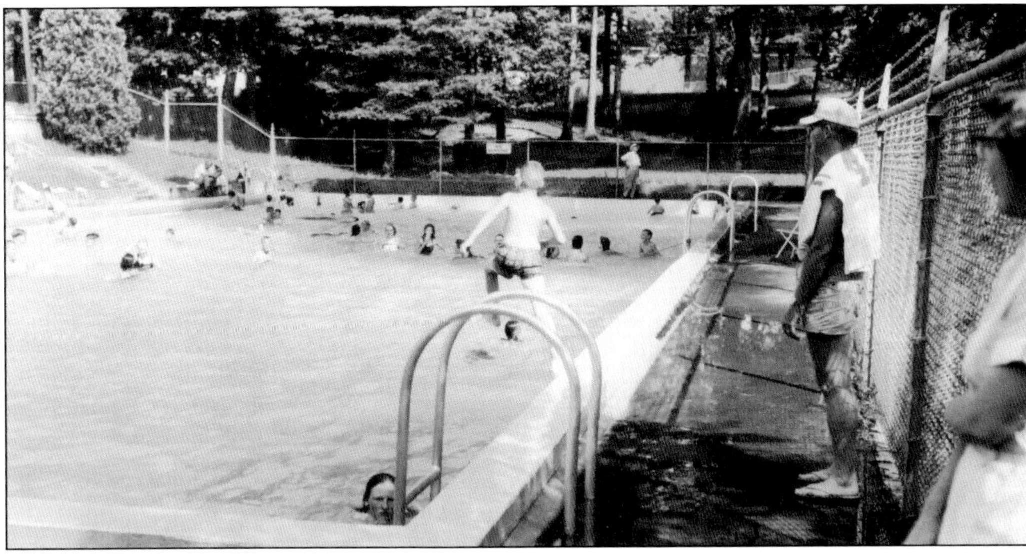

Billy Sam Nolan was a coach at Benjamin Russell High School and a Red Cross lifeguard at Avondale's J. Fletcher and Helen B. Comer Memorial Swimming Pool. In this 1960s photograph, children of Bevelle employees swim in the community pool and participate in the summer fun activities. Instructors were employed to provide the swim lessons required of schoolchildren in the summer months. (Courtesy of MainStreet Organization.)

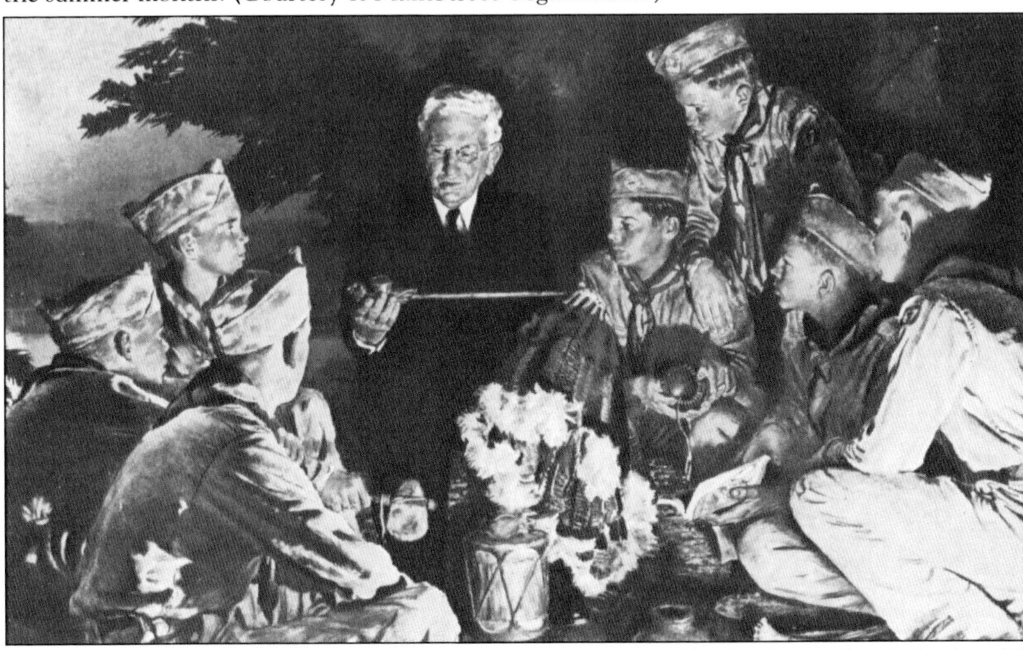

Reprints of the 1946 Douglass Crockwell painting commissioned by the Comer family for the 1952 *Avondale Calendar* were given to Avondale employees for Christmas in 1951. Featuring employees and their families, the image here shows Bevelle Boy Scout leader and, from left to right, scouts Lloyd Sellers, Paul Talley, Clyde Forbus, General Noble, Wayne Lyles, Freddie Turner, Buddy Dean, and Dan Kimbrough. The following quotation accompanied the picture: "To help produce more self-reliant citizens for America, every eligible boy and girl in Avondale communities is urged to join a Boy Scout or Girl Scout Troop." (Courtesy of Laura Oliver.)

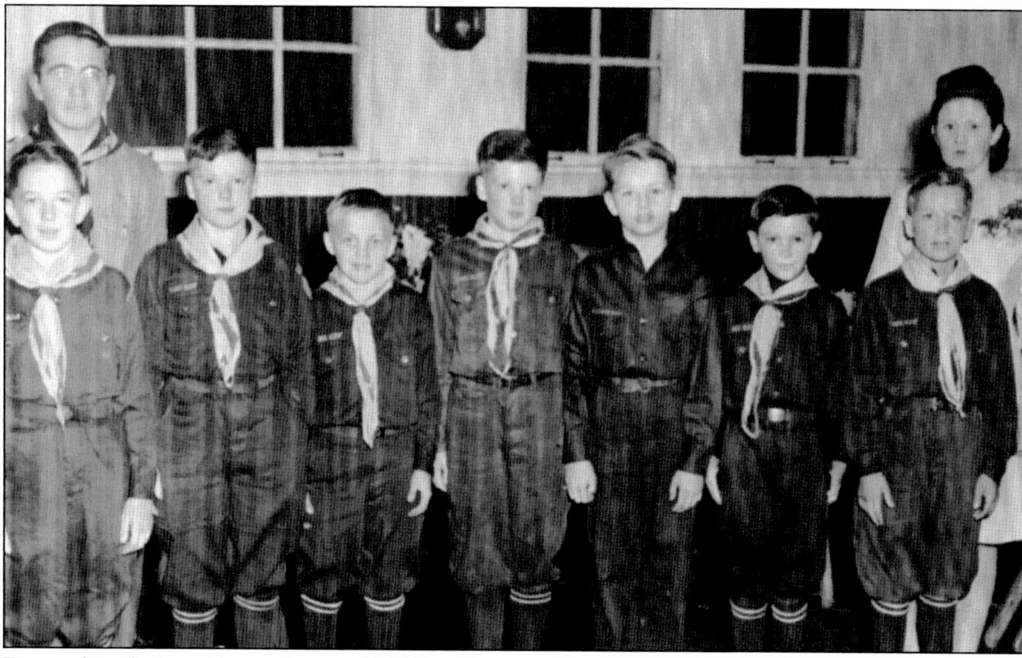

Dressed in their uniforms for a c. 1945 Boy Scout troop picture, den chief Bobby Whetstone and den mother Mrs. W.O. Vickers frame the line of scouts that include, from left to right, Jimmie Scott, Ray Vickers, Yvonne Whetstone, Clay Vickers, Billy Johnson, Edwin Davis, and Douglas Merritt. (Courtesy of Laura Oliver.)

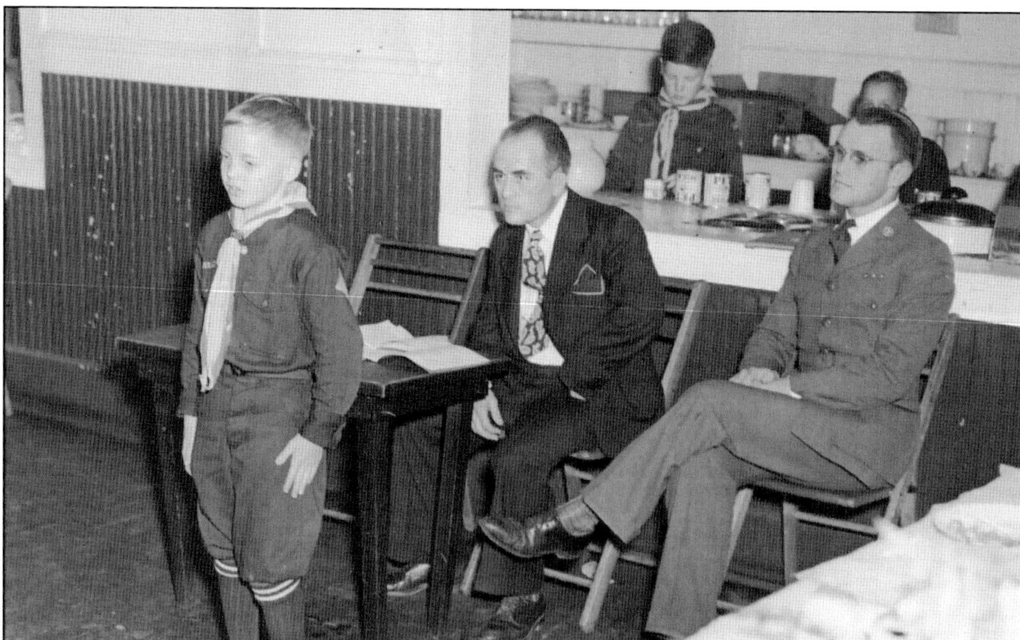

Scout tests require demonstrating skills at different levels to qualify for advancement within the troop. Yvonne Whetstone is observed by cub master W.D. Brown and scout executive Charles Hooker (right). Other scouts work in the kitchen area. The event takes place in the mid-1940s in the Boy Scout hut in Alexander City. (Courtesy of Laura Oliver.)

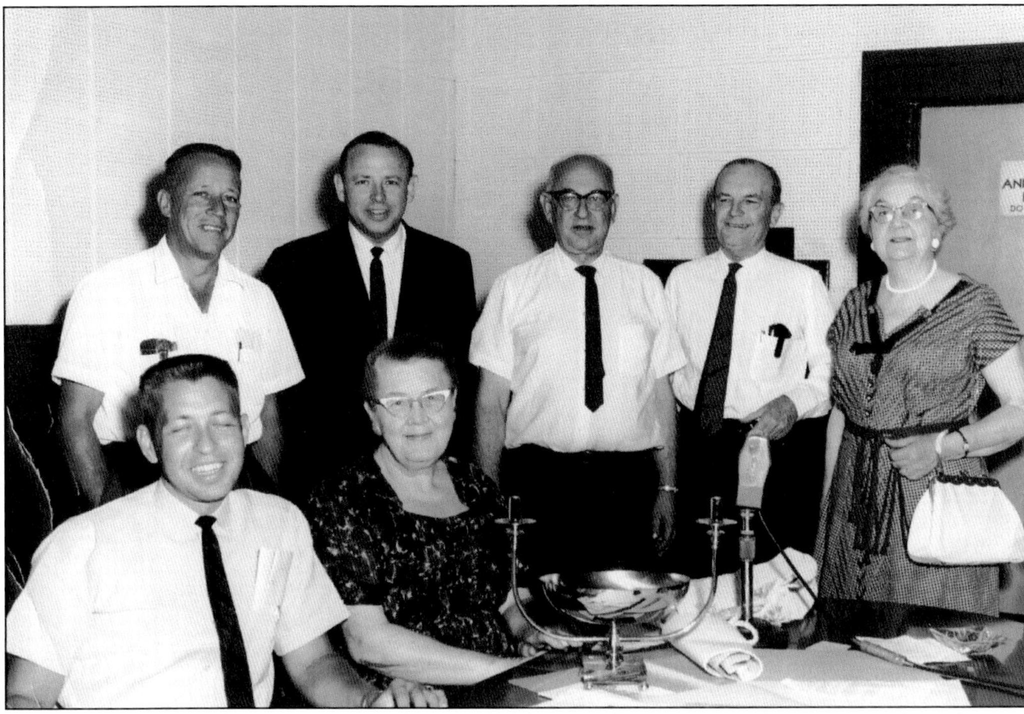

From left to right are (first row) attorney Tom Radney and WRFS announcer Louise Day; (second row) Billy Radney, Dr. Moss Robertson (First Baptist minister), Ralph Frohsin, Judge Clinton Jackson Coley, and Katie Gross. Other WRFS announcers were Henry Waites, Bill Buchannon, Bob McKinnon, and Louise Day. Day's program, *Daily Doings*, was a favorite of those who tuned into WRFS to learn about local events. WRFS was the first radio station in Alexander City and was located upstairs in a Main Street building. (Courtesy of MainStreet Organization; photograph by Brooks Studio.)

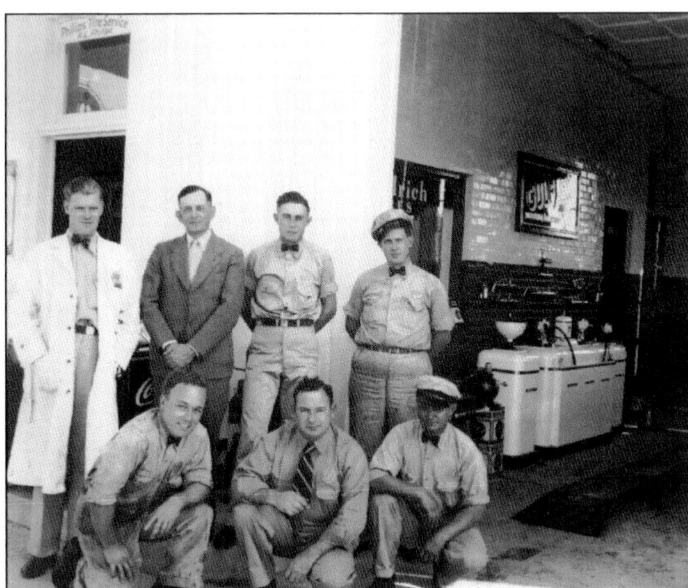

Russell Foshee, owner of the new Gulf service station, poses for a picture with his employees and representatives of the Gulf Oil Company. Shown from left to right are (first row) Abe Phillips (grease control specialist from Gulf Oil), Clifford Thomas (Gulf Oil representative), and unidentified; (second row) unidentified, Carey Harlan, Russell Foshee, and unidentified. (Courtesy of Scotty Foshee.)

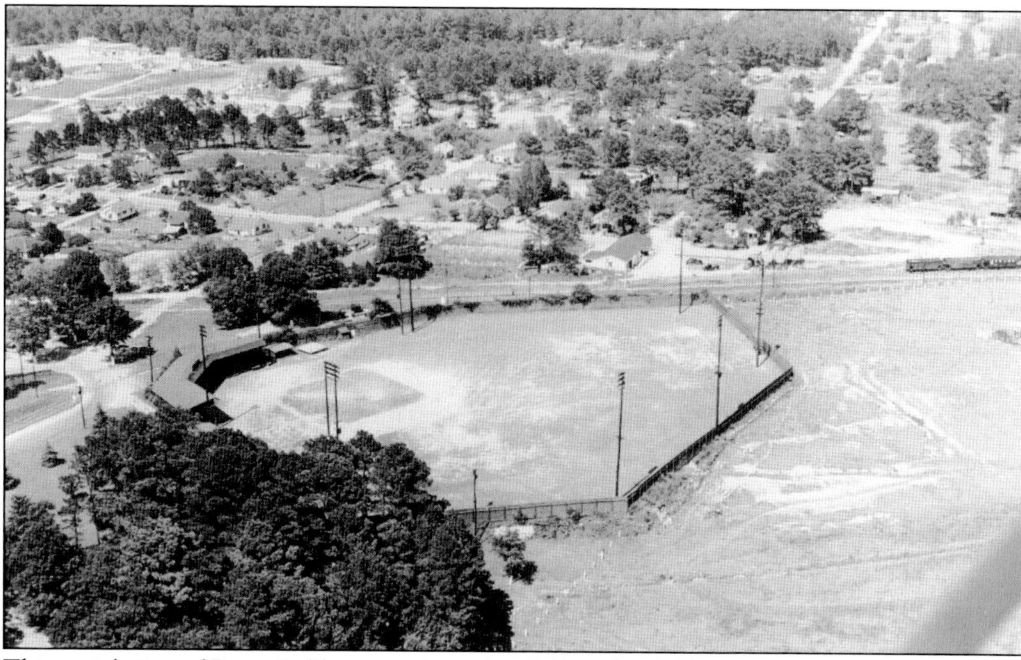

This aerial view of Byers Field was made in the 1950s. The field was named for superintendent Jimmy Byers. The Avondale ball team practiced on the field and hosted games with visiting teams from other Avondale plants. A covered seating area and bleachers were constructed for fans to sit and enjoy baseball games. (Courtesy of Laura Oliver.)

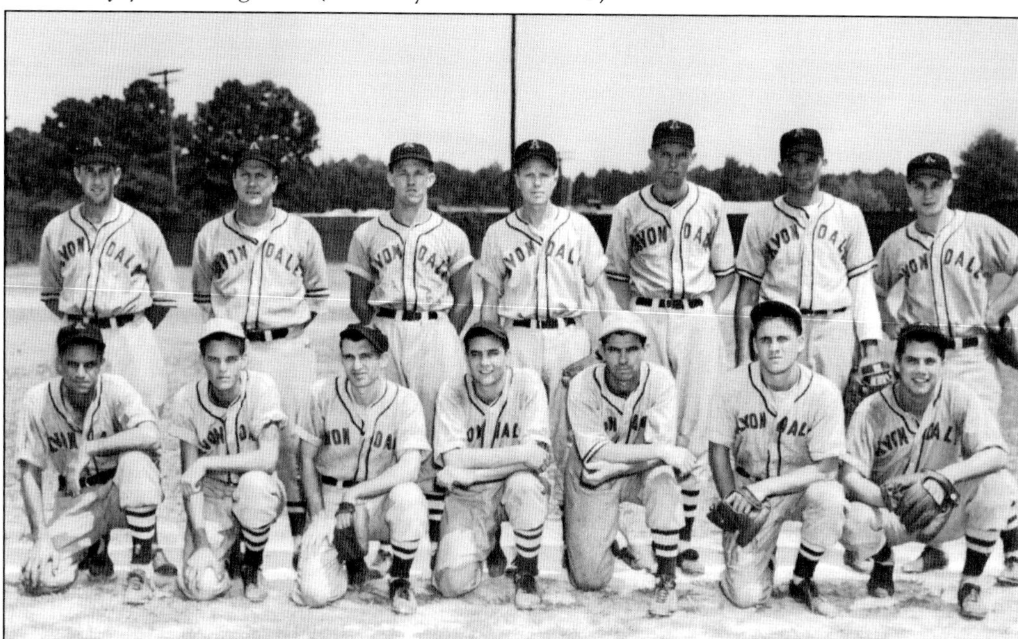

Avondale baseball team members posing for a picture are, from left to right, (first row) Troy Holley, Marlin Holman, Johnny Trussell, Nolen Price, Joe Florine, Doug McGill, and unidentified; (second row) Stanley Sprayberry, James Limbaugh, David McCullough, Elmer Hassett, F.C. Holman, Howard Rhodes, and Jimmy Smith. (Courtesy of Laura Oliver.)

Six

School Days

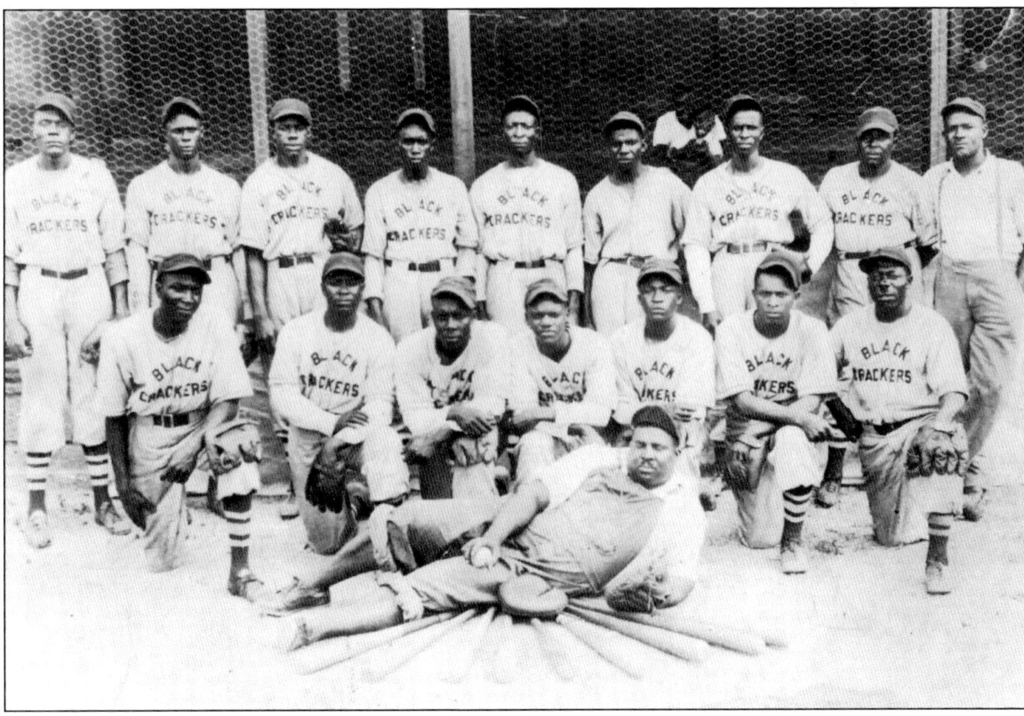

The Black Crackers, comprised of Bevelle employees, was Alexander City's first organized black, baseball team. The winning team, listed on the photograph from left to right, included: (first row) Melton Tucker; (second row) Ross Harris, Steve McIntire, Robert Murry, Que Boleware, Pap ?, J.T. Reese, and Curly William; (third row) Earlie Henderson, Buster Henderson, Eddie Lee, Lindsey Turdis, Sandle Hill, Jab McIntire, John Lindsey, Johnny Reese, Junior Harris, and Jim Brown. One of the Black Crackers' big wins was against the Birmingham Barons and star player Willie Mays. (Courtesy of Mary Wyckoff.)

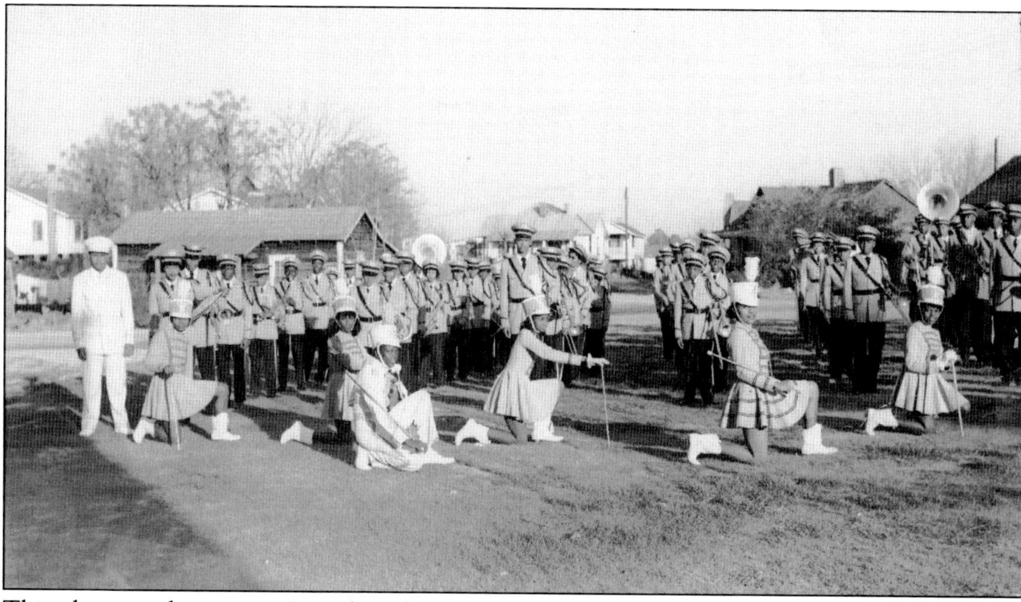

This photograph captures Laurel High School majorettes and the band in a dress rehearsal for a game. Band director Harry Sweetwine stands at front left. The picture was made in the early 1950s, before integration of schools. Benjamin Russell High School was the first Alexander City High School that served all high school students—children from Laurel and from both Russell and Avondale mill villages. (Courtesy of MainStreet Organization; photograph by Robert Graves.)

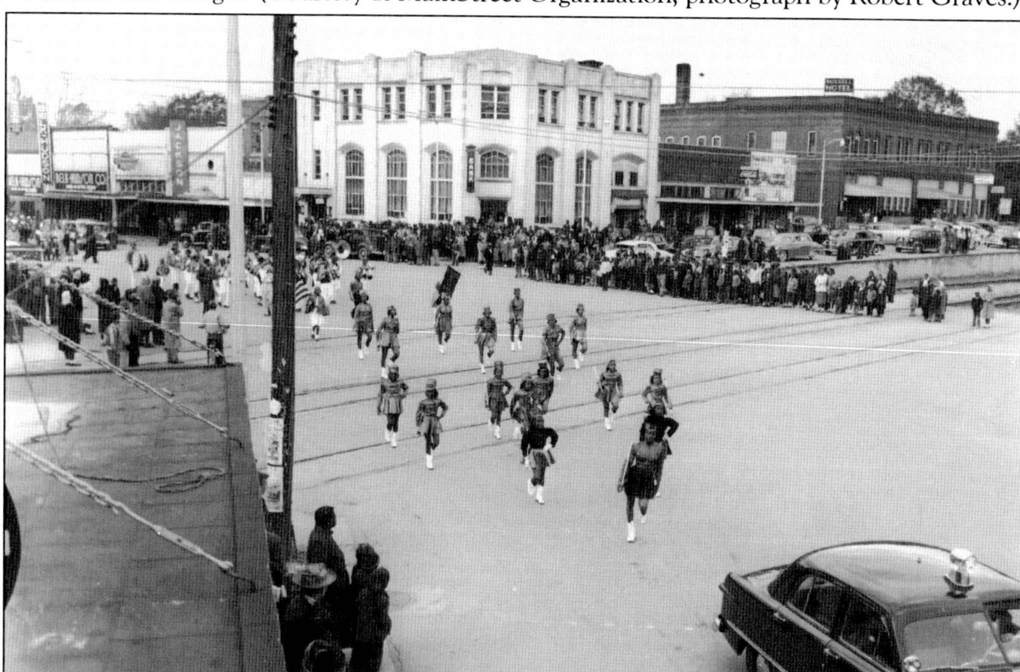

With the Alexander City Bank and Russell Hotel behind them, the Laurel High School majorettes march over the railroad tracks that run through the center of town. Laurel High School was constructed in 1952 and renovated in 1970. (Courtesy of MainStreet Organization; photograph by Robert Graves.)

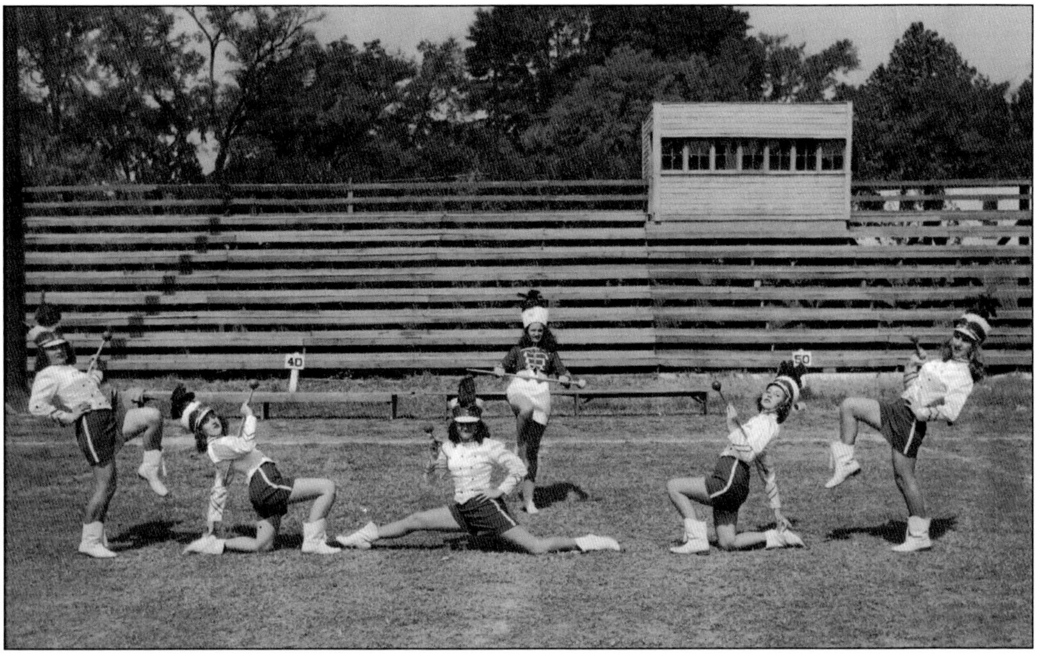

Alexander City majorettes practice their routine at the Hamp Lyon Stadium. The structure at the top of the bleachers was reserved for newscasters and special guests. From left to right are majorettes Gay Ingram, Gay Blair, Hilda Waites, Betty Tate, Betty Jo Grant, and Bobbie Bishop. (Courtesy of MainStreet Organization.)

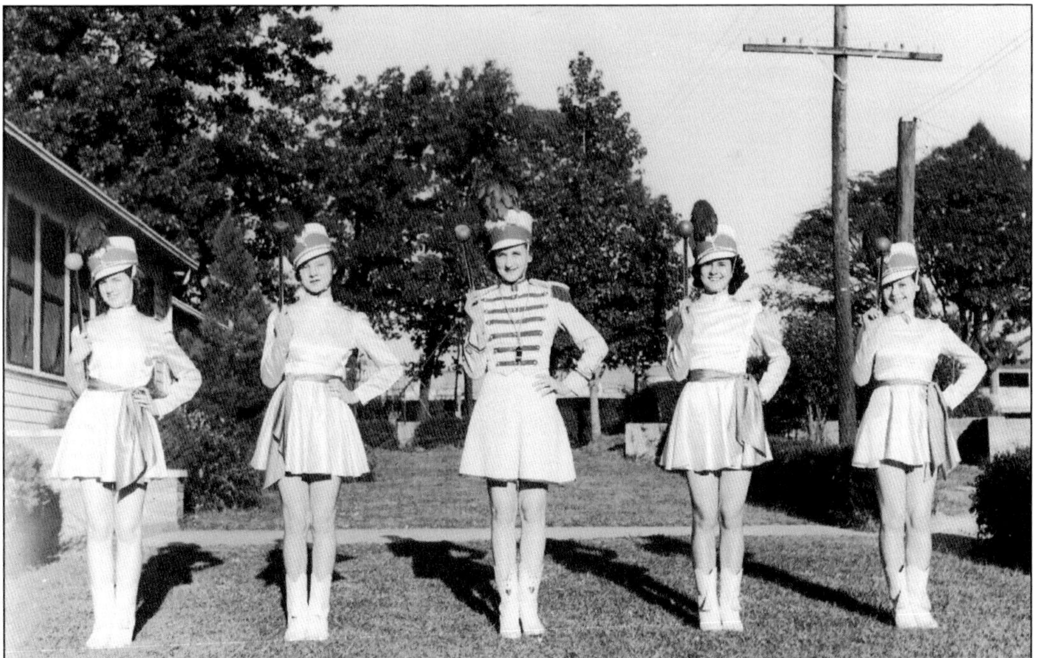

Bevelle majorettes meet for a practice and photograph session in preparation for an upcoming game in the 1950s. From left to right are Mary F. Scott, Billy Wayne Ray, Jean Boos, Martha Pike, and Virginia Cooley. (Courtesy of Laura Oliver.)

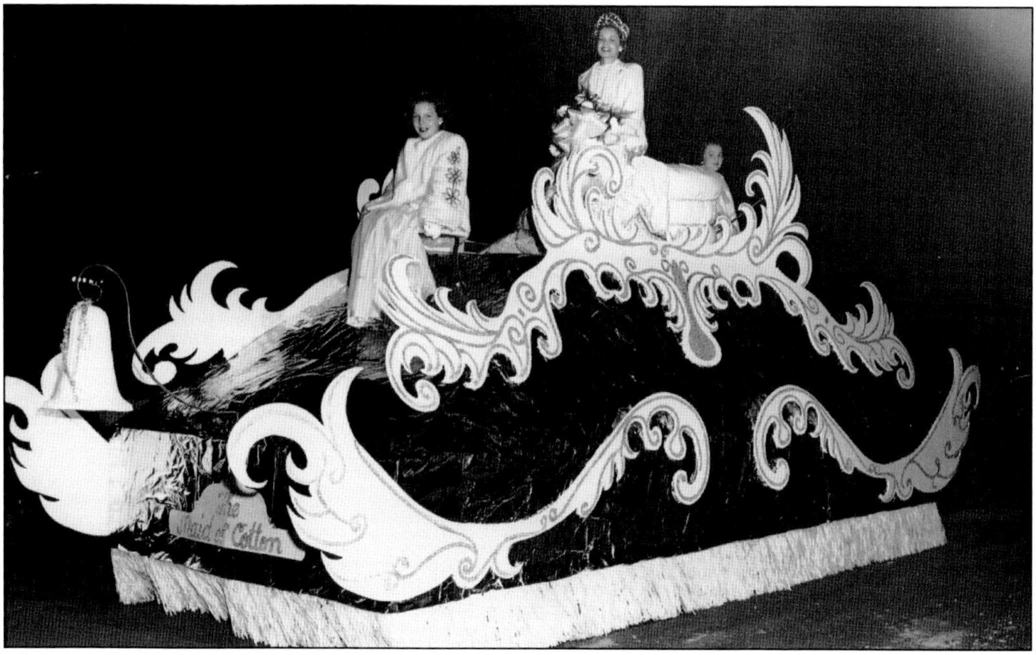

The 1950 National Maid of Cotton, Ann Adams, rides in the Alexander City Christmas parade while surrounded by her court. Each year, a county Maid of Cotton was chosen from a group of eligible girls. Ann Adams represented Tuscaloosa in the state competition, won the title "Alabama Maid of Cotton," and went on to win the national title. All participants wore dresses sewn from cotton material, consistent with the competition rules. They later modeled their dresses at a fashion show for family and local supporters. (Courtesy of MainStreet Organization.)

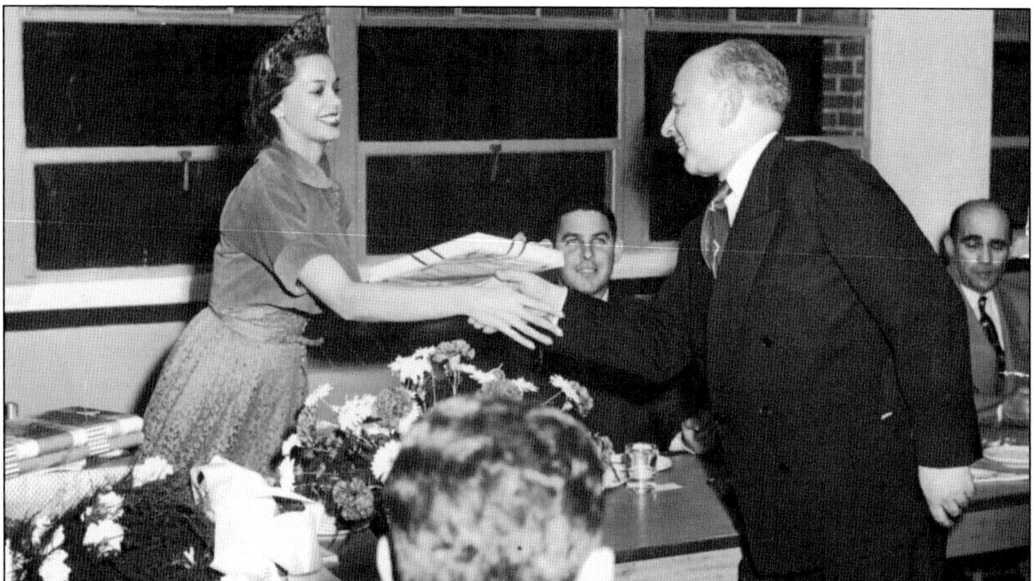

The 1950 National Maid of Cotton, Ann Adams, receives congratulations from Ralph Frohsin Sr. Attendees include Bud Hodo (left) and Joe H. Robinson, seated in the background, during a civic ceremony in Alexander City held in Adams's honor. (Courtesy of MainStreet Organization.)

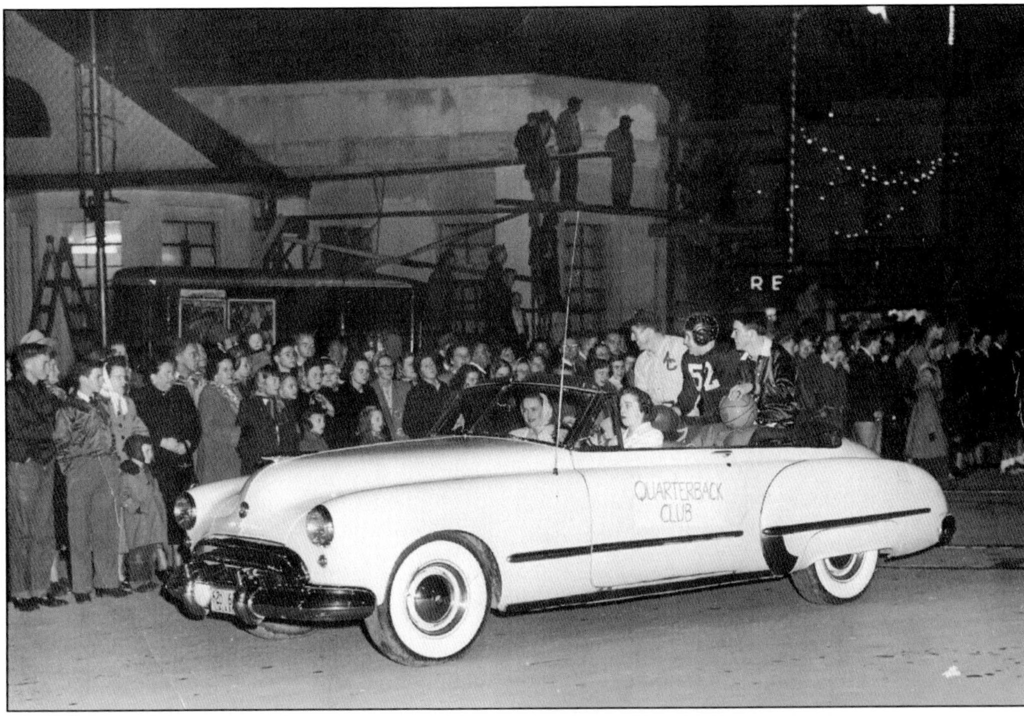

Sponsored by the Quarterback Club, football player Royce Jay Bird Weddle (left) and Merrell Hill (far right) ride in a car on loan from a local dealership for this parade in the 1950s. Wooden structures were erected to provide elevated places from which to view the Christmas parade. Local organizations, such as the Kiwanis and the Civitans, had their own floats but also helped to sponsor student organizations, such as the Junior Civitans. (Courtesy of MainStreet Organization.)

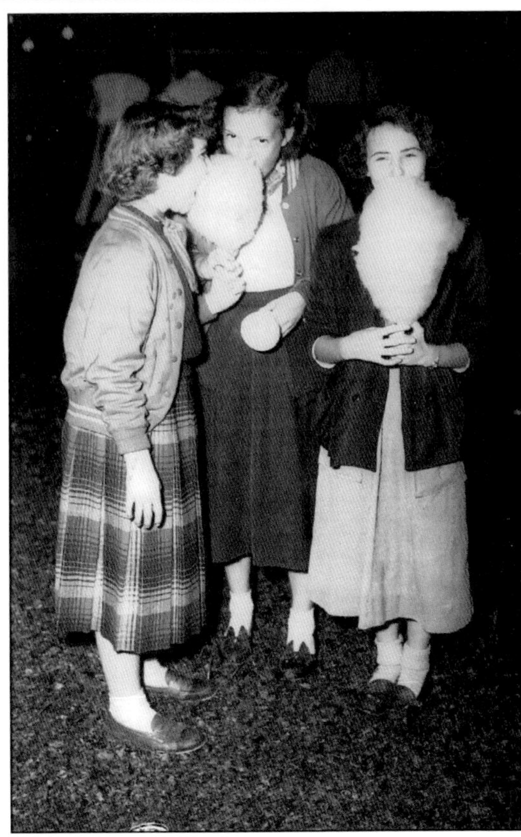

The arrival of a carnival was a special occasion for the city with the many activities and treats that were available. Cotton candy was a favorite. The carnivals usually rolled into town each June and pitched tents on the fairgrounds, the present-day site of the Benjamin Russell High School and Bennie Russell athletic field. Children saved their pennies throughout the year to spend on the merry-go-round, the Bullet, Scream Machine, and Ferris wheel. They tried their luck at pitching pennies, aiming to ring carnival glass bowls and take home a prize. (Courtesy of MainStreet Organization.)

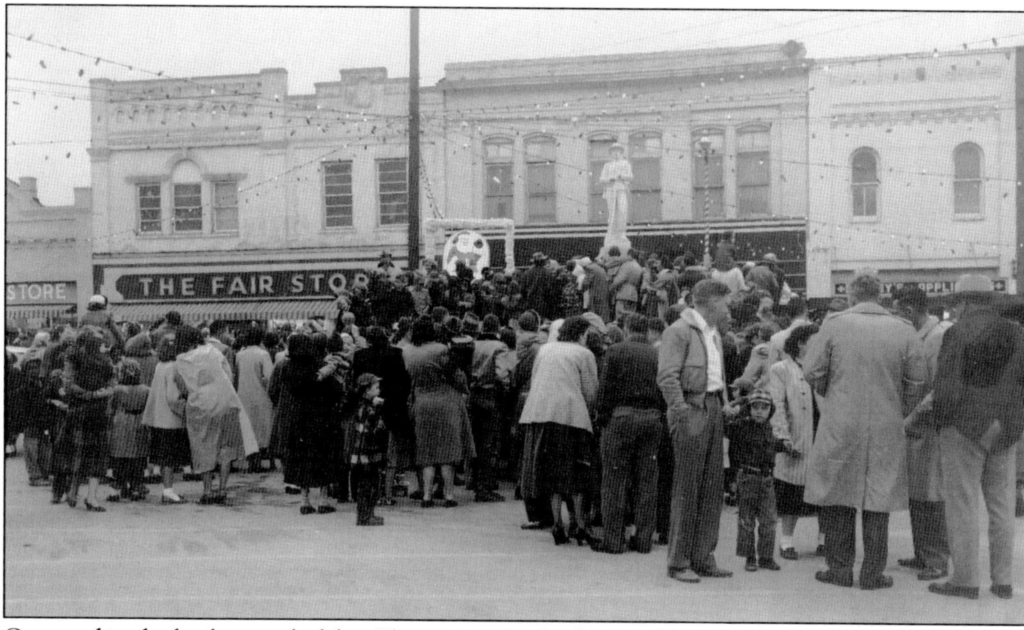

Captured in the background of this Christmas parade photograph are the Fair Store and its bargain basement—favorite shopping places for local citizens. Dave "Mr. Pat" Cohen came to Alexander City from Lithuania. In 1913, he peddled his wares door to door before opening a clothing store on Broad Street. Two sons, Leon and Oscar, continued operating the business for half a century. (Courtesy of Jane McLeod.)

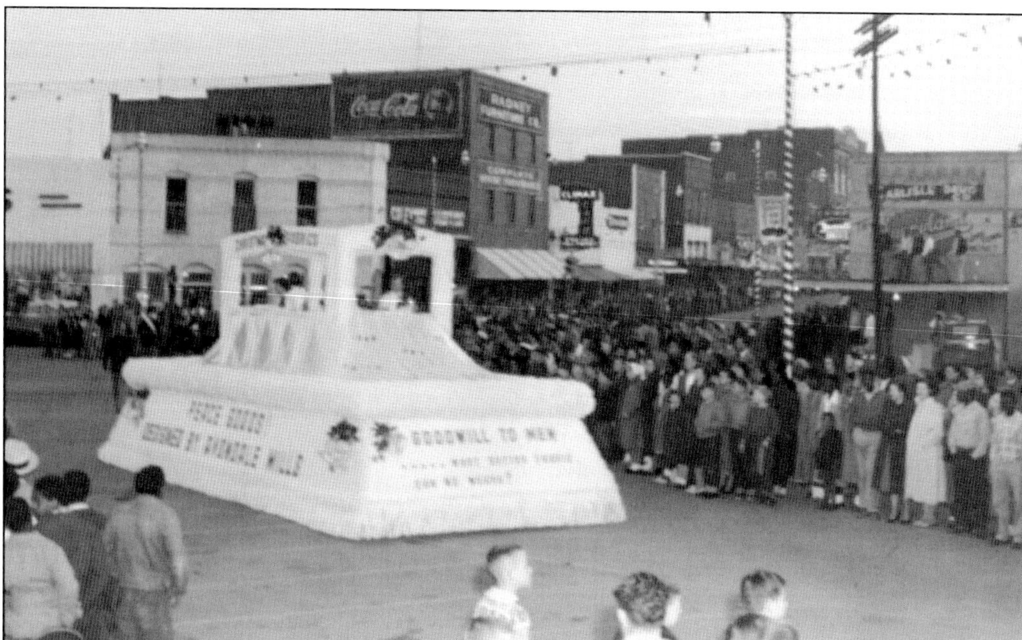

Christmas floats in the 1940s and 1950s were elaborate. Students, organizations, and businesses worked for months on their floats. Crowds from neighboring communities lined the streets as they waited for the sound of drums from the band leading the parade. Young children waited anxiously for the final float that held Santa in a high snow sleigh. (Courtesy of Fletcher Adamson.)

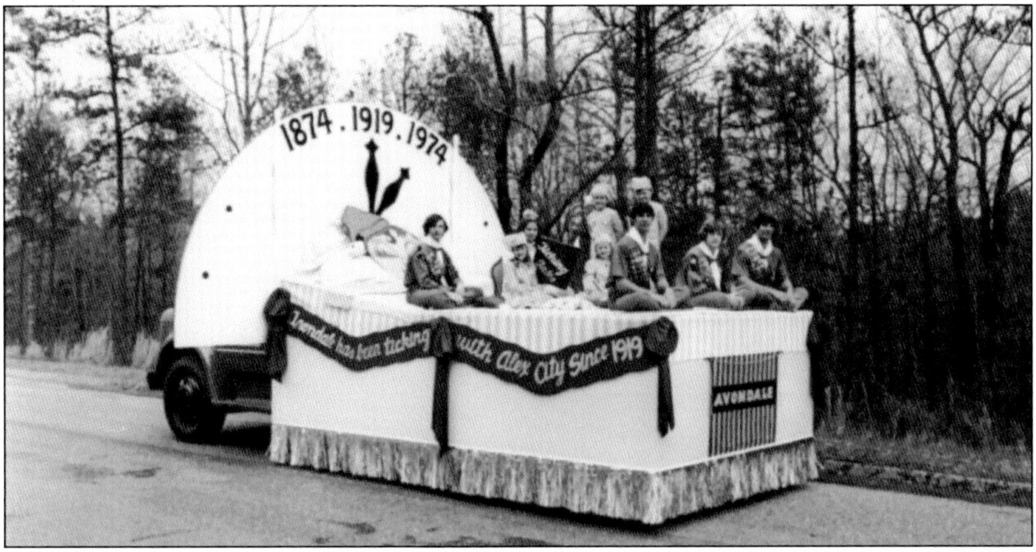

Avondale has been ticking with Alexander City since 1919. The ticking theme is reflected in the children's sleepwear and garment covering the float bed. The year 1874 marks the change of the town's name from Youngsville to Alexander City, and 1974 marks the year of the parade celebrating Alexander City's 100-year anniversary. Bevelle Scout Troop No. 67 is shown. Twins Larry and Barry Boddie are seen on each end of the float directly above "Avondale." (Courtesy of Laura Oliver.)

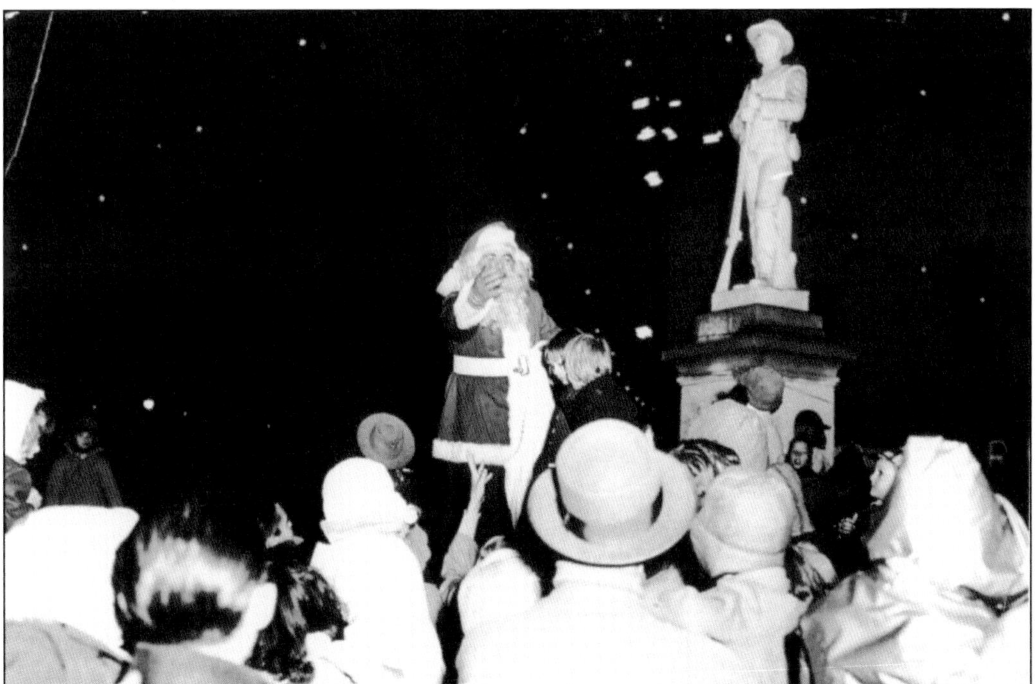

Santa Claus stands on the platform near the Confederate soldier statue, throwing candy to the crowd. He listens to the children tell what they want for Christmas and asks if they have been good or bad. Clutching a handful of candy, each child rejoins an awaiting family nearby. (Courtesy of MainStreet Organization.)

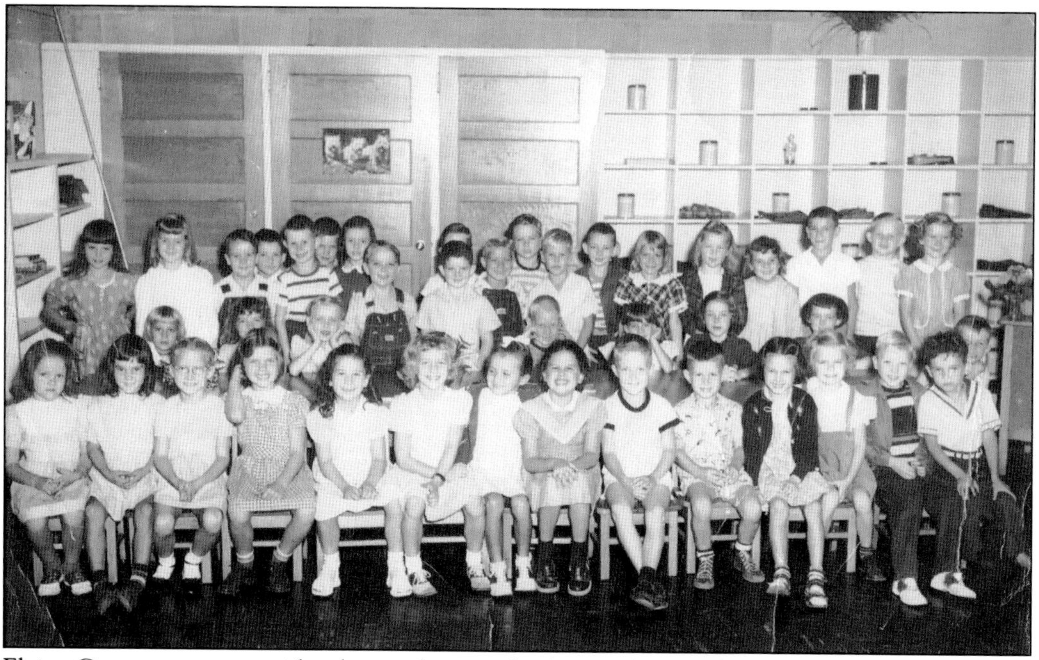

Elaine Cameron appears with other students in the first grade. Mrs. Ralph Blythe was the teacher. In the 1949–1950 school year, one of the legislators wanted his little girl to start to school early, so the age cutoff was set back to January to qualify her. The result was an enormous first-grade class. (Courtesy of Eleanor Carlisle; photograph by Gale Little.)

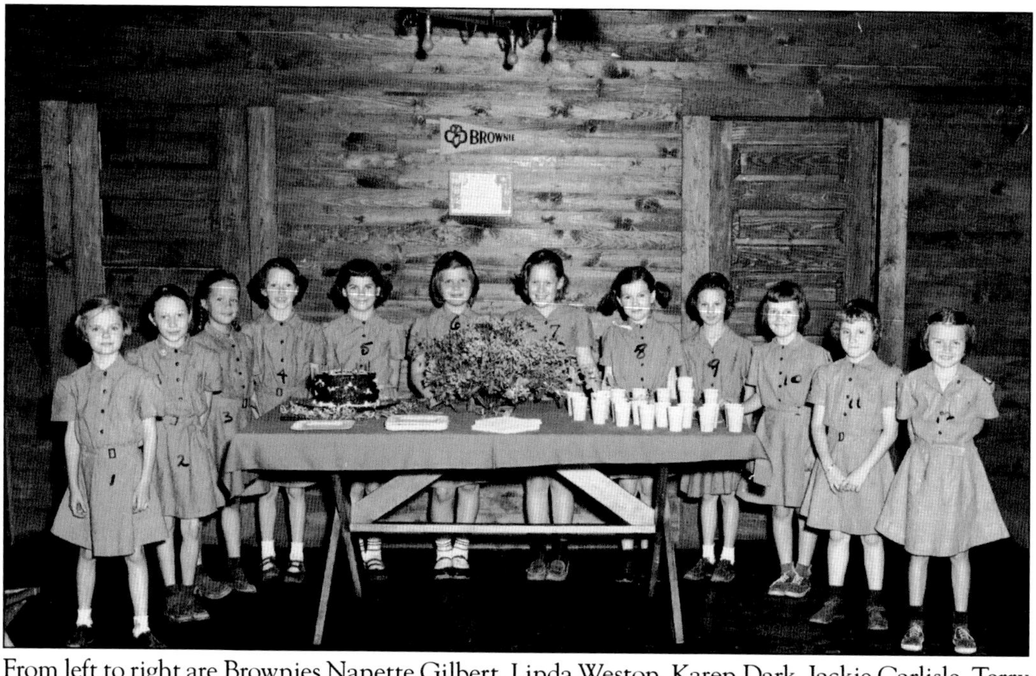

From left to right are Brownies Nanette Gilbert, Linda Weston, Karen Dark, Jackie Carlisle, Terry Yeargan, Elaine Cameron, Patricia Henderson, Nancy Wilbanks, Delia Duncan, Susan Hunter, Nell Askew, and Roberta Alison. The group met at Elizabeth Alison's Elkahatchee Creek cabin in 1951 for a combined troop meeting and birthday party. (Courtesy of Eleanor Carlisle.)

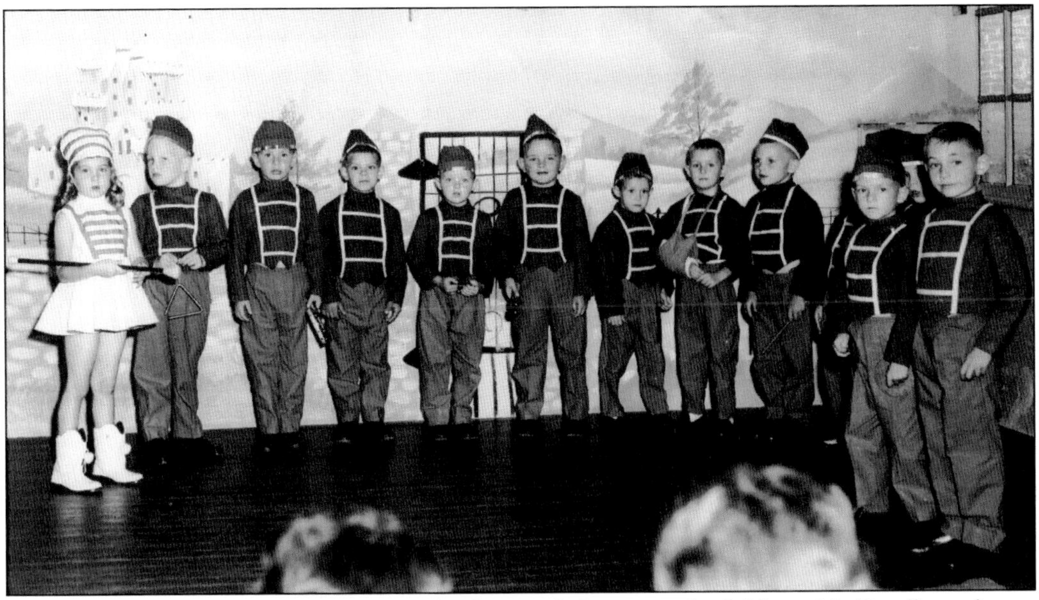

Mary Holbrook was employed by the Comer family to teach dancing to the children of the Bevelle employees. She worked with their dance routines to prepare them for the annual inspection programs. The costumes were designed to reflect the theme of the play, which sometimes portrayed book characters. Toy soldiers are lined up on stage for a preformance of "Through the Garden Gate." (Courtesy of Laura Oliver.)

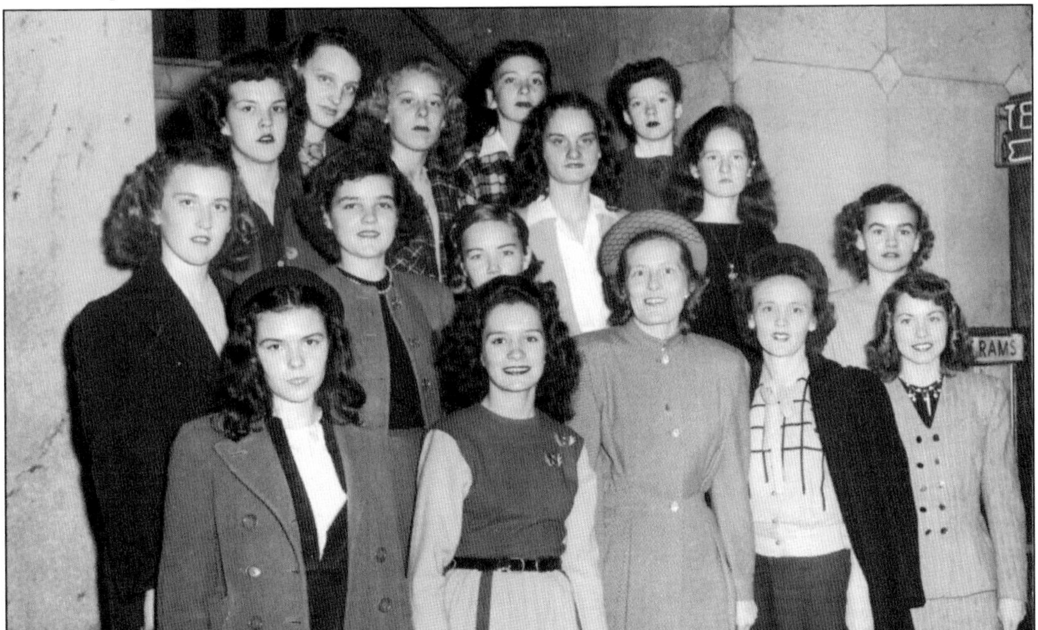

Mary Holbrook took members of her dance class on a tour to perform at conferences in other cities, such as Chattanooga and New Orleans. Pictured from left to right are (first row) Monnie Jo Price, Helen Blankenship, Mary Hallbrook, Lucille Box, and Jo Strickland; (second row) Eva Clyde Jones, Ealene Price, Jean Strickland, and Frankie Nell Ray; (third row) Sue McCollough, Jeanette Rape, Lorene Stephens, and Marie Stephens; (fourth row) Luvenia Dykes, Wilma Prophitt, and Patti Hickman. (Courtesy of Jane McLeod.)

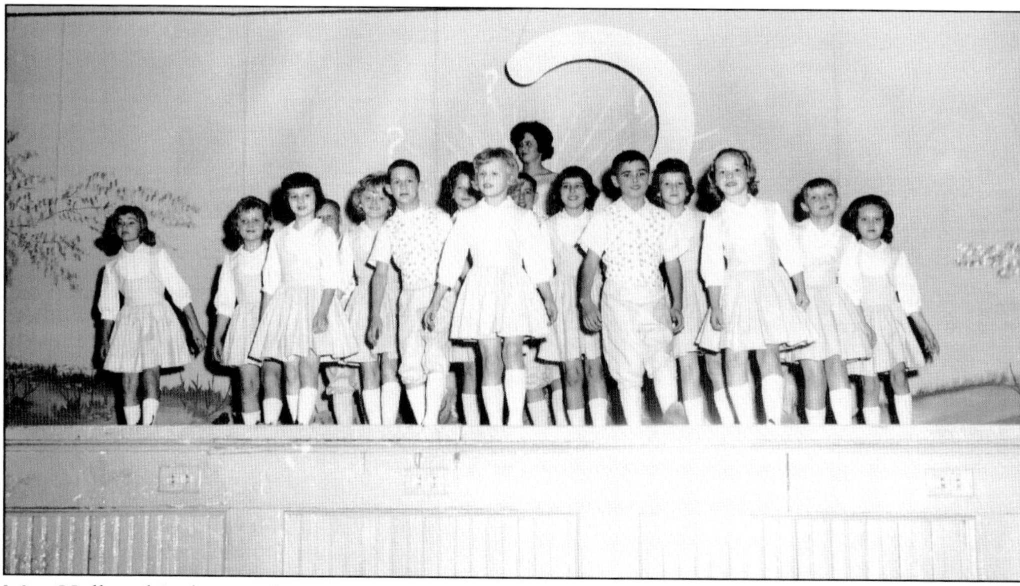

Miss Holbrook's class performs at an annual Bevelle inspection program. Students include, from left to right, Rhonda Thornton, Anita Cromer, Sue Price, James Hand, Patricia Kirk, Terry Price, Jackie Fuller, Teresa Baker, Randall Stephens, Kathy Nester, Bobby Johnson, Barbara Patterson, Mona Peppers, Carolyn Blanks, and Kathy Prickett. (Courtesy of Laura Oliver.)

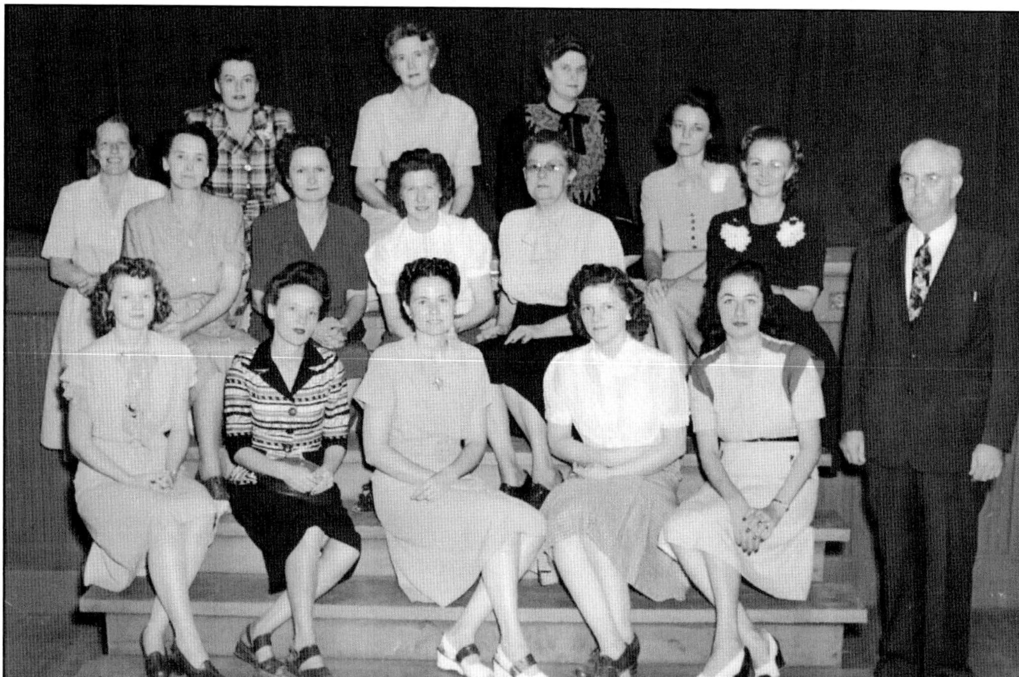

T.D. Kimbrough, principal of Bevelle School, stands by his faculty. From left to right are (first row) Mary Helen Thompson, Lucille Box, Gussie Mae Kennedy, Mary Campbell, and Vera Nabors Harris; (second row) Mary Hallbrook, Gaynell Turner Tankersley, Lucille Carlisle, Majorie Jarrell, Sarah Dark, and Mable Mason; (third row) Josephine Harris, Maude Ford, Mary Kimbrough, and Pauline Weddle. (Courtesy of Jane McLeod.)

Appearing in a Bevelle operetta in the 1940s, Helen Blankenship stands in front of the large basket of cotton printed on a poster. Helen's siblings include Freddy, Dorothy, and Bernard Blankenship. (Courtesy of Laura Oliver.)

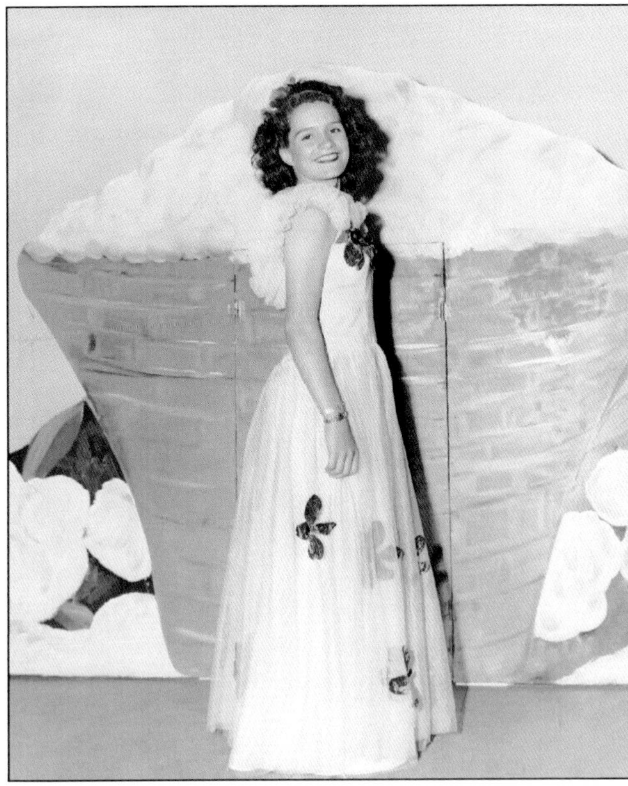

The 1937 Bevelle Trophy winning team was comprised of, from left to right, Fred Boos, Roscoe Slagle, Red Payne, David Long, Troy Holley, Phillip Avery, Vercho Carter, Bill Evans (captain), and Robert Graves (coach). (Courtesy of Jane McLeod.)

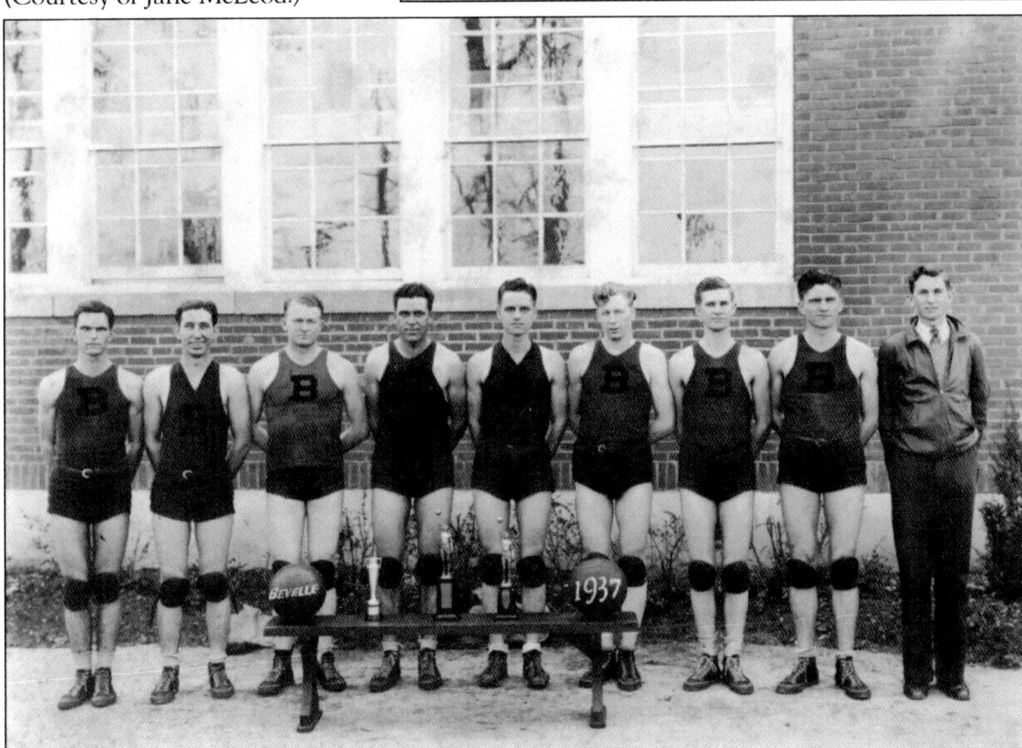

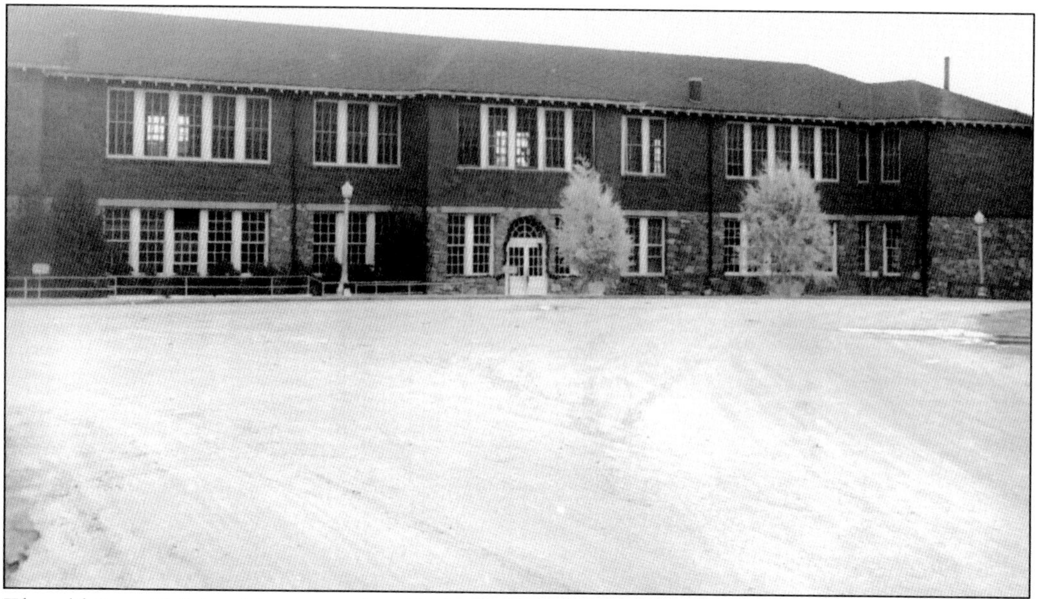

The old Russell School is pictured in 1925. The building was behind the Russell Mills plant and near the Russell Church, which was comprised of Baptists and Methodists in its early days of serving the Russell village community. (Courtesy of Robert Martin; photograph by Robert Graves.)

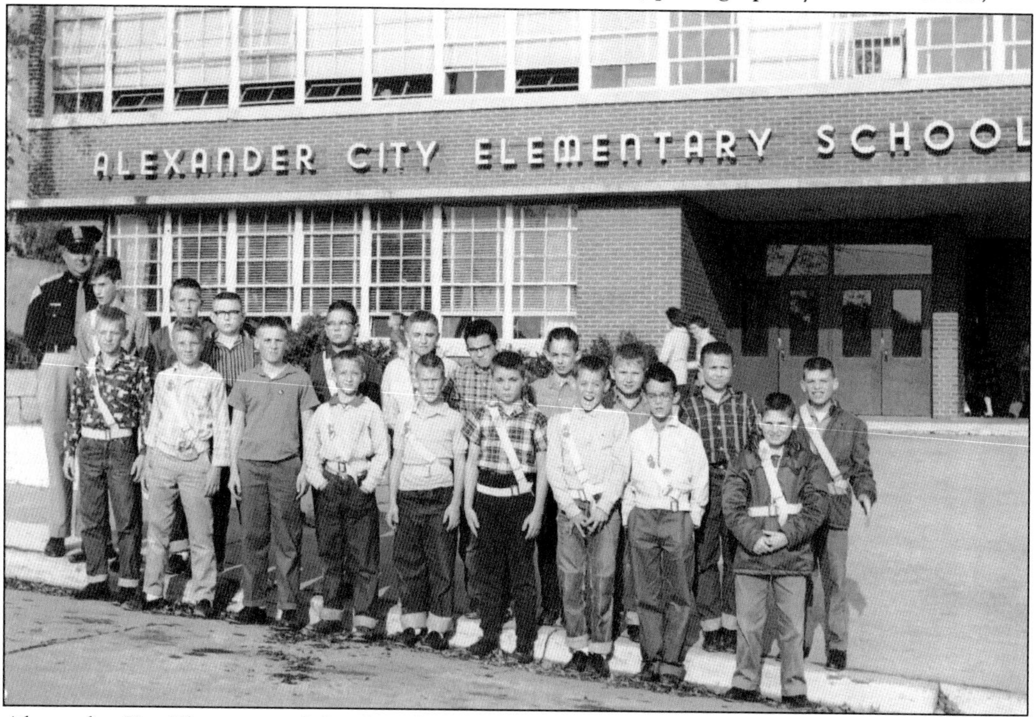

Alexander City Elementary School students pictured from left to right are (first row) Lee Jackson, Lewis Lamberth Jr., Walton Jackson, Mike Jordan, John Meacham, Buster Warren, Jim Hodo, John Coley, and Larry Wedgworth; (second row) John Petrey, Mike Duncan, unidentified, Jack Smith, Chesley Neely, Dannie Culberson, Bill Watley, unidentified, Tommy Gunn, and Ben G. Coken. (Courtesy of Sandra Wilson.)

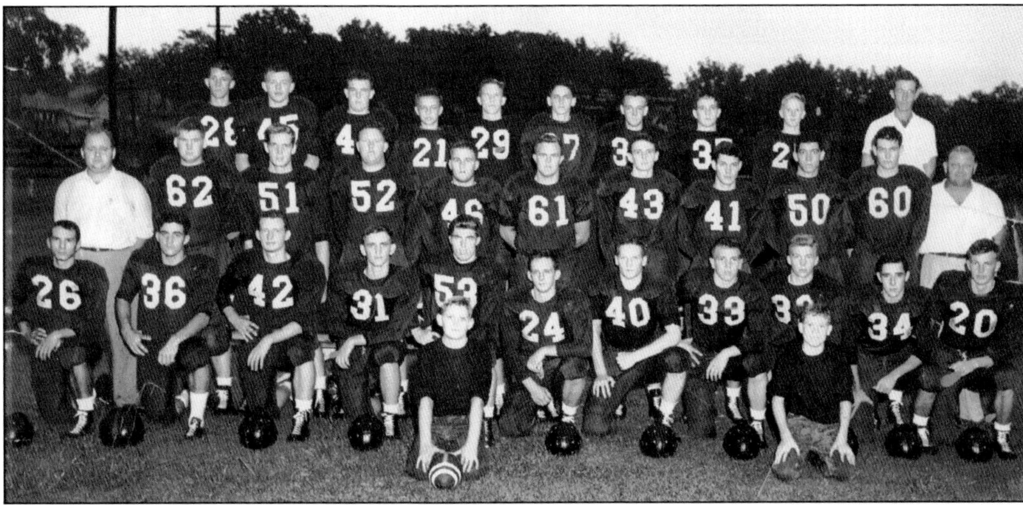

The 1951 Benjamin Russell High School football team lines up for a yearbook photograph. The mascots at front are Jimmy Carter (left) and Ronnie Smith. From left to right are (first row) Frank Foy, Glen Brown, Charles Wilson, Charles Huey, Merrell Hill, Jimmy Smith, Joe Tom Roberts, Thomas Davis, Dwight Carlisle, Fletcher Adamson, and Lawrence Meadows; (second row) coach Smith, Bill Blankenship, Louis Veazey, Bennie Self, Talmon Davis, Versie Smith, Billy Vaughn Headley, Eugene Britton, James Jones, Roy Forbus, and coach Hamp Lyon; (third row) Charles Smith, Jimmy "Red" Phillips, Tommy Ogletree, Johnny Thompson, Jack Duncan, Don Holley, Gerald Joiner, J.H. Guthrie, Merrell "Ba Ba" Turner, and coach Murray Hammond. (Courtesy of Sandra Wilson.)

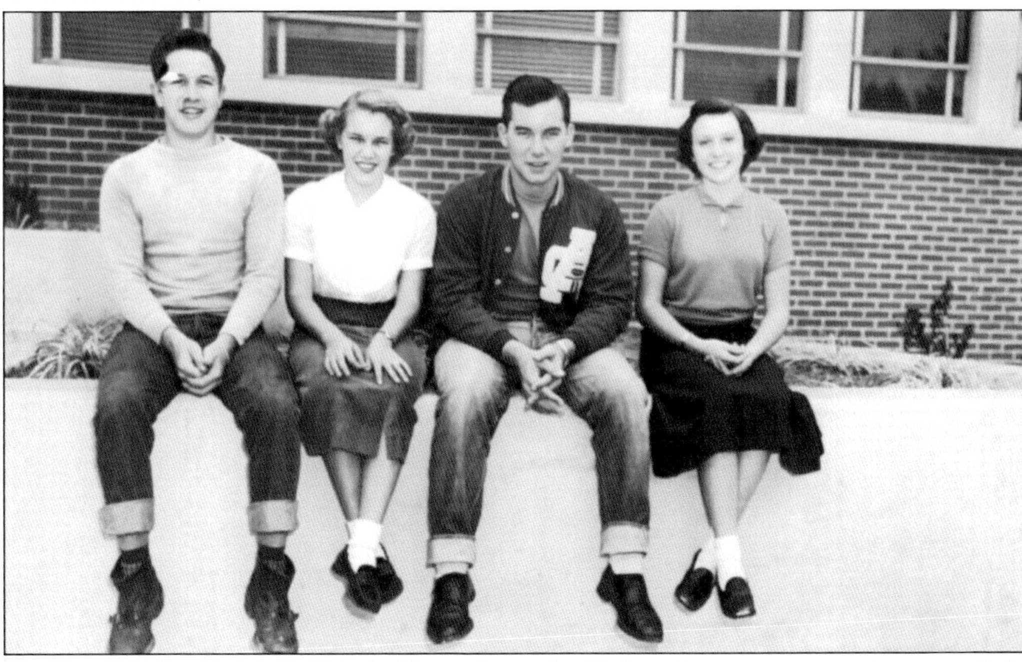

The sports jacket, penny loafers, bobby socks, and rolled up dungarees are reminiscent of the James Dean era. The four friends posing for a picture outside the Benjamin Russell classroom are, from left to right, Buddy Phillips, Amanda Simpson, Kenneth Johnson, and Virginia Shaw. (Courtesy of Sandra Wilson.)

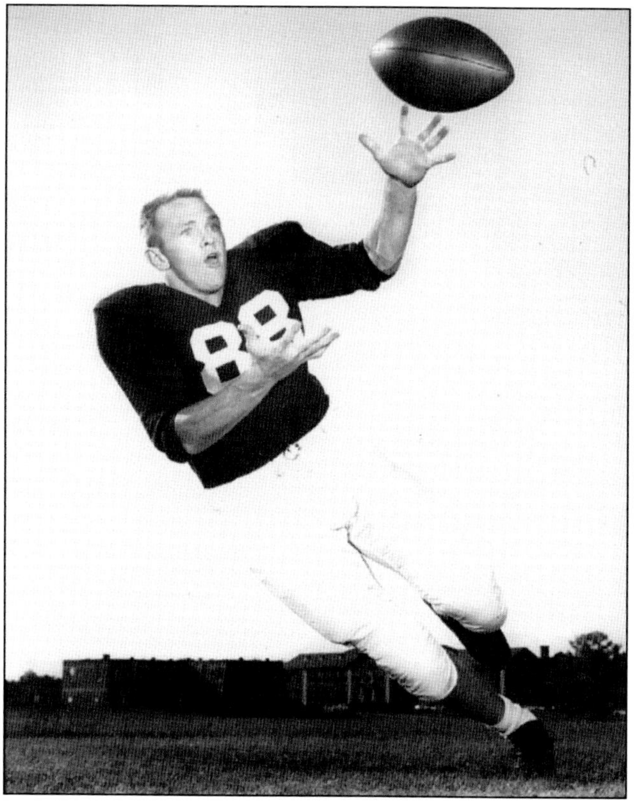

Jimmy "Red" Phillips, was wide receiver for Auburn University and cocaptain of Auburn's 1957 national championship team. He was selected as the best right end in the nation, setting a record for votes from 21 All-American selectors. After the 1958 National Football League (NFL) draft, Phillips played for the Los Angeles Rams and the Minnesota Vikings from 1958 to 1967. (Courtesy of Beverly P. Henry.)

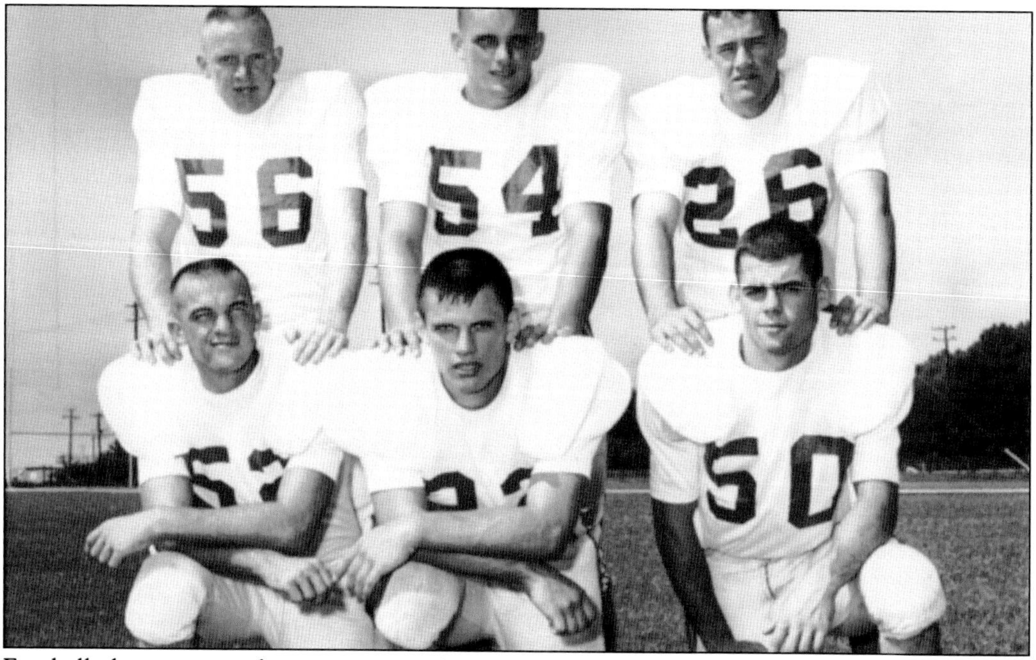

Football players posing for a picture are, from left to right, (first row) Mack Brown, Bill Sharpe, and Russell ?; (second row) Evans Wilson, David Ray, and Lynwood Strickland. (Courtesy of MainStreet Organization.)

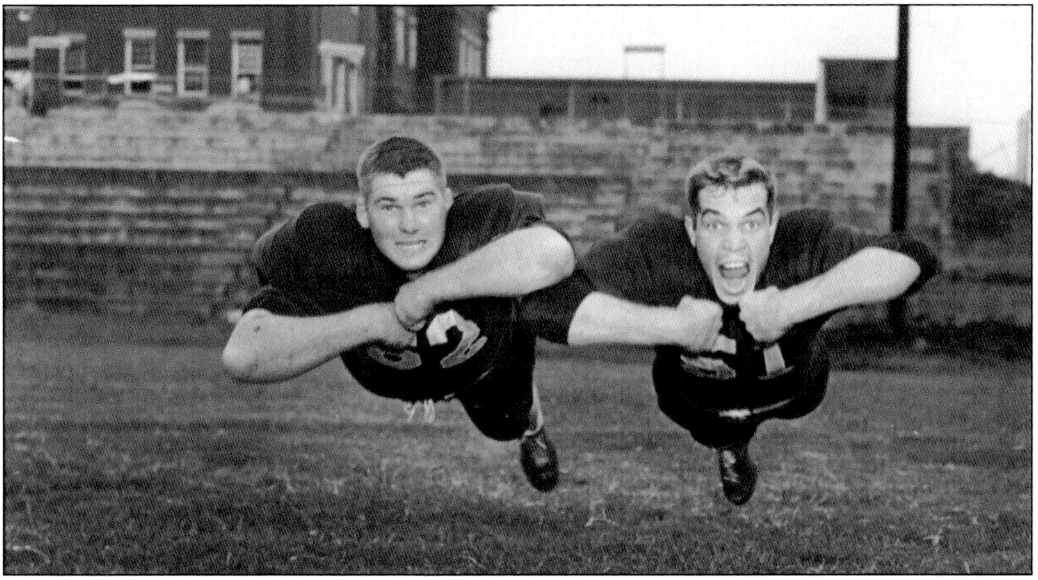

Displaying their athletic prowess for the photographer are football players Bill Blankenship (left) and Louis Veazey. Hamp Lyon Stadium was named in honor of S.H. (Hamp) Lyon, who was coach at the Alexander City High School and Benjamin Russell High School before being named athletic director for the school from 1937 to 1972. (Courtesy of MainStreet Organization.)

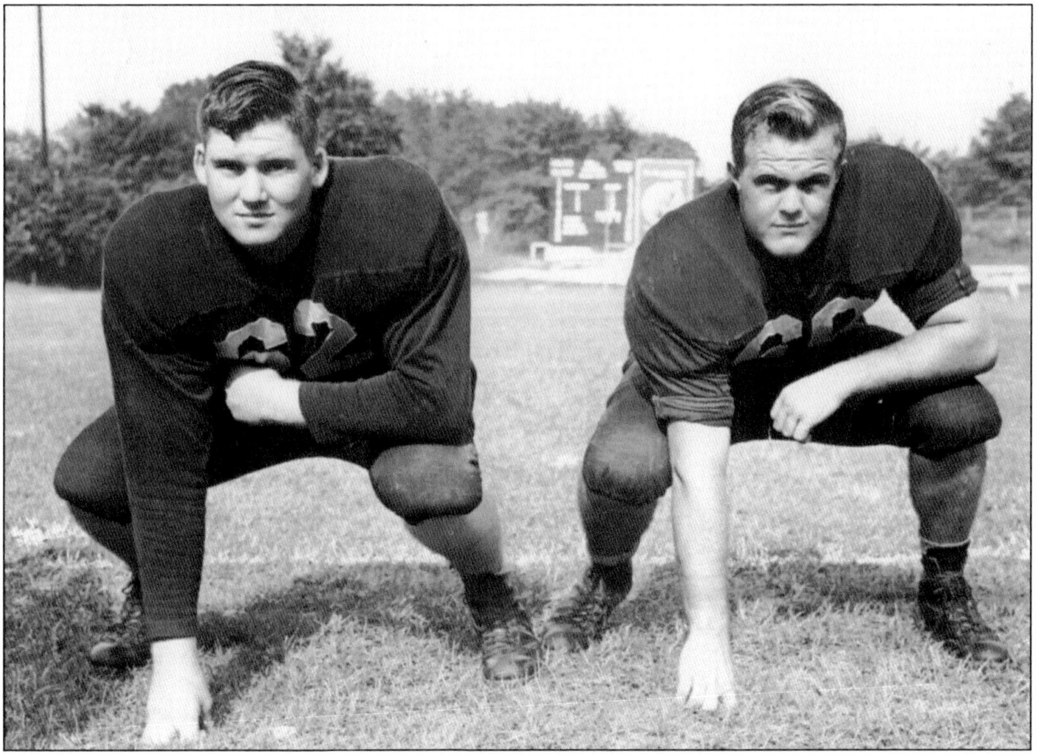

With the scoreboard behind them, Alexander City football players Bill Blankenship (left) and Versie Smith are ready to play ball at the old Hamp Lyon Stadium in the 1950s. The Alexander City High School was built on "The Hill" in 1909. (Courtesy of MainStreet Organization.)

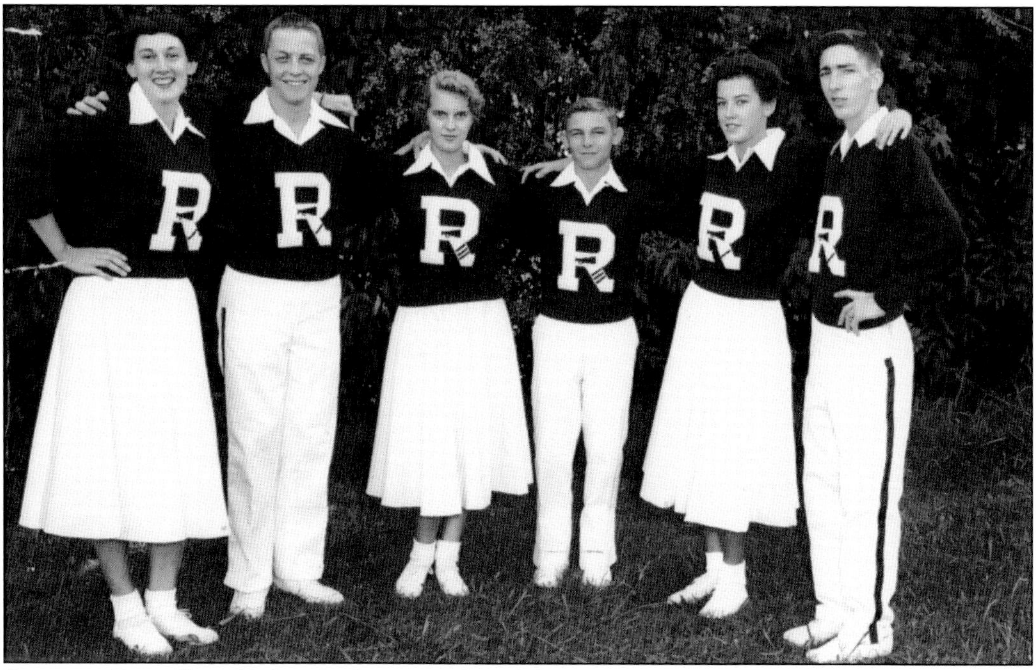

Benjamin Russell's 1956 cheerleaders were, from left to right, June Smith, Marion Neighbors, Jean Segrest, Jerry Oneil, Doris Miller, and Charles McLeod. (Courtesy of Sandra Wilson.)

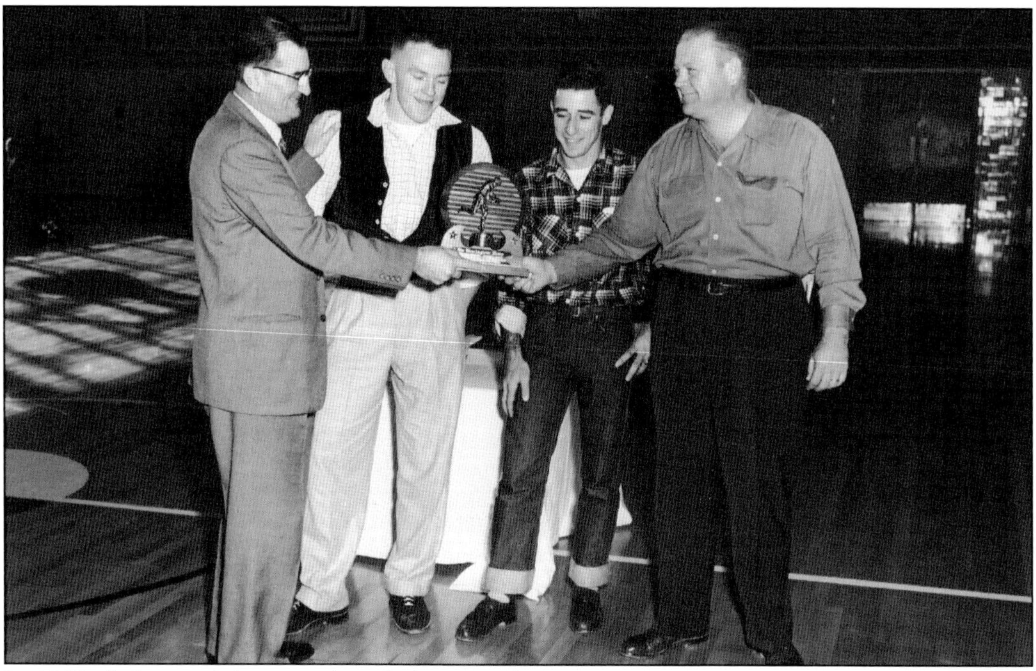

In 1953, (left to right) an unidentified *Birmingham News* representative, Jimmy "Red" Phillips (1957 Auburn All-American), Fletcher Adamson, and Hamp Lyon were among those celebrating Benjamin Russell High School's state championship in the AA division of Alabama high schools. The *Birmingham News* presented the school with the trophy to commemorate the championship. (Courtesy of Fletcher Adamson.)

Seven

ORGANIZATIONS

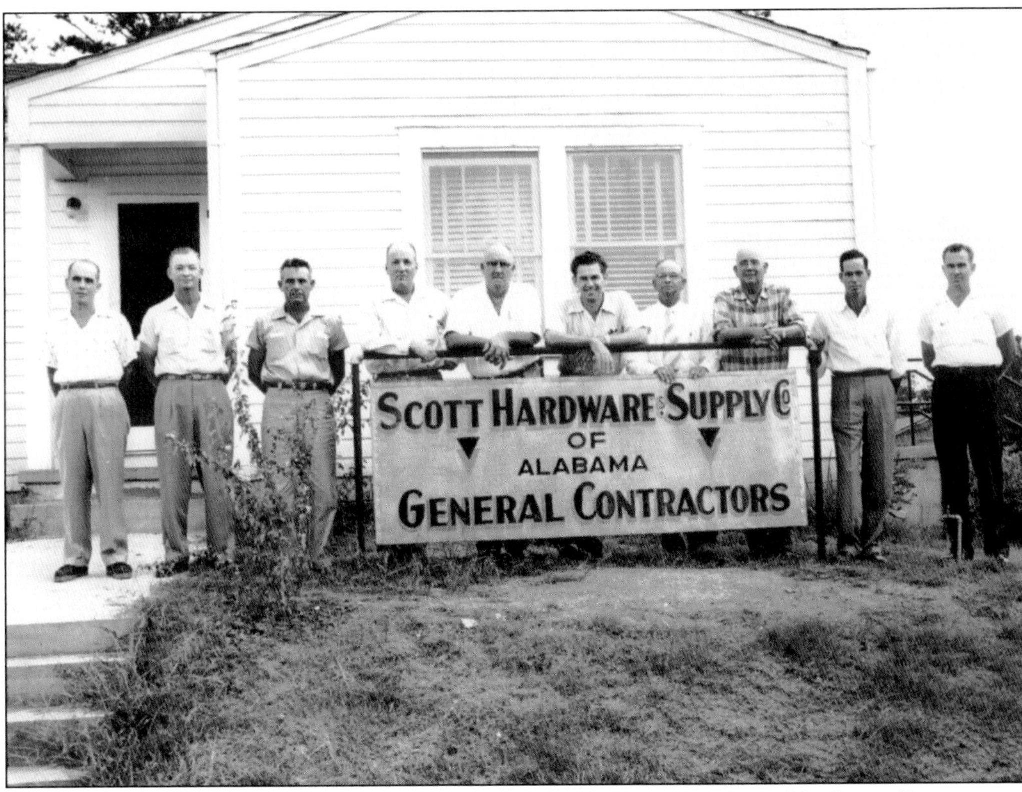

Before large chain stores made their inroad into the local commerce, Scott Hardware Construction Company, located on Scott Road, was owned and operated by the Scott family. The business was a favorite shopping place for builders with large construction contracts, small home repair projects, and general maintenance jobs. From left to right in this 1950s picture are ? Yates, ? Yates, Joe Locke, Claude Chappell, Carey Newman, Emmett Scott, Mr. Grice, Clyde Britton, unidentified, and Joe Scott. (Courtesy of Sandra Wilson.)

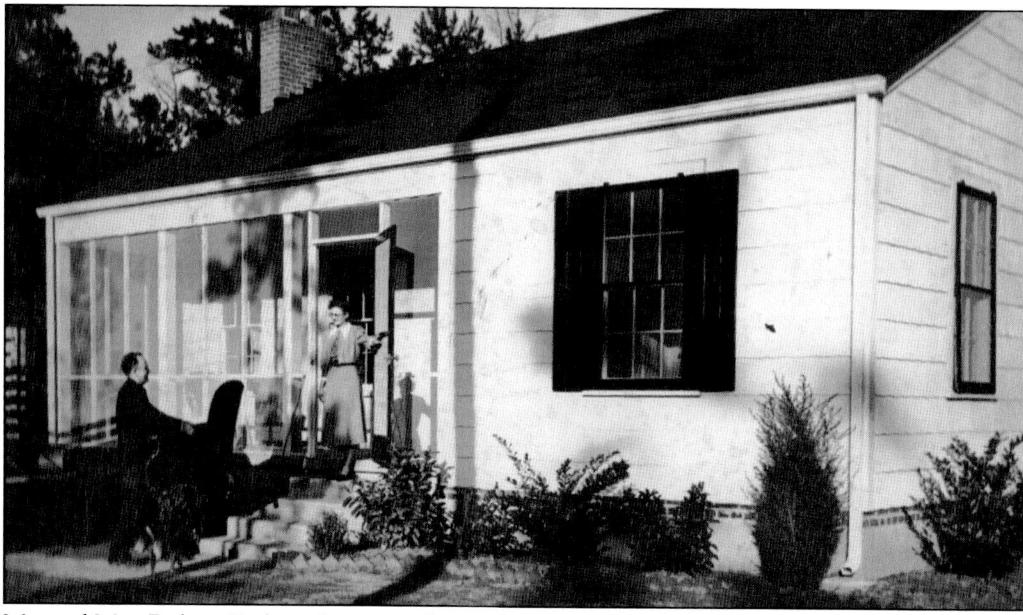

Mr. and Mrs. Robert Forbus, shown in this 1950s picture, were the first couple to move into the Russell Springhill subdivision. (Courtesy of Jacob Henderson.)

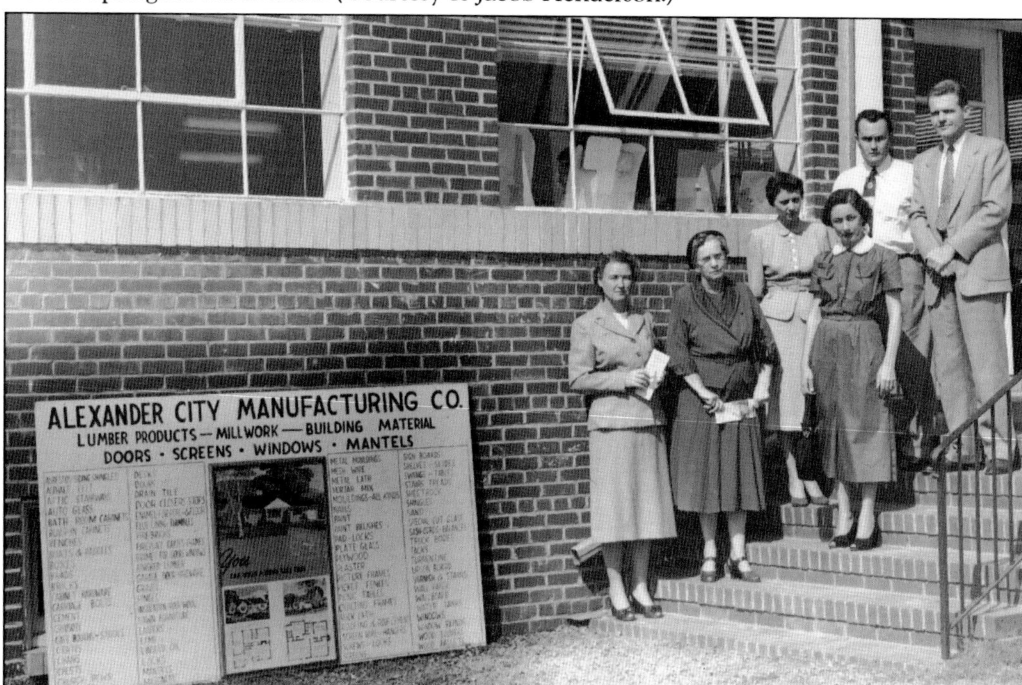

In a 1950s advertisement of the Alexander City Manufacturing Company, Alexander City High School faculty and workers line the building steps. From left to right are (first row, closest to the building) unidentified, Lucy Page Fuller (BRHS teacher), Georgia Darden (secretary), Byron Causey (teacher); (second row) Vera Nabors Harris (teacher) and S.C. Doss (principal). The sign lists diverse products related to constructing and furnishing homes, from desks and doors to benches and lawn furniture. (Courtesy of Sandra Wilson.)

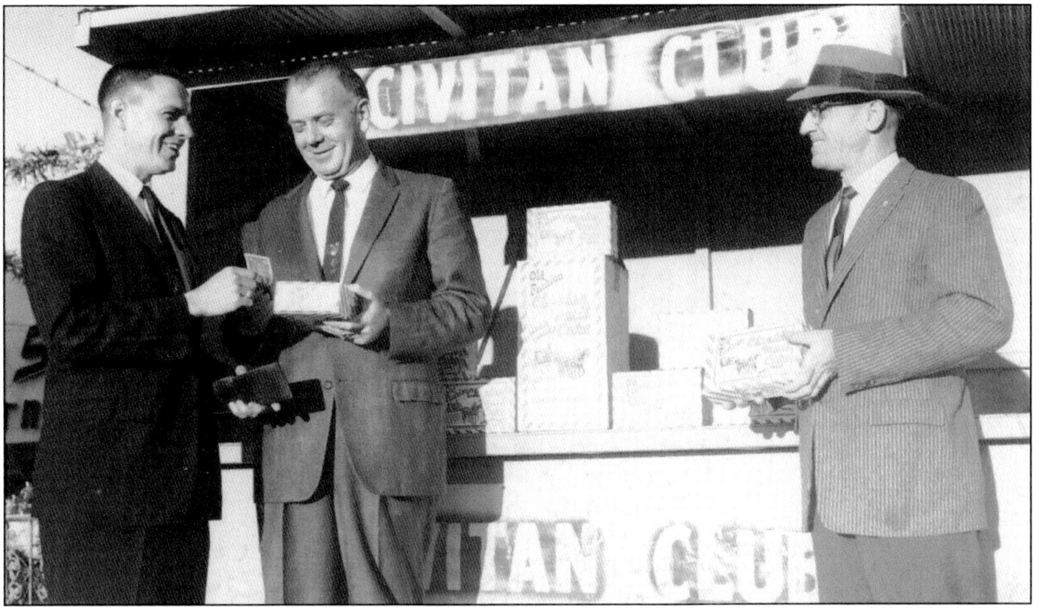

David Ginn, owner of Ginn Jewelry Store on Broad Street, purchases a Claxton fruitcake from "Red" Cheaney (center) as fellow Civitan Troy Veasey (right) displays a fruitcake. In the background, boxes of "Old Fashion Claxton Fruit Cake" are ready for the annual Civitan fundraiser. (Courtesy of Sandra Wilson.)

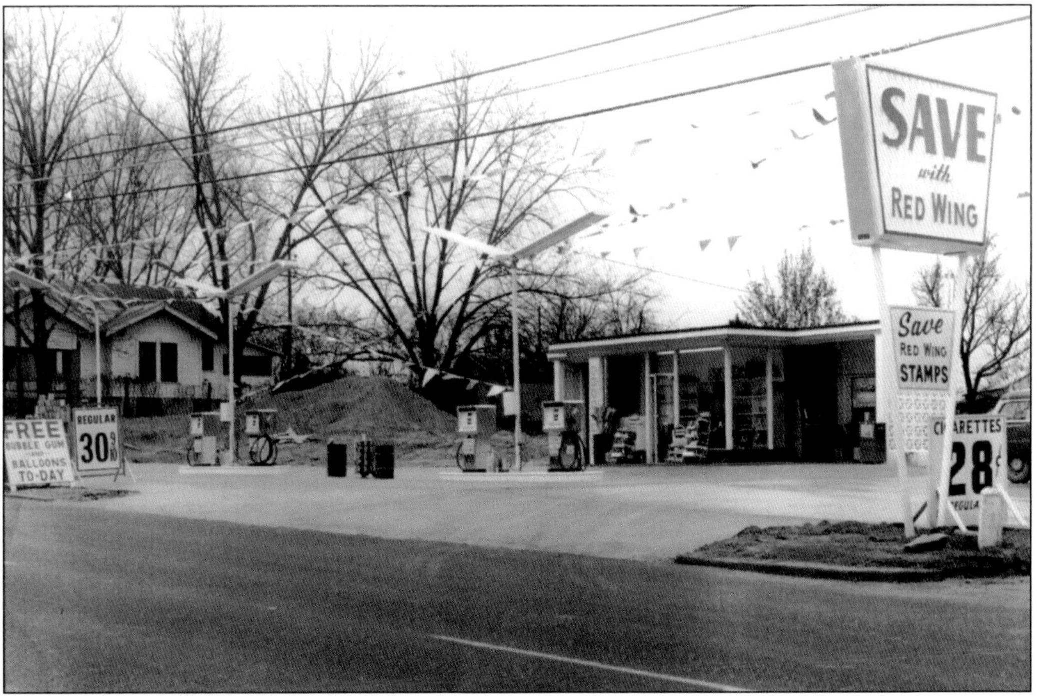

Shown in this 1960s picture, Red Wing Service Station on Cherokee Road sold gas for 30.9¢ a gallon and cigarettes for 28¢ a pack. To attract families, the station gave free bubble gum and balloons to the children and Red Wing stamps for discounted gas prices to the adults. (Courtesy of MainStreet Organization.)

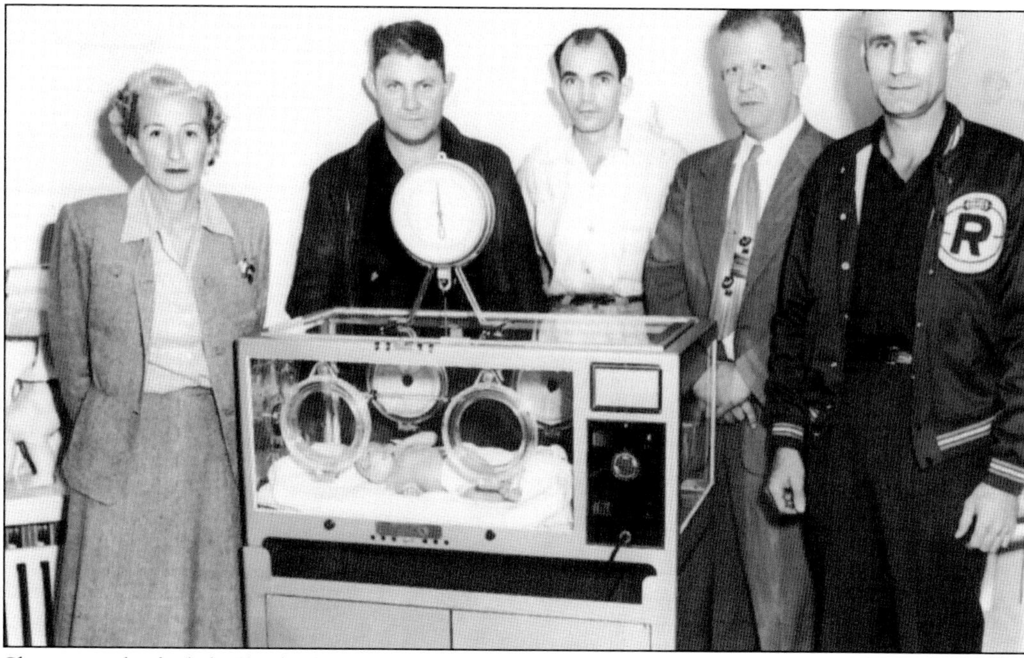

Shown on the far left, Elizabeth Russell Alison, the only daughter of Benjamin and Roberta Russell, was devoted to the care of the city's youngest citizens and worked successfully to add the incubator to Russell Hospital care for infants. She was vice president of Russell Manufacturing Co. and served as president and chairman of the Russell Hospital board. (Courtesy of MainStreet Organization.)

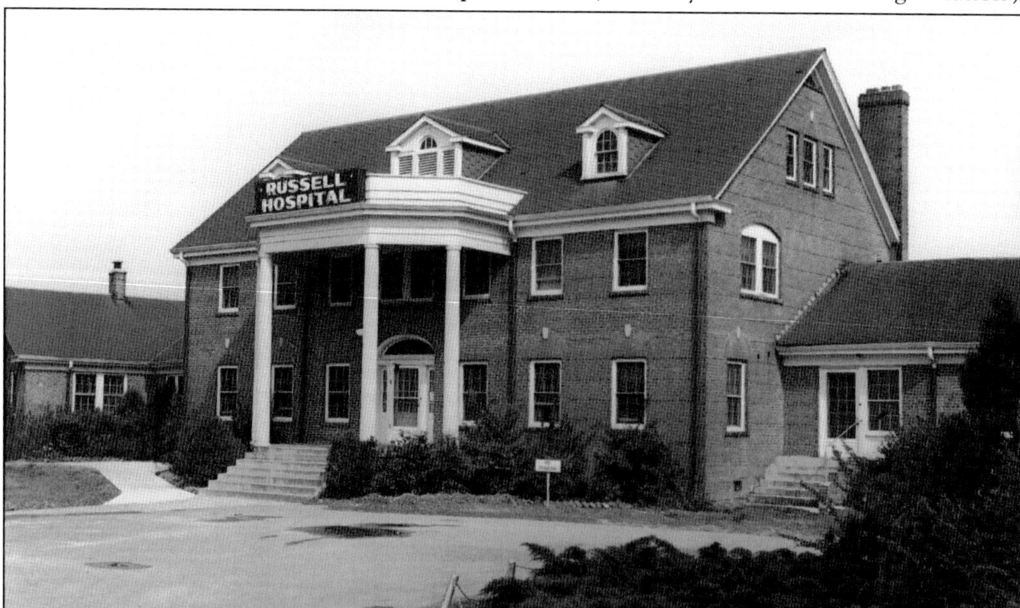

In 1923, Benjamin Russell built a hospital on Lee Street to meet the medical needs of Alexander City. The hospital was equipped with 35 beds and inpatient care staff. Russell Hospital remained at this site for 41 years, expanding to meet the needs of the community. In 1964, the hospital equipment and employees were moved to a new facility on Highway 280 to serve the people of Alexander City and surrounding towns. (Courtesy of Robert Martin; photograph by Robert Graves.)

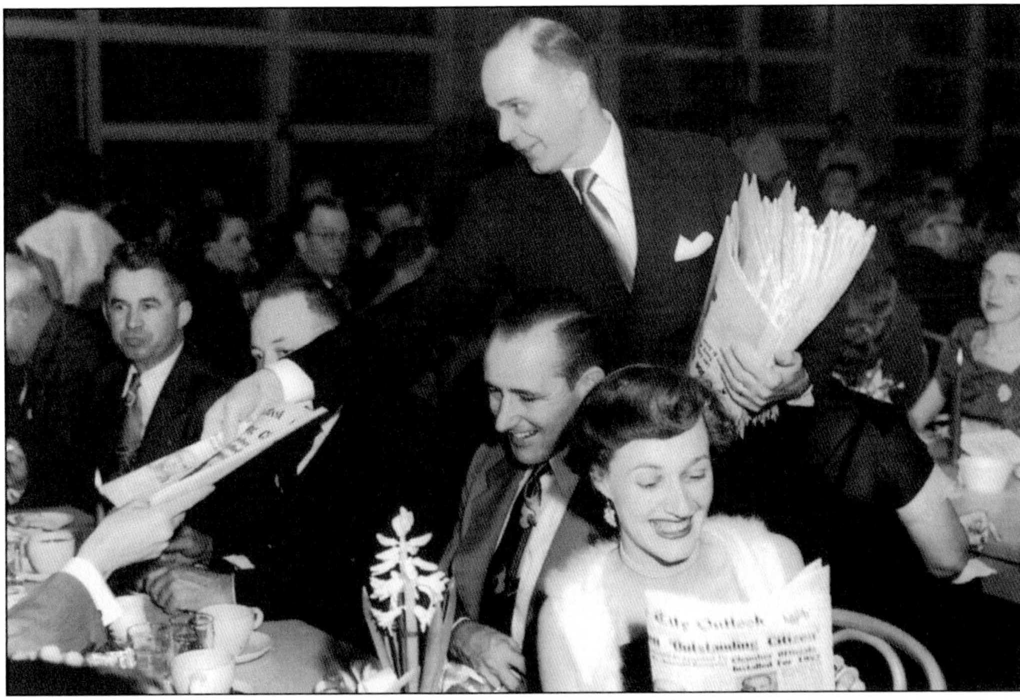

J.C. Henderson, editor and publisher of the *Alexander City Outlook*, distributes an "Extra" edition of the paper to Robert A. Russell. The occasion was a banquet held by the chamber of commerce to honor Russell, who was chosen as the "Man of the Year." Jimmy and Clara Ewing read the headlines. (Courtesy of Jacob Henderson.)

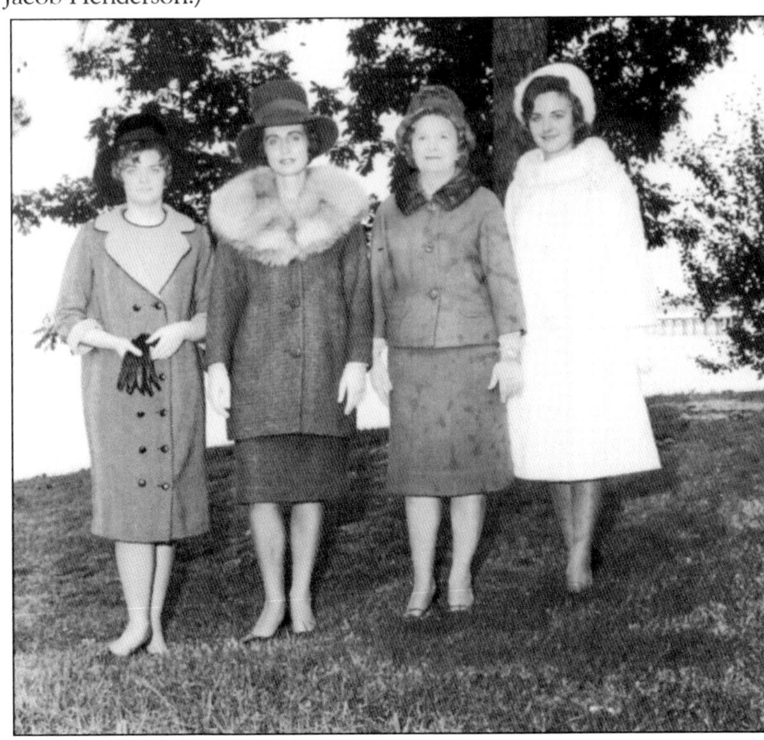

The lovely ladies modeling 1963 fall fashions from Frohsin's Department Store are, from left to right, Clara Cribb Hagan, ? Valentine, Edith Cameron, and Frances Latimer. (Courtesy of Eleanor Carlisle.)

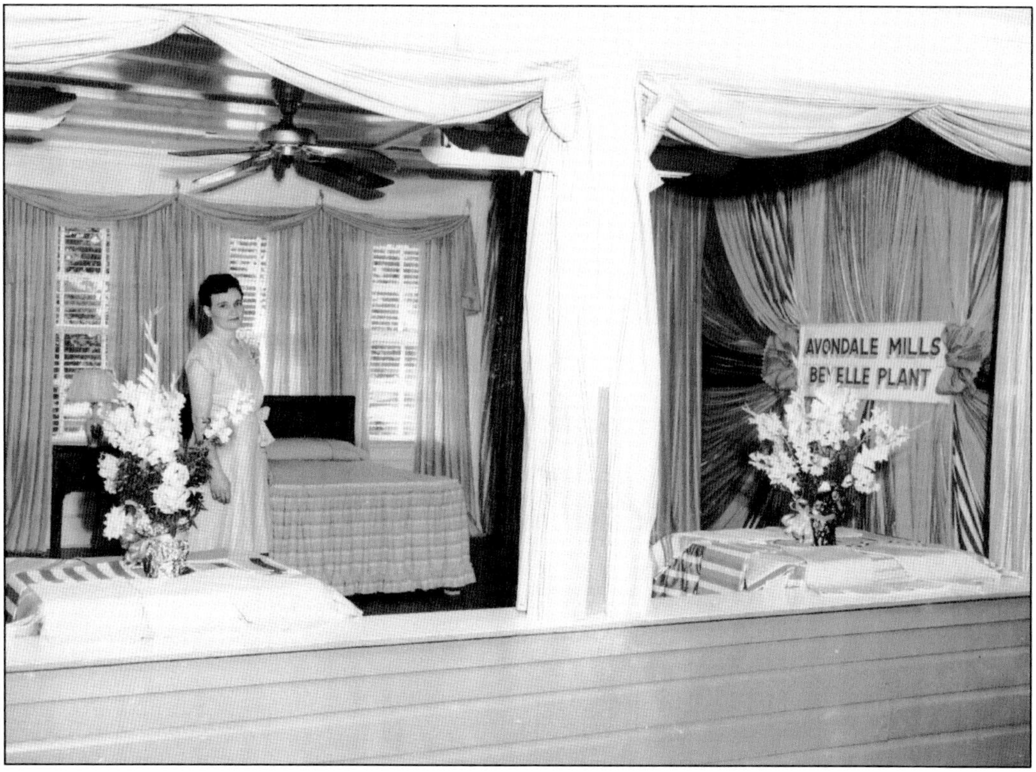

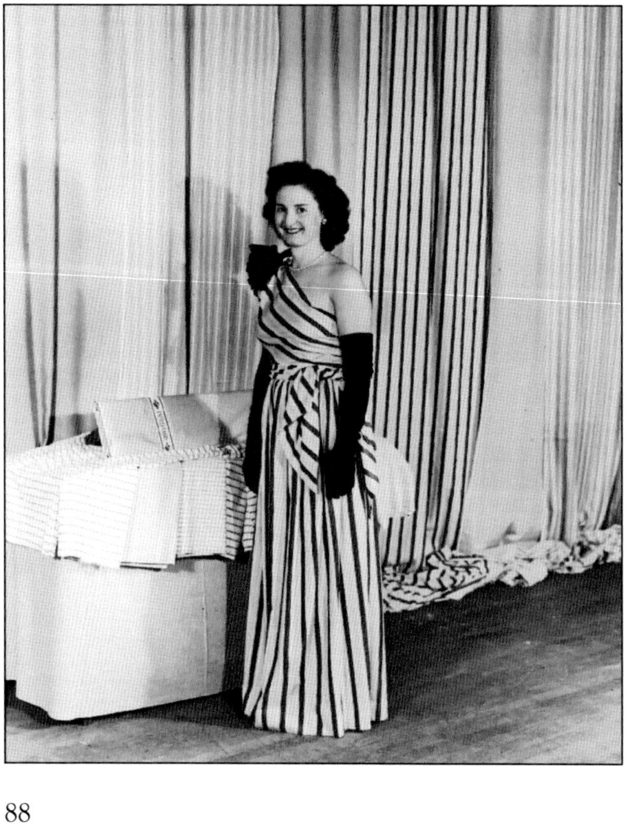

Shown here is a display of Avondale fabric in the 1946 inspection tour. Kathleen Hyde models clothing made from Avondale material and stands in front of cotton products that include curtains, a bedspread, table cover, and folds of different colors. The tour was open to Bevelle associates, as well as visitors from the city and other parts of the state. (Courtesy of Laura Oliver.)

Ruby Maxwell models a yellow and black striped evening dress made from Avondale's Marlin Chambray. Avondale products were featured in fashion events, state fair exhibits, and magazine advertisements, promoting products and offering modeling experience for selected associates. (Courtesy of Laura Oliver.)

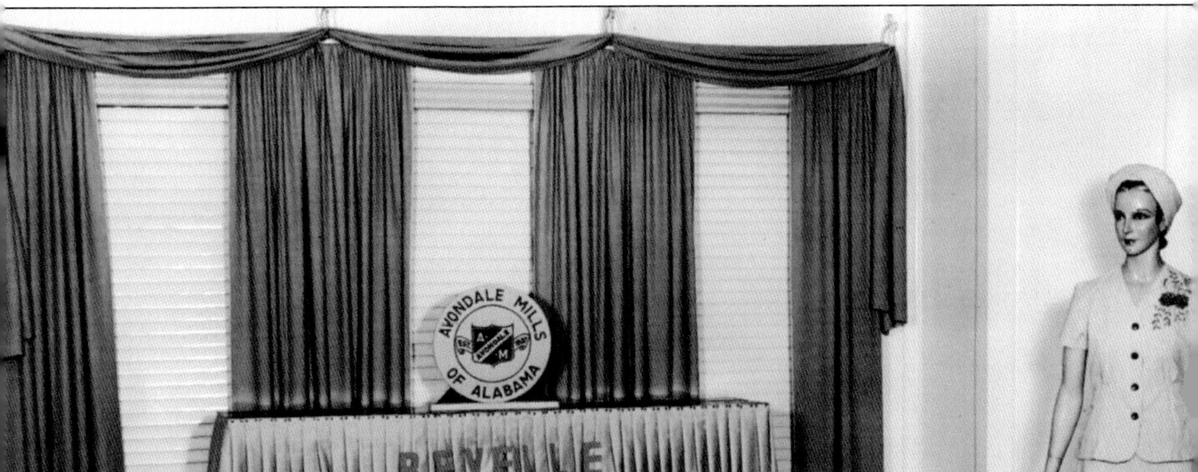

The Bevelle Community Center display marks 50 years of progress by Avondale Mills of Alabama. Braxton Bragg Comer's career as an industrialist began in Birmingham in 1897, the same year that the Alexander City Cotton Mill came to Alexander City. In 1919, Comer (governor from 1907 to 1911) bought the little mill and employed workers from the city and surrounding areas. Avondale Mills did not start in Alexander City, but the Bevelle plant, employing over 700 workers at one point, made a significant contribution to making Avondale Mills the world's leading producer of ticking. (Courtesy of Laura Oliver.)

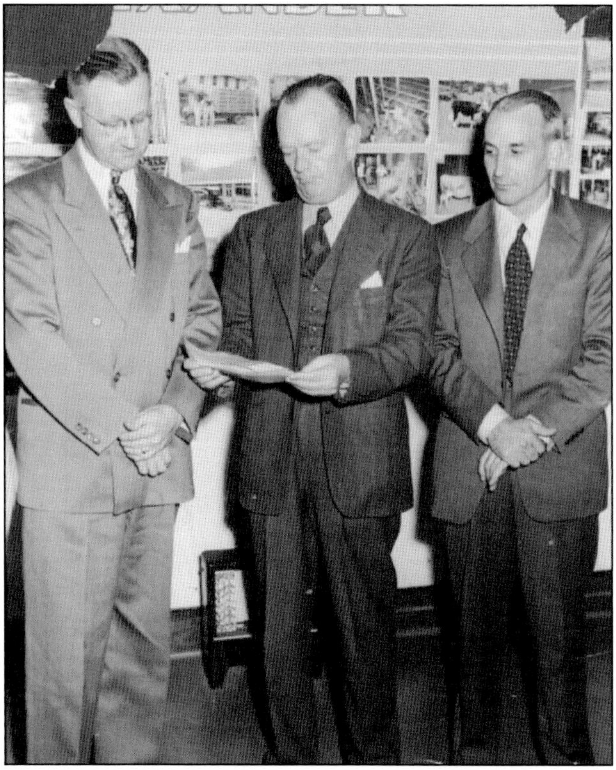

Businessmen Temple Coley (center) and Robert A. Russell (right) meet with an unidentified man to discuss a city project. Behind the men, a collage of local enterprises—including automotive, farming, and iron businesses—can be observed. Robert A. Russell was a vice president and engineer with Russell Manufacturing Co. (Courtesy of MainStreet Organization.)

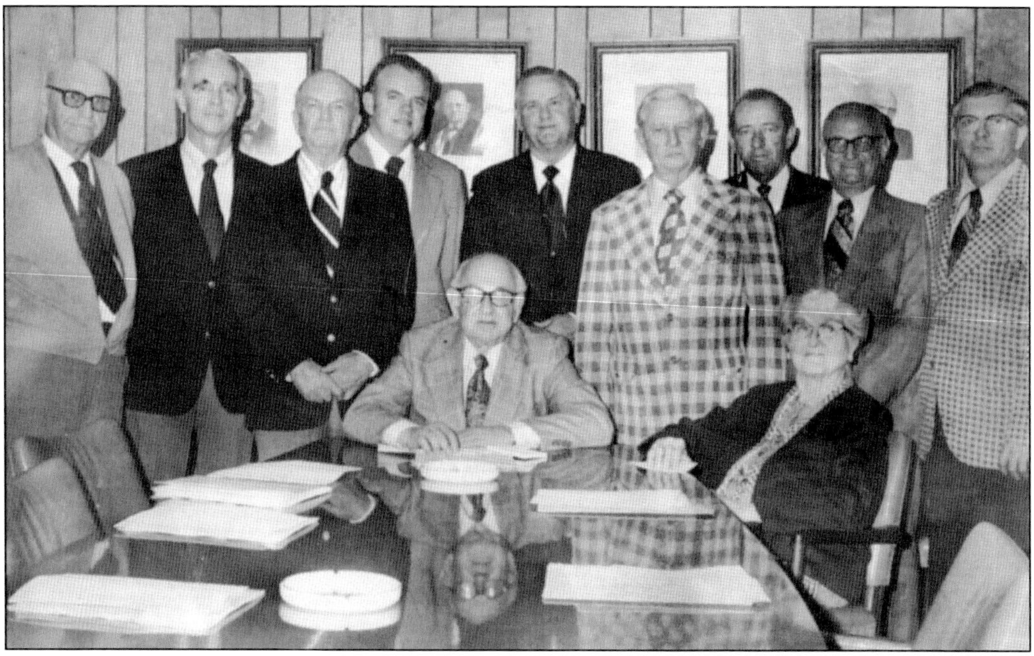

From left to right are Alexander City Chamber of Commerce members (first row) Ralph Frohsin Sr. and Jeanie Herzfeld; (second row) W.C. Adams, Mack Horton, Judge C.J. Coley, Pres. Hugh Neighbors Jr., L.E. Sellers, Charles Wayne Davis, James Ewing, Charles Cohen, and Robert Harris. (Courtesy of MainStreet Organization.)

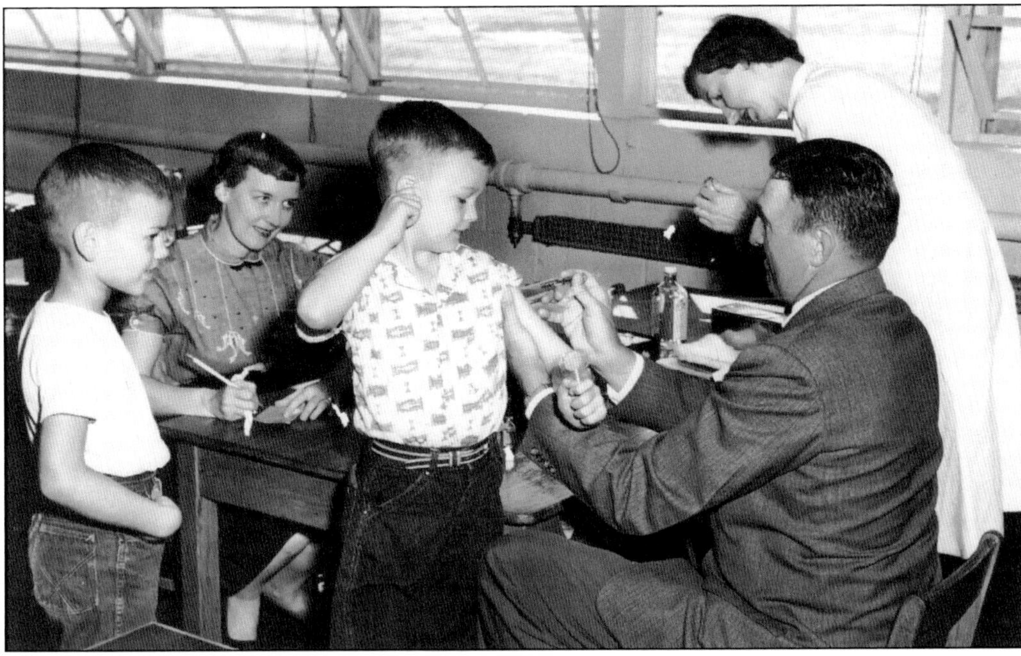

Jimmy Cameron receives the first polio vaccine shot in Tallapoosa County from his father, Dr. James Cameron, on April 18, 1955, as other children and two assistants watch. The first polio vaccine was developed by Jonas Salk in 1952 and announced to the world on April 12, 1955. (Courtesy of Eleanor Carlisle.)

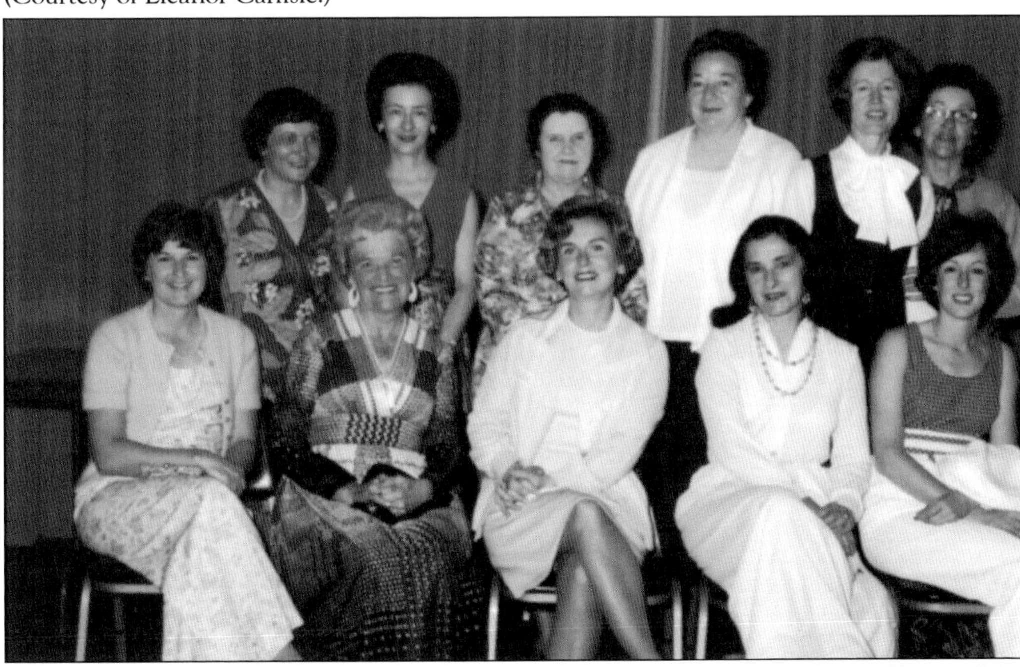

At an Auxiliary party at the Horseshoe Bend Restaurant are local doctors' wives (first row) Lee Stimson, Edith Cameron, Blanche Warr, Frances Harrison, and Betty Hamilton; (second row) Dr. Emma Swindall, Faye Temple, Margaret Chapman, Helen Heidenpriem, Marian Gaba, and Mrs. Farguson. (Courtesy of Eleanor Carlisle.)

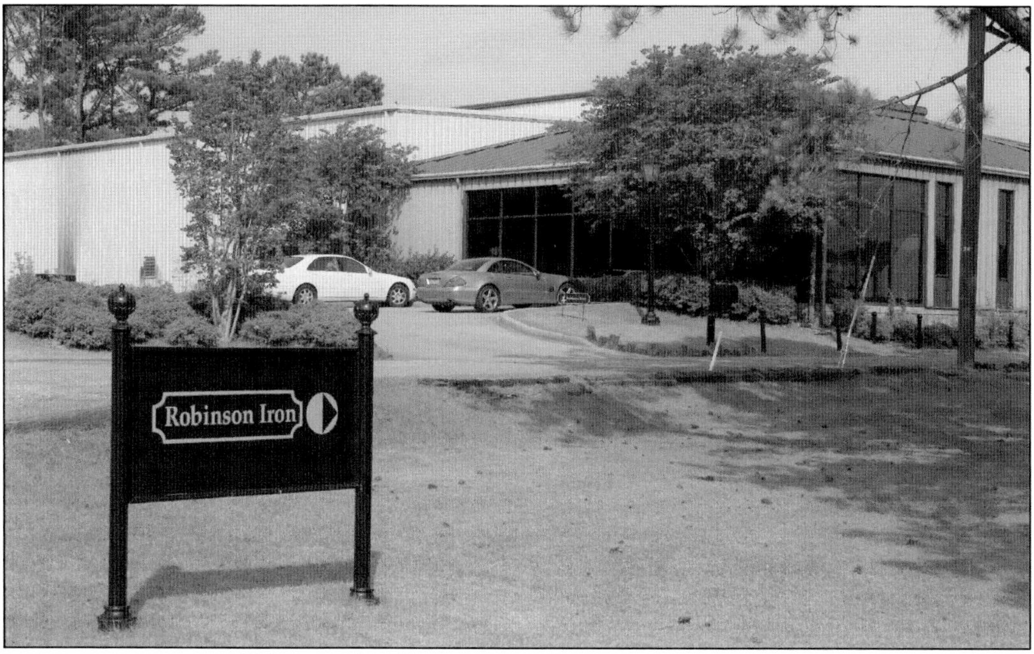

Robinson Iron is world famous for their iron products, decorative fountains, and restoration projects, such as the Vulcan in Birmingham and the cast-iron balcony on the Lincoln Cottage in Washington DC. Robinson Iron's artistic skills are demonstrated in the creation of Victorian statues for museum exhibitions. (Courtesy of Peggy Walls.)

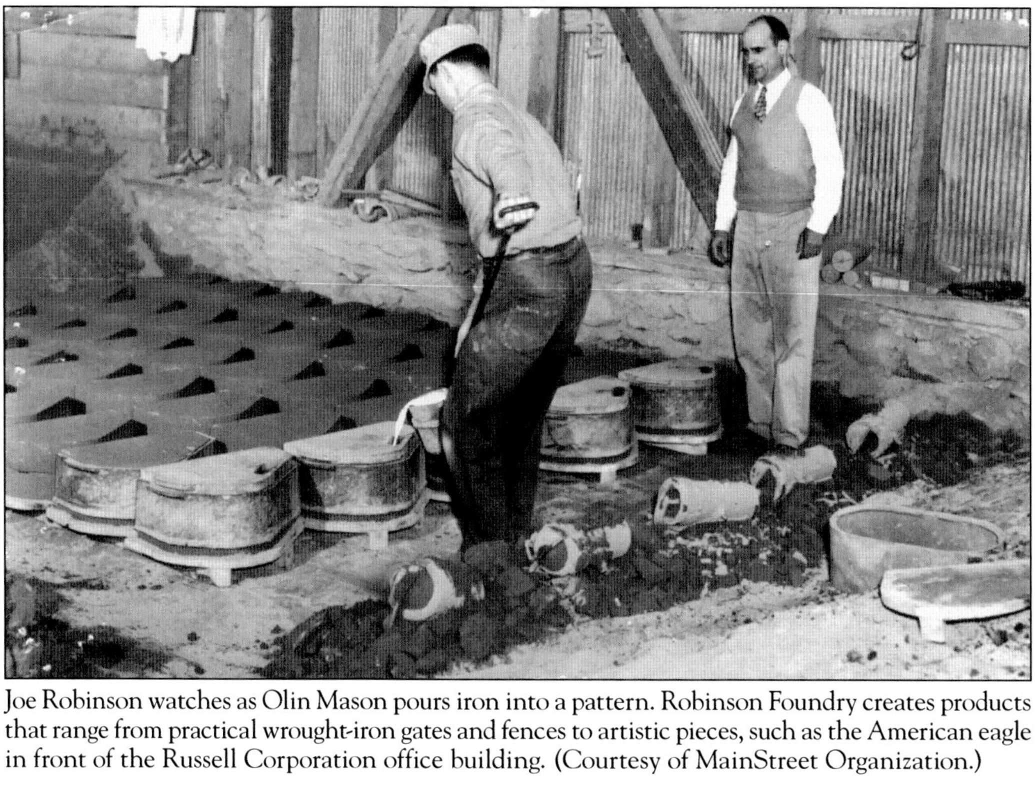

Joe Robinson watches as Olin Mason pours iron into a pattern. Robinson Foundry creates products that range from practical wrought-iron gates and fences to artistic pieces, such as the American eagle in front of the Russell Corporation office building. (Courtesy of MainStreet Organization.)

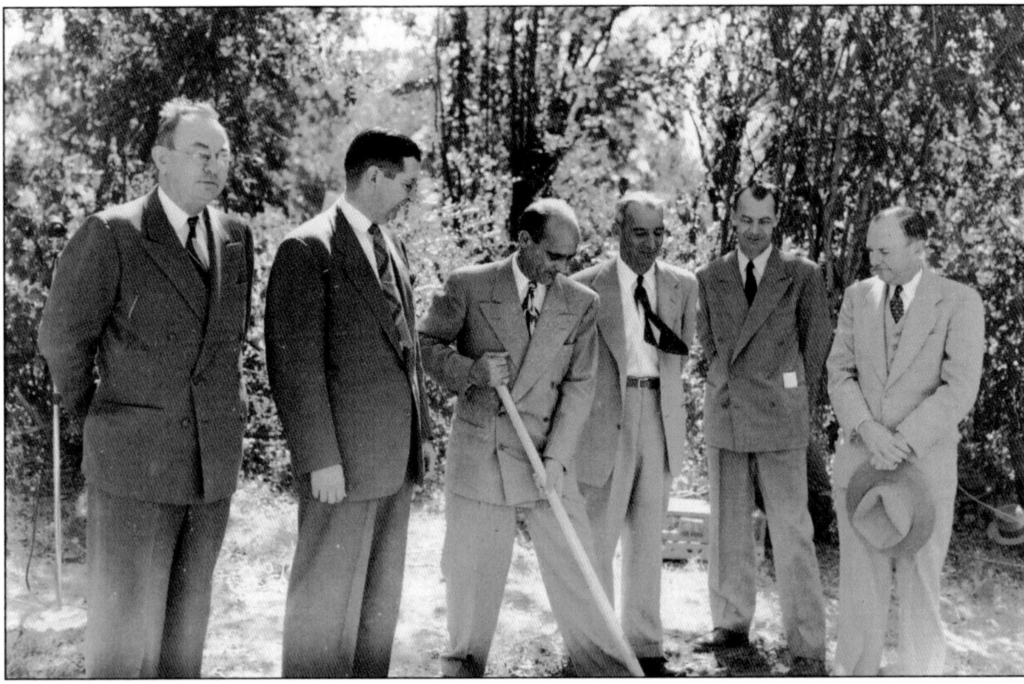

Local businessmen meeting to break ground on a new city project are, from left to right, Ewell Gunn, unidentified, Joe H. Robinson, Robert A. Russell, Jim Callahan, and Jack Coley. (Courtesy of MainStreet Organization.)

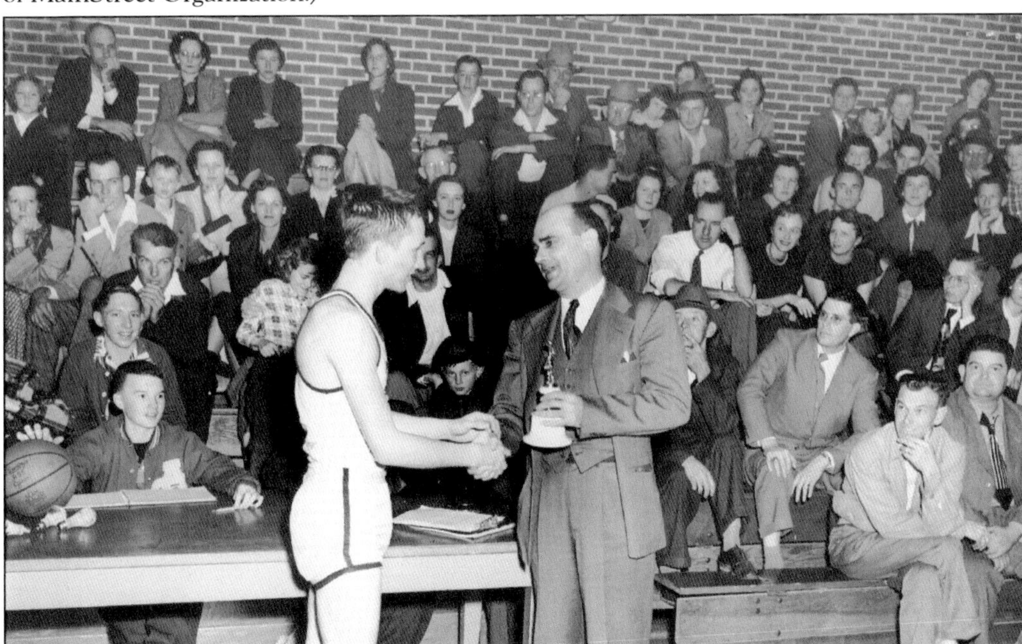

In the Benjamin Russell High School gymnasium in the 1950s, Joe Robinson awards a basketball trophy to the school's outstanding player. Scorekeeper Buddy Willis sits at the table on the left. Royal Spears, the second man sitting in the first row on the right, is a supporter of local athletics. (Courtesy of MainStreet Organization.)

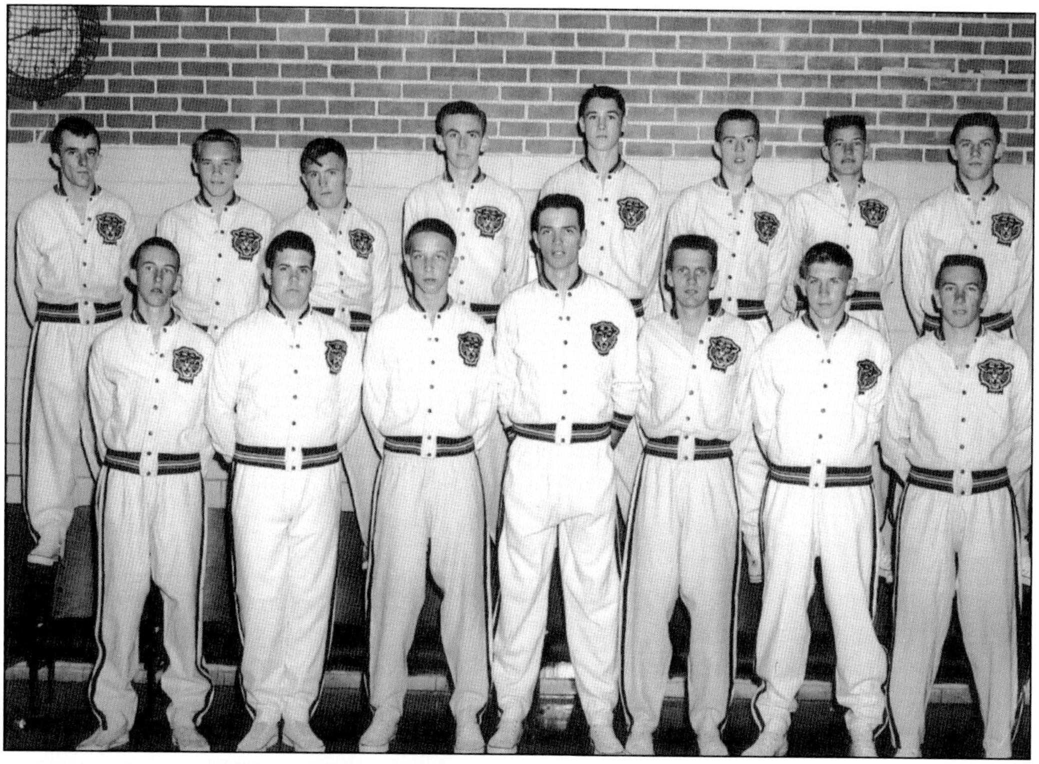

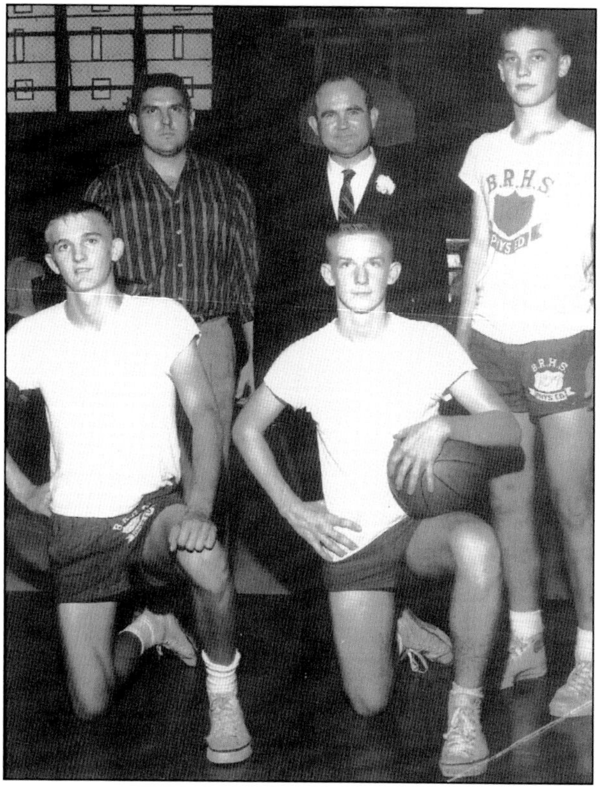

The 1959 Benjamin Russell High School basketball players pose in warm-ups for a team picture before the game. From left to right are (first row) Clint Langley, Billy Yates, Herman Robinson, Charles Robinson, Kennedy Foshee, James Parsons, and Bill Spivey; (second row) Jimmy Nicholson, Jimmy Box, Hershel Hicks, Crayton Forbus, Glen Gilbert, James Sanders, Ewell Smith, and Donald Rush. (Courtesy of MainStreet Organization.)

The two star basketball players in front are Othell McCain (left) and Jimmy Freeman. Standing in the back, from left to right, are Dr. Ted Spears, principal of Benjamin Russell High School; John Patterson, 44th governor of Alabama (1959–1963); and a third star basketball player, Steve Crowe. (Courtesy of MainStreet Organization.)

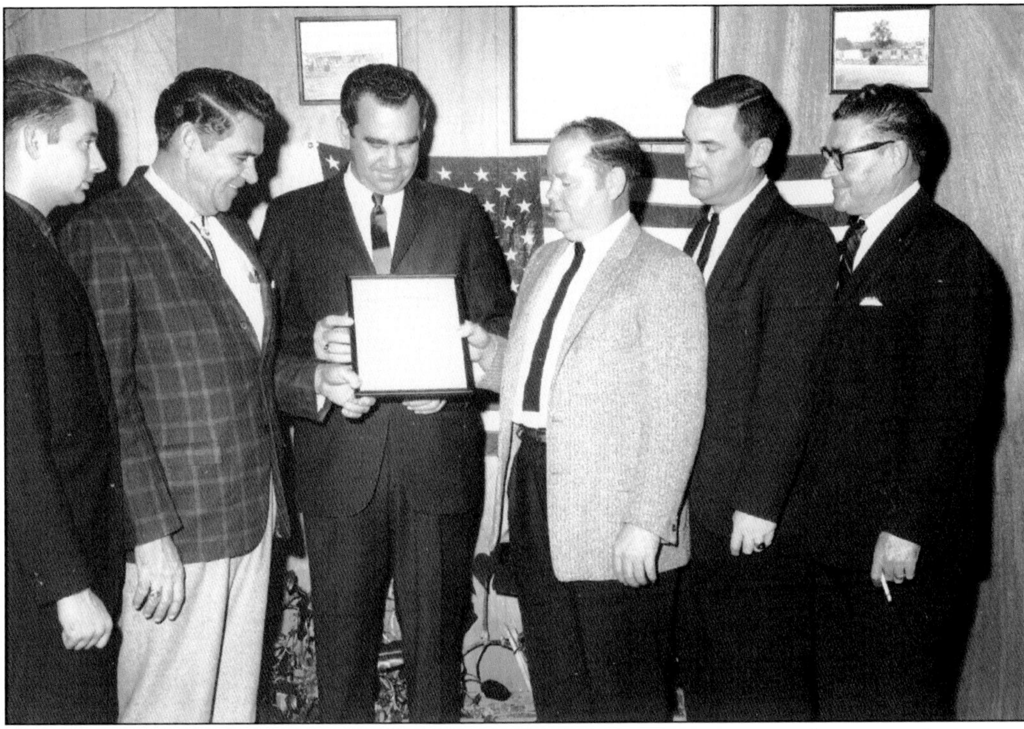

In 1962, the Scott brothers, Emmett and Joe, and their employees received commendation and patriotic recognition from the Veterans of Foreign Wars for their outstanding display and use of the US flag. From left to right are Mickey Watts, Emmett Scott, Joe Scott, unidentified representative of Duncan Still Post 1701, Al Tapley, and Lamar McDonald. (Courtesy of Sandra Wilson.)

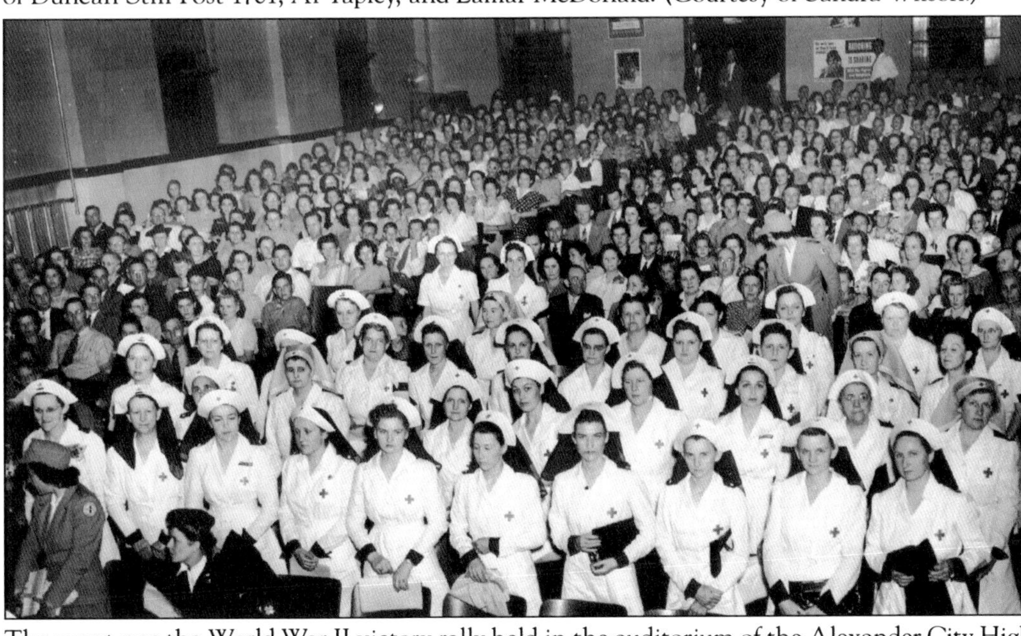

The event was the World War II victory rally held in the auditorium of the Alexander City High School. The Victory Ball performance by Bevelle School students was the highlight of the program. In the foreground is a group of volunteer Red Cross workers. (Courtesy of Laura Oliver.)

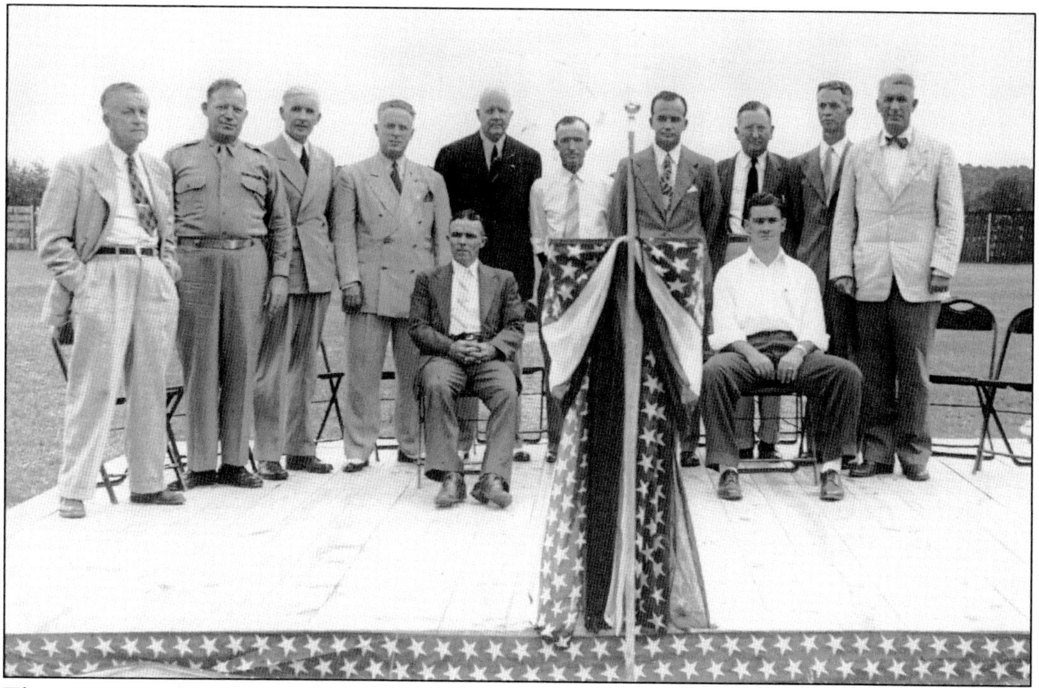

The group is gathered to honor veterans at Byers Field. The men include Chal Adamson, Ezell Forbus, Grover Hamilton, W.A. Turner, Rev. Corley, Rev. Stanley H. Guyton, Shorty Bush, Gaines Coker, and Hugh Comer (far right). (Courtesy of Laura Oliver.)

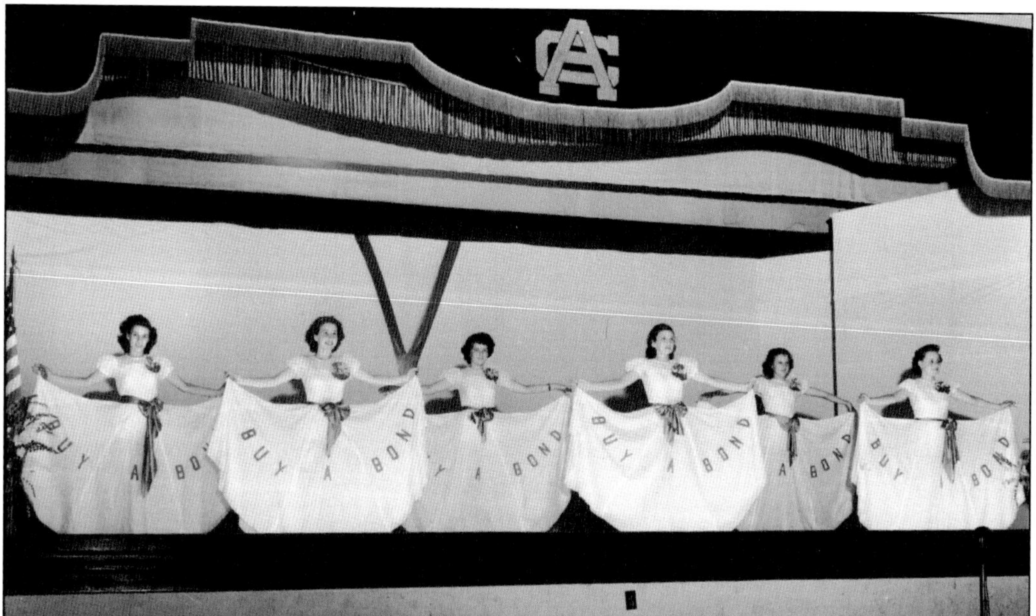

The Bevelle operetta closed each year with a waltz. This dance promoted the "Buy a Bond" theme during World War II. Identified in the picture are Betty Jo Adamson (far left) and Jackie McCollough (second from left). Promotion of the Buy a Bond program resulted in a near 100 percent of Avondale employees participating in the program. (Courtesy of Laura Oliver.)

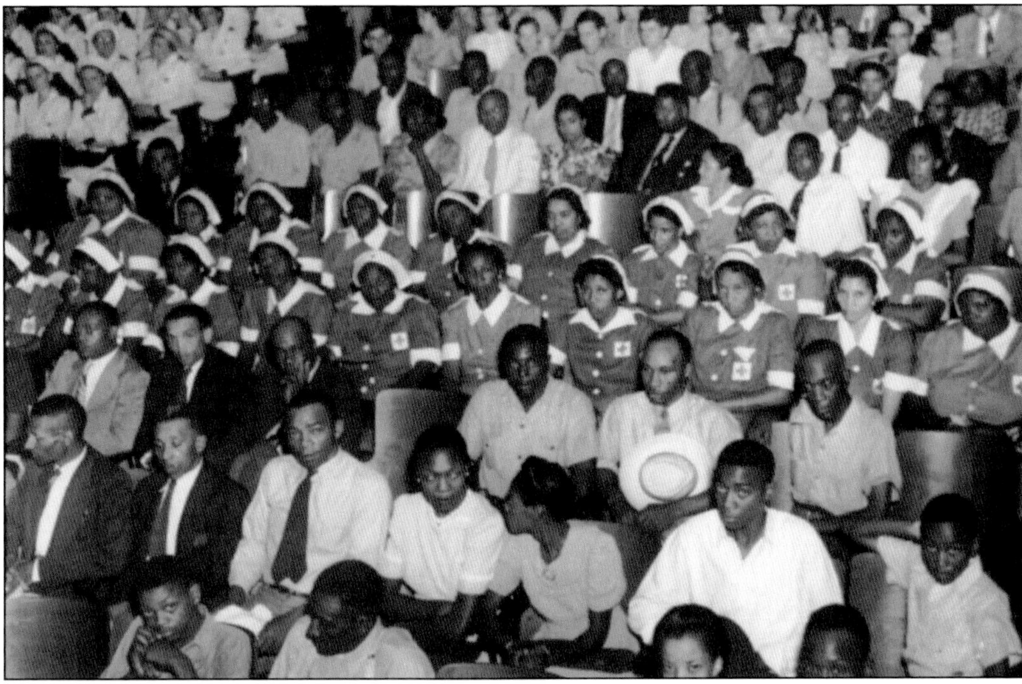

The Alexander City High School auditorium was filled with Red Cross volunteers, patriotic organizations, and community and school supporters to celebrate the end of World War II and to enjoy the performances of Mary Holbrook's dance students. (Courtesy of Laura Oliver.)

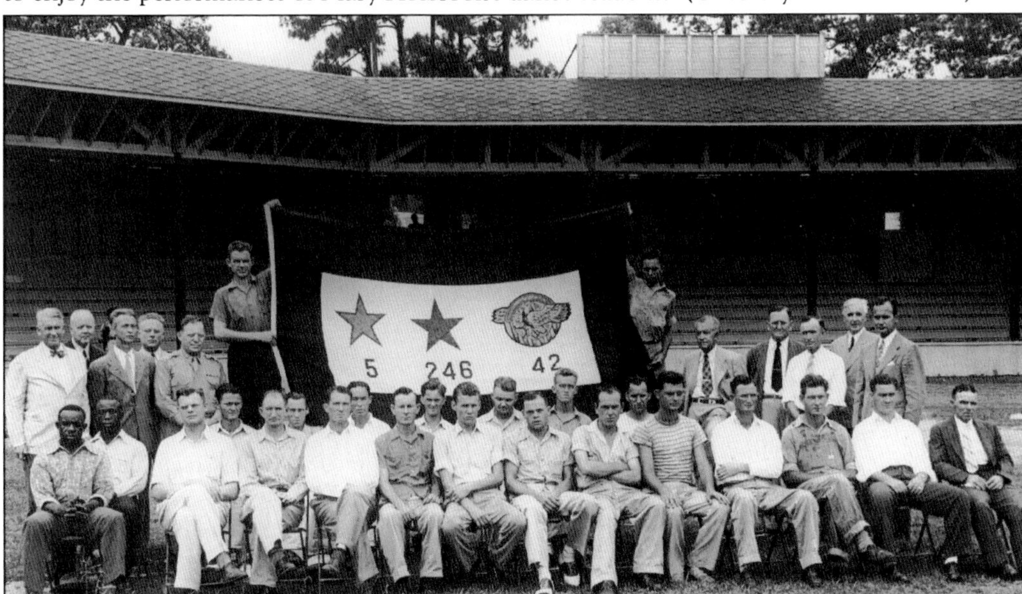

Representatives of the Comer family and Bevelle community leaders turn out to honor the Bevelle soldiers in a ceremony at Byers Field. The names of the Gold Star soldiers were engraved on a monument and placed in front of the Bevelle plant. Gold star soldiers were Carl Baxter, Austin Belyeu, Eddie L. Brown Jr., James R. Green, Louis McGill, Thomas J. McGill, Wallace D. Pate, James D. Robinson, and Douglas and Jiles Smith. (Courtesy of Laura Oliver.)

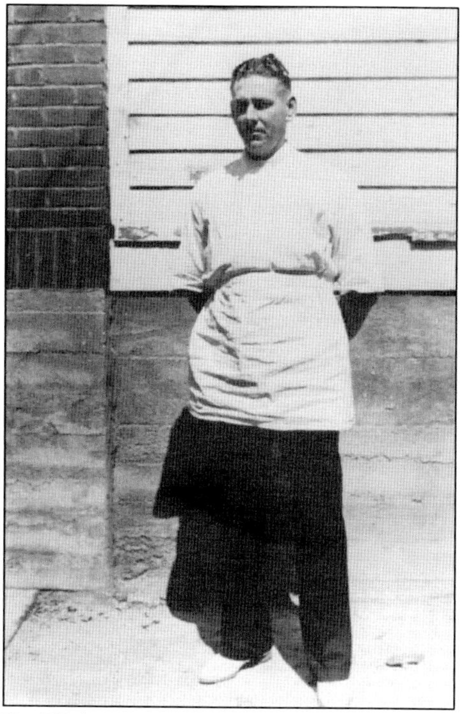

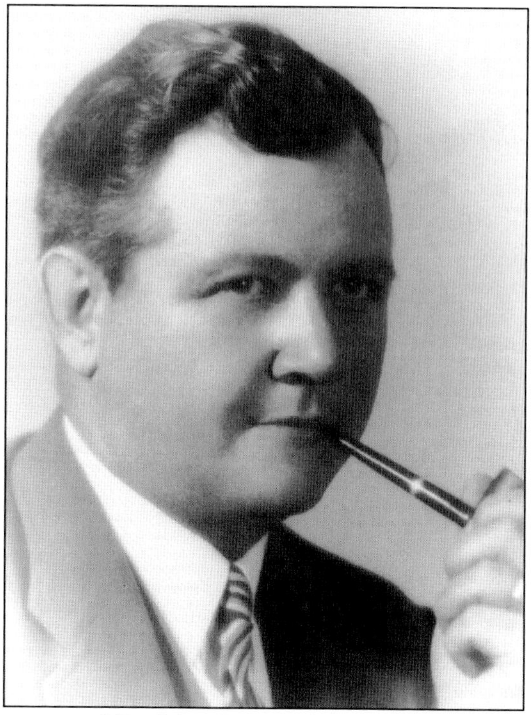

Dr. Walter Mayfield, DDS, the Bevelle plant dentist, and Dr. John Denny, the company doctor, had offices in the elementary school, where employees could take a break from work to visit the doctor or dentist and return with little interruption if not severely ill. (Left, courtesy of Melba Mayfield; right, courtesy of Laura Oliver.)

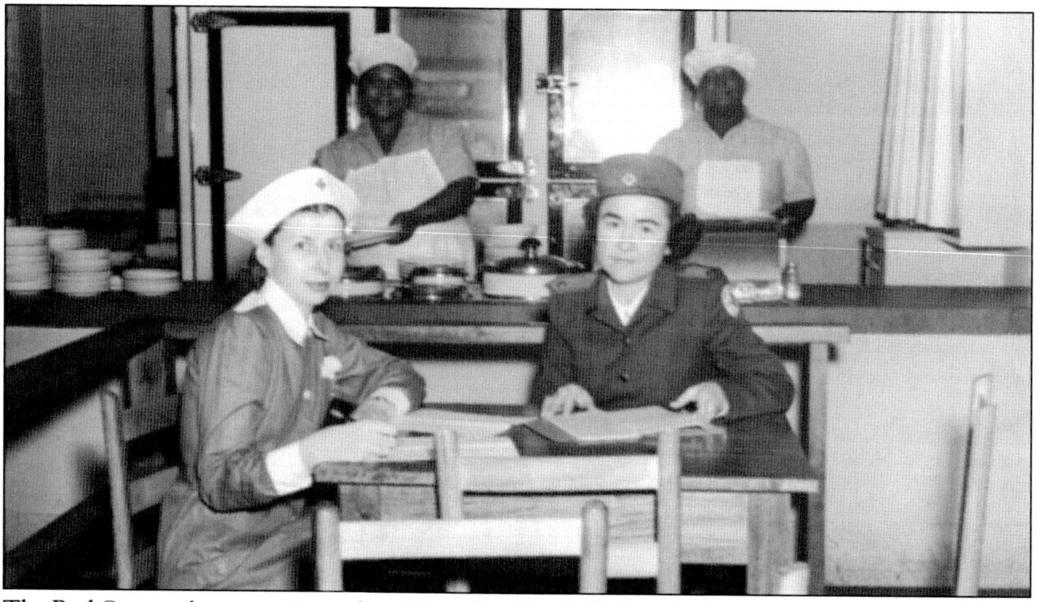

The Red Cross volunteers pictured are Elane Lamberth (left, wife of Dr. Wade Lamberth) and Lila Nolen Graves (W.D. Graves Jr.'s wife). The spirit of patriotism ran high during the World War II period, with many volunteers rolling bandages, addressing envelopes, and preparing packages for the hometown boys fighting in the war. (Courtesy of MainStreet Organization.)

Eight

Worship and Play

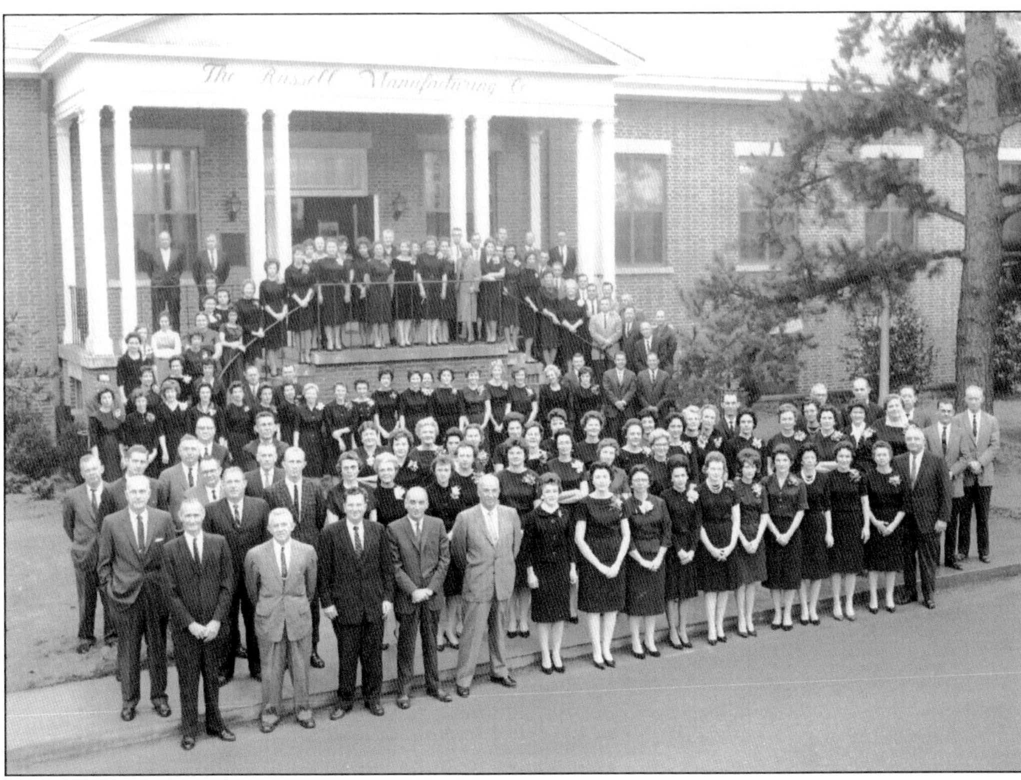

Executives and employees stand in front of the Russell Manufacturing Co.'s main office building in the 1960s. (Courtesy of Russell Lands.)

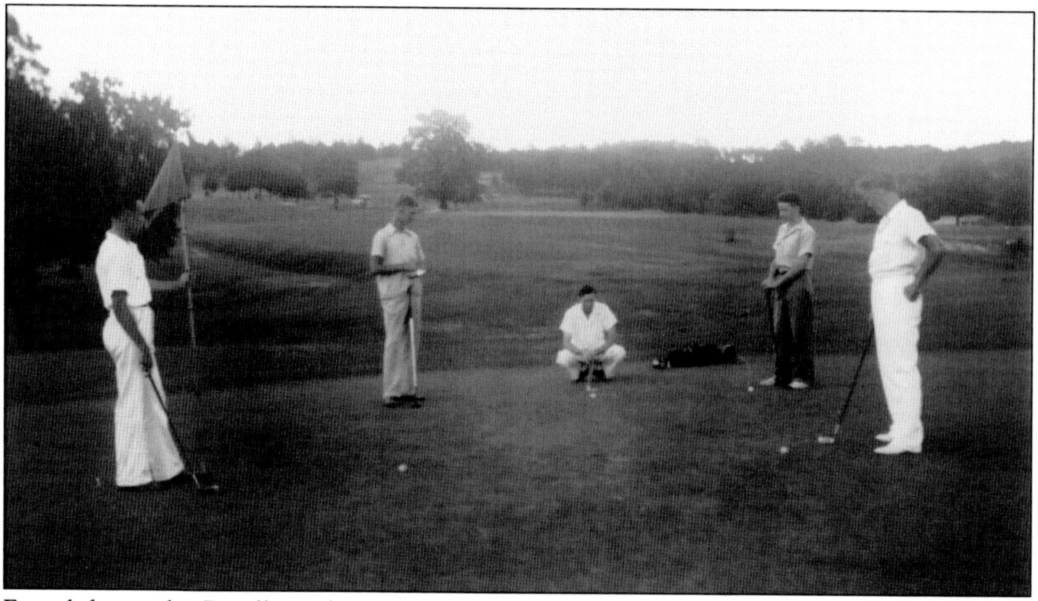

From left to right, Bevelle workers Carl Dean, Pete Rhodes, Elmer Hassett, Jessie Cannon, and Lawton Rich play the sixth hole at the Alexander City Country Club in 1941. The country club was converted to the Alexander City Junior College in September 1966. (Courtesy of Jane McLeod.)

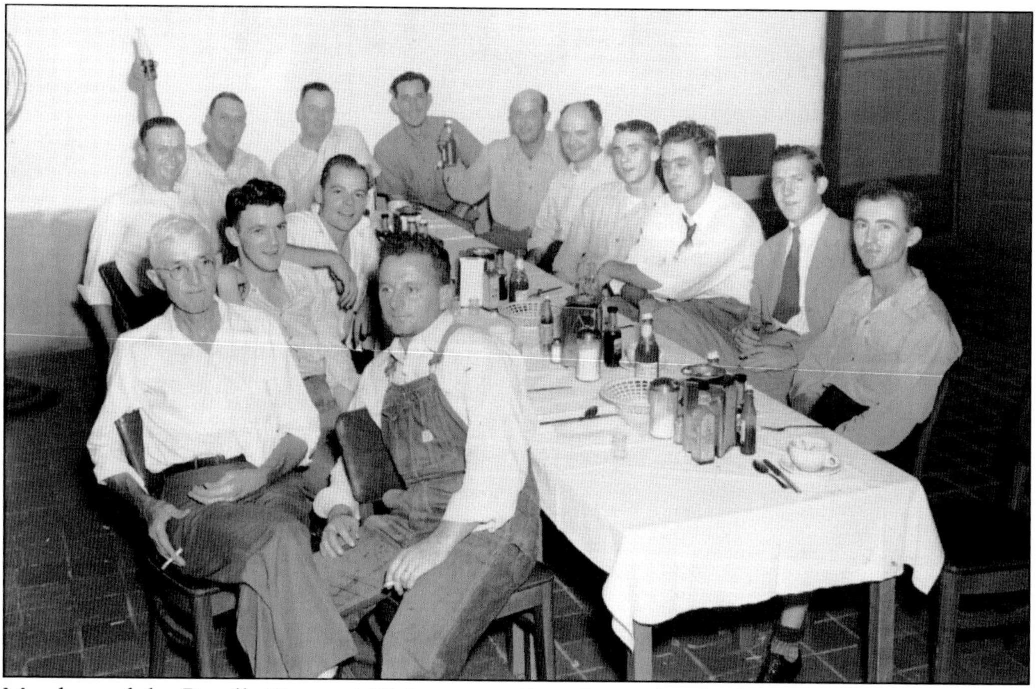

Members of the Bevelle Hunters' Club enjoy a Saturday night chicken supper in the 1940s or 1950s. From left to right, clockwise, are James Corley (wearing overalls), Roy Thompson, Desmond Blanks, Grant Gordon, Buck Hardy, Andy Adcock, Roy Moore, Roscoe Slagle, Harvey Ware, Hubert Kennedy, Hovey Cromer Jr., Essie McCollough, Jasper McCollough, and Red Sellers. (Courtesy of Jane McLeod.)

Local bathing beauty Patsy Bevis poses by the Cara Nome display case. Cara Nome was a successful business as early as 1922, featuring favorite fragrances, face powder, and rouge. Maude Tate was the Cara Nome beauty consultant for the local Rexall dealership. Carlisle Drugstore was owned and operated by the Carlisle family, which included brothers Homer, Hoyt, David, and Dwight. (Courtesy of MainStreet Organization; photograph by Robert Graves.)

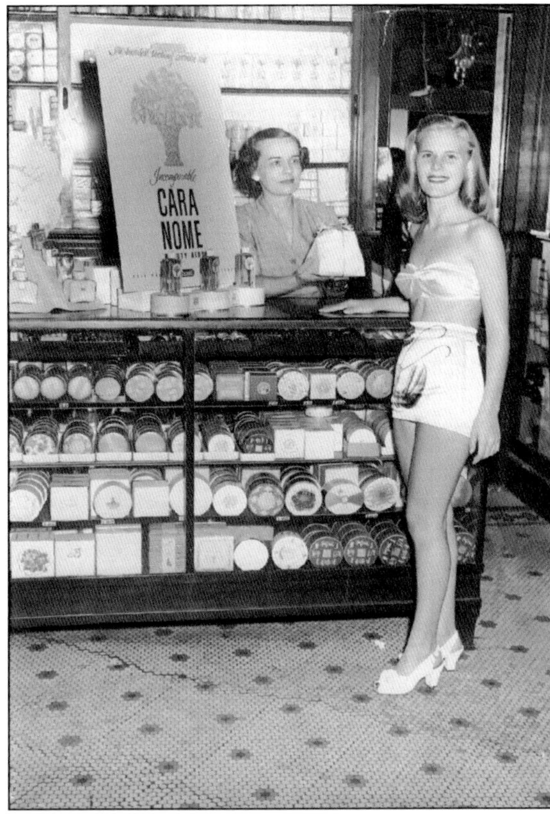

The Tallapoosa River Bridge originally was a narrow two-lane bridge with over-deck trusses. The River Bridge restaurant was located next to the Tallapoosa River Bridge in the early years of its operation. Lawton and Helen Pemberton were managers, followed by their daughter, Sybil, and her husband, Kenneth Johnson. The restaurant was moved to the top of the hill across the highway, where the view of the lake was broadened. (Courtesy of Robert Martin; photograph by Robert Graves.)

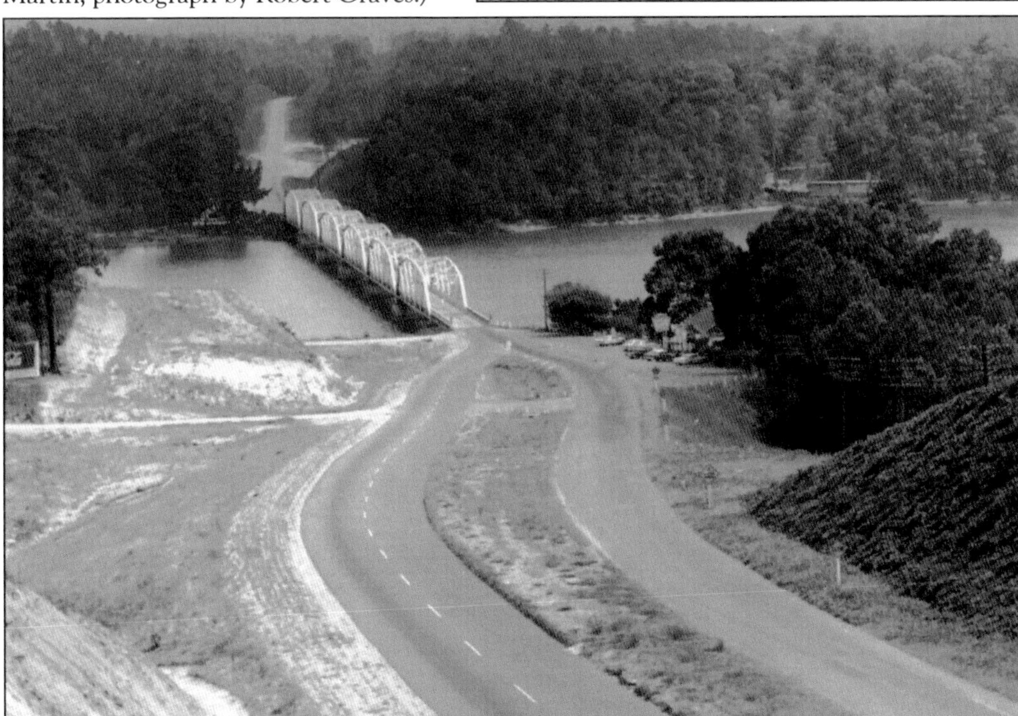

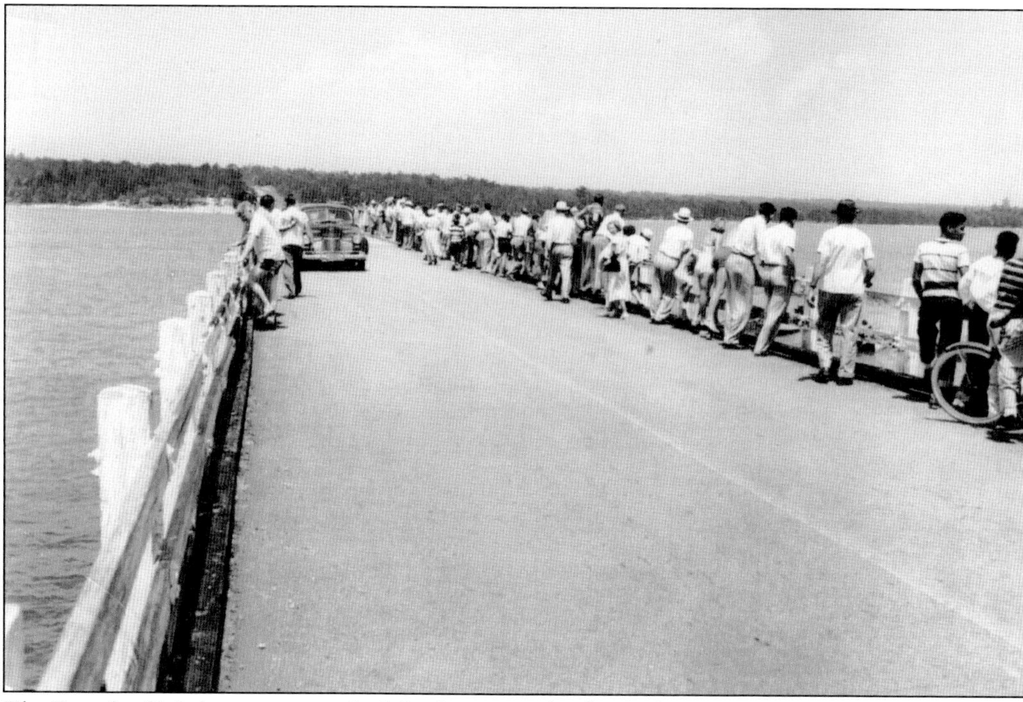

The Fourth of July boat races on the lake drew crowds of onlookers to Kowaliga Bridge, where they lined up on either side to yell encouragement and wave at people in the boats before they passed under the bridge. Below, Dr. James Cameron, businessman Frank Penton, and educator and athlete Hamp Lyon wave as they pass the Kowaliga Bridge. (Both, courtesy of Eleanor Carlisle.)

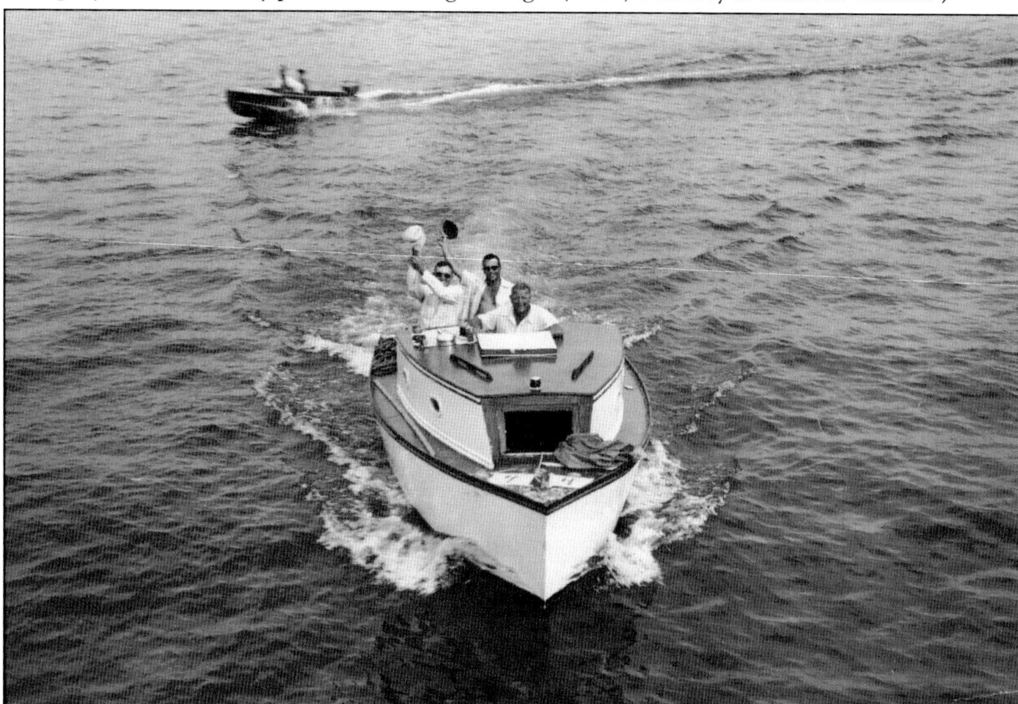

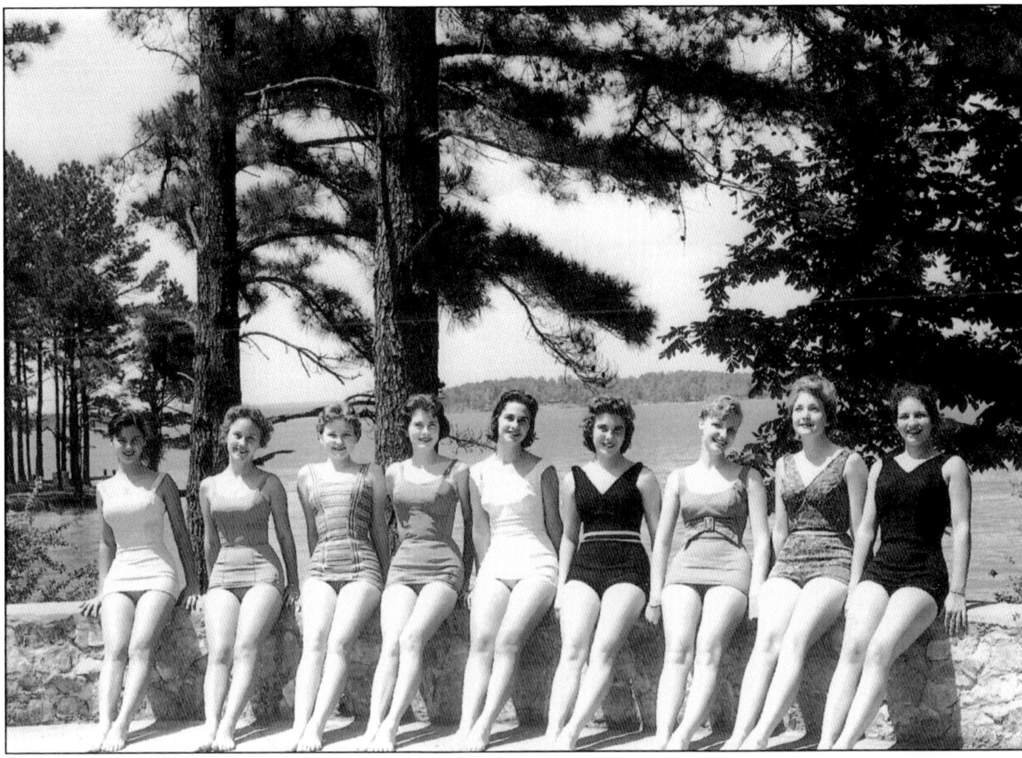

1960 Bathing beauties pose on the Kowaliga Bridge for a picture to be made into a postcard, copies of which were sold in the old Kowaliga Store. From left to right, the girls are Delia Duncan, Ruth Radney, Barbara Blair, Mary Hillman Forbus, Beverly Turner, Carolyn Carlisle, Tillie Dobbs, Nell Wood, and Nancy Lindsey. (Courtesy of Eleanor Carlisle.)

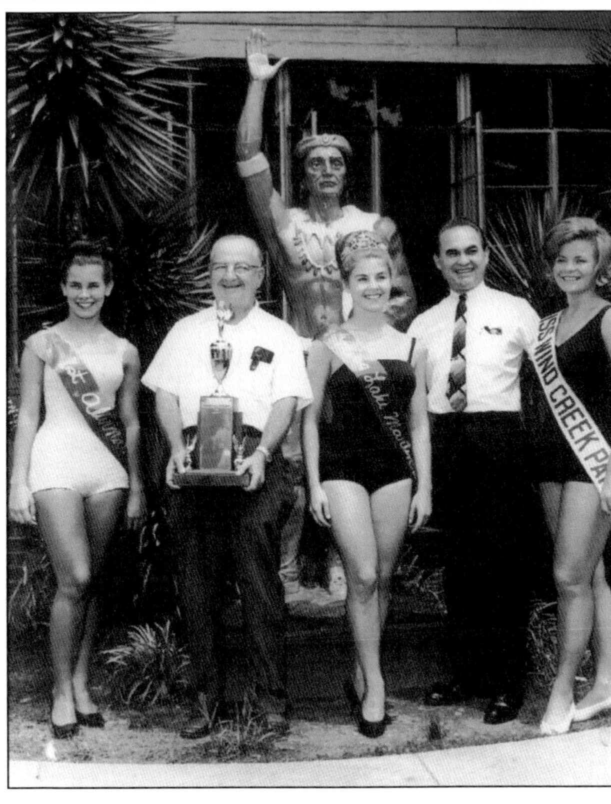

With Kowaliga Restaurant in the background, Gov. George Wallace stands between Miss Lake Martin (left) and Miss Wind Creek in the 1960s. At left, Miss Alabama stands next to an unidentified man holding the trophy. The old wooden Indian that inspired Hank Williams's famous "Kaw-Liga" hit record stands behind the group. (Courtesy of MainStreet Organization.)

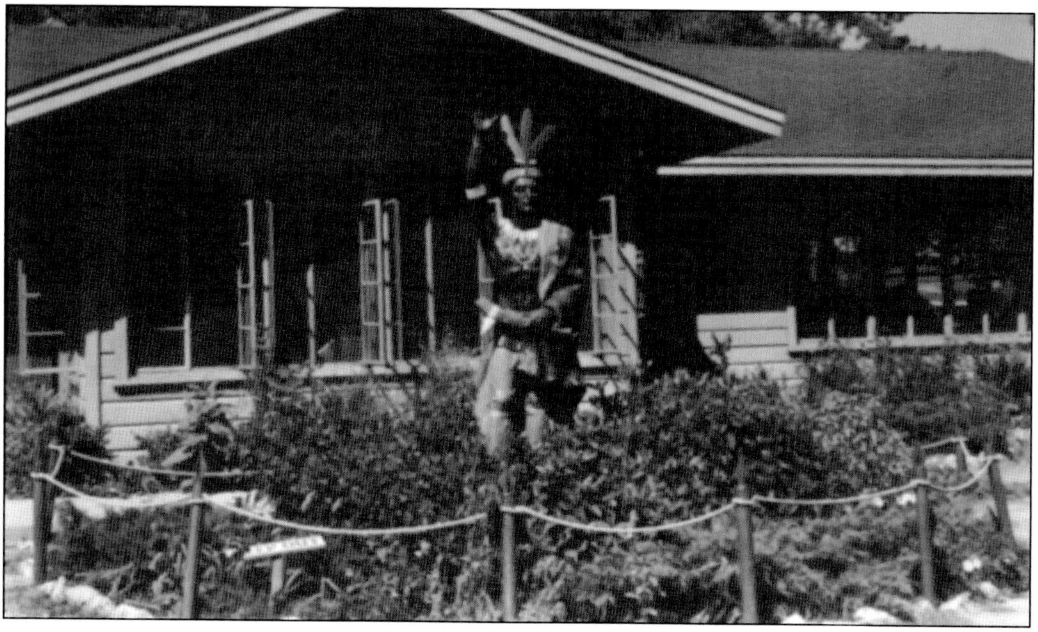

Kowaliga Restaurant provides a view of Lake Martin and the Kowaliga Bridge. The famous wooden Indian is a tourist attraction, especially for country music fans who know the lyrics and origin of Hank Williams's No. 1 hit record "Kaw-Liga," landing at the top of the charts in 1952. (Both, courtesy of MainStreet Organization.)

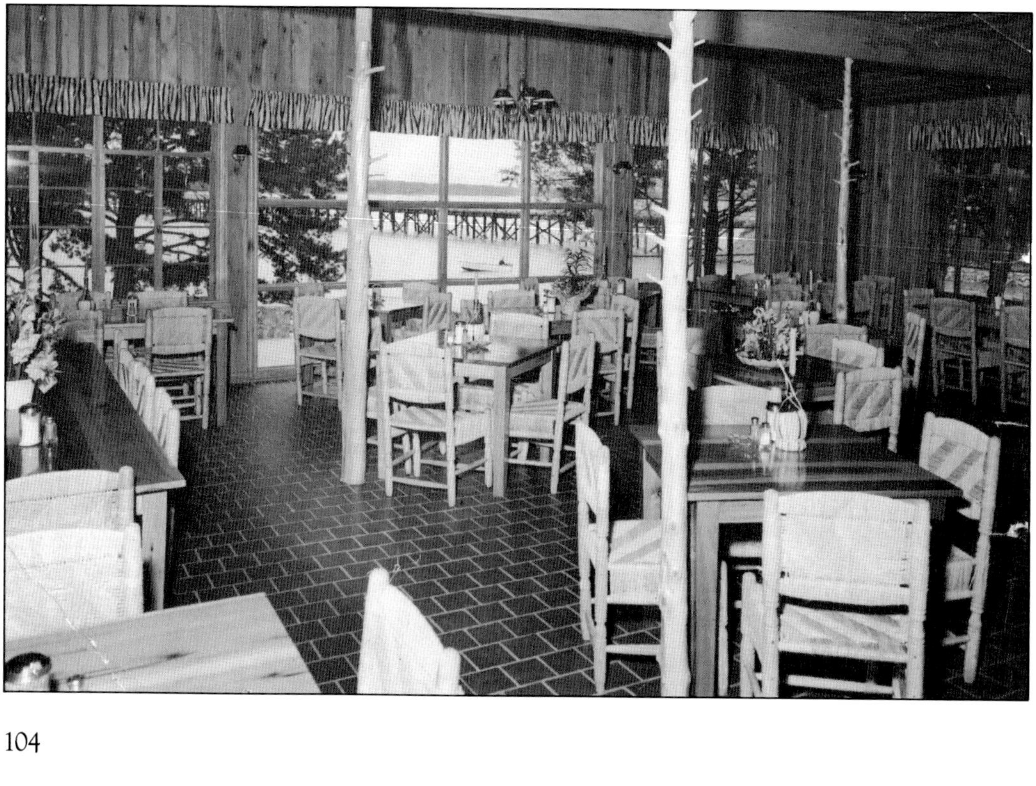

Hank Williams was a personal friend of local people, such as Darwin Dobbs, owner of a local car dealership, and Bob McKinnon, WRFS radio announcer. Hank relaxed at the Dobbs lake cabin when he was in the area and wrote two of his biggest hits, "Your Cheating Heart" and "Kaw-Liga," while at Lake Martin in August 1952. (Courtesy of Hank Williams Museum, Montgomery, Alabama.)

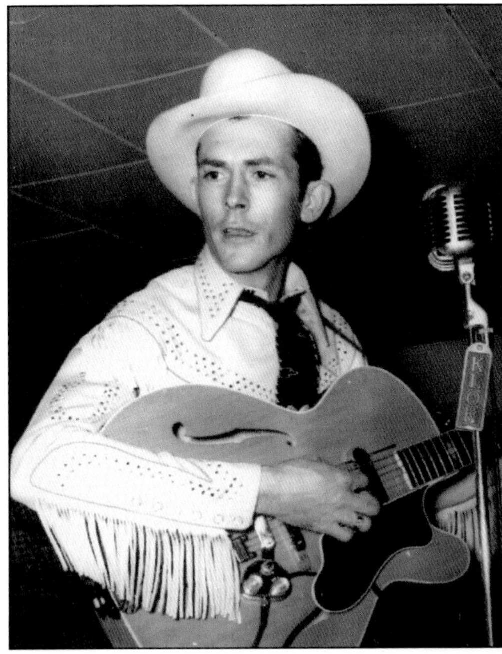

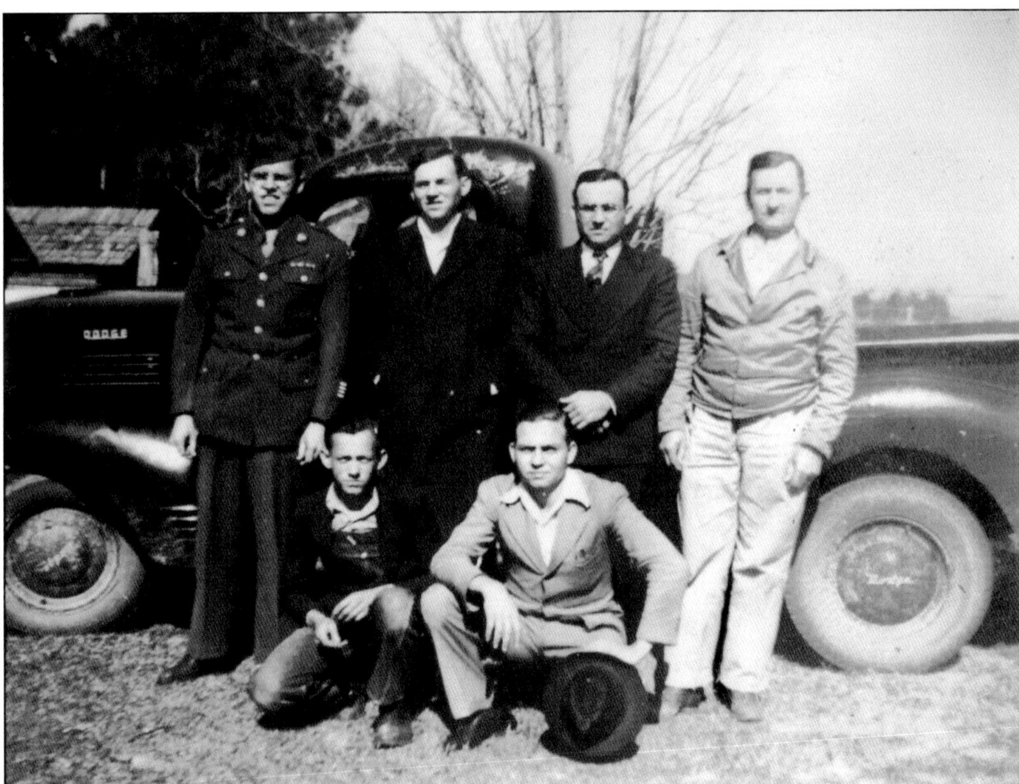

Standing second from the left is Doug "G.W." Moody, Hank Williams's taxi driver when he was in the Lake Martin/Alexander City area. Doug drove for the Herzfeld Taxi Service. (Courtesy of Linda Meadows.)

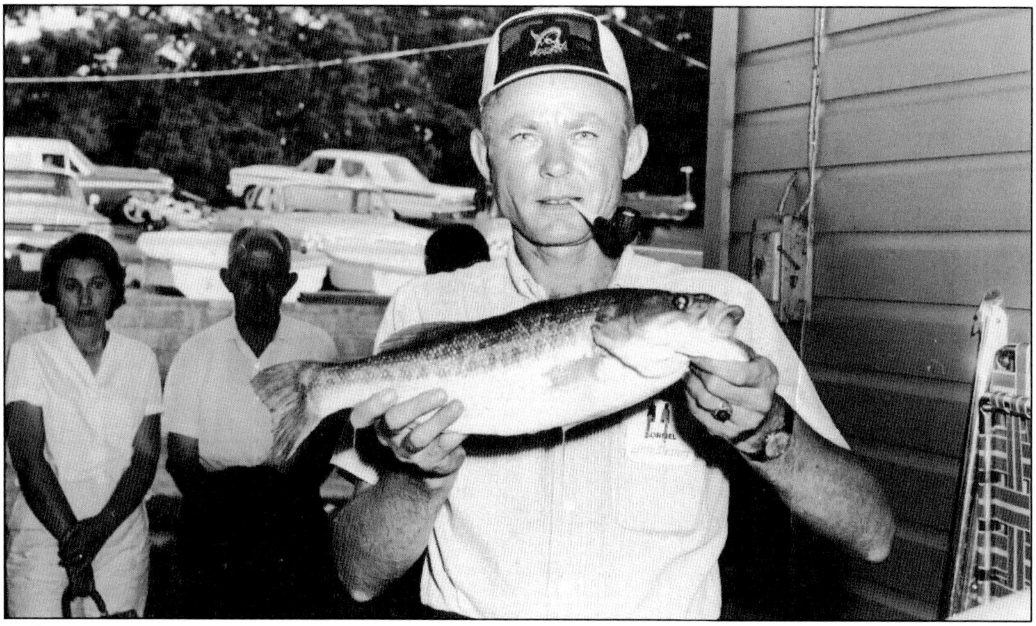

Billy Boone proudly displays the catch of the day. Lake Martin is a favorite place for amateur and professional fishermen from all over the United States. Fishing contests with prizes, trophies, and bragging rights are a regular sporting activity around the lake. In the picture below, from left to right, are Gerald McGill, Aubrey Stevens, ? McCalendar, and Omer McGhee. (Both, courtesy of MainStreet Organization.)

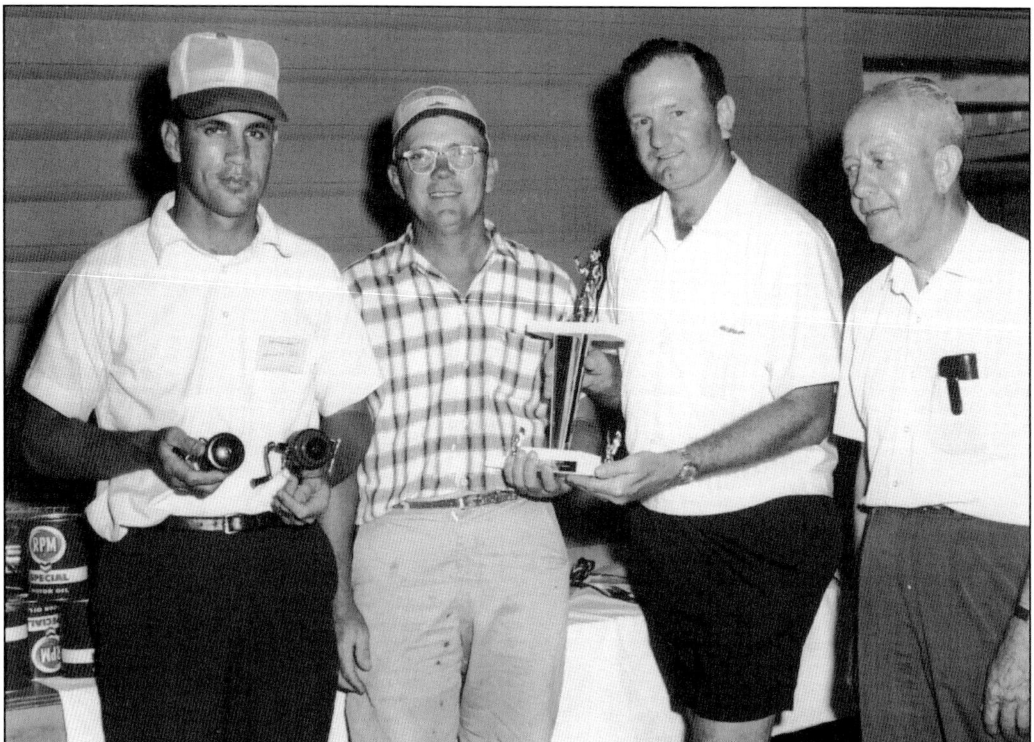

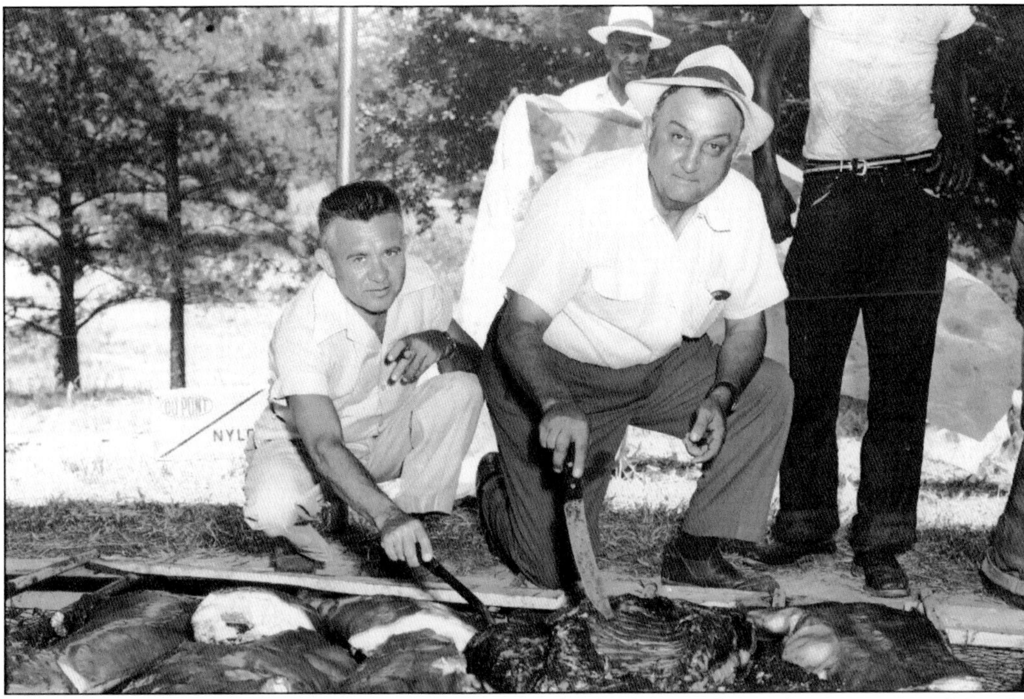

Lewis Askew and Allan Ponder keep an eye on the barbecue that is being prepared for the annual Russell Mills picnic for the company's employees and their families. (Courtesy of MainStreet Organization.)

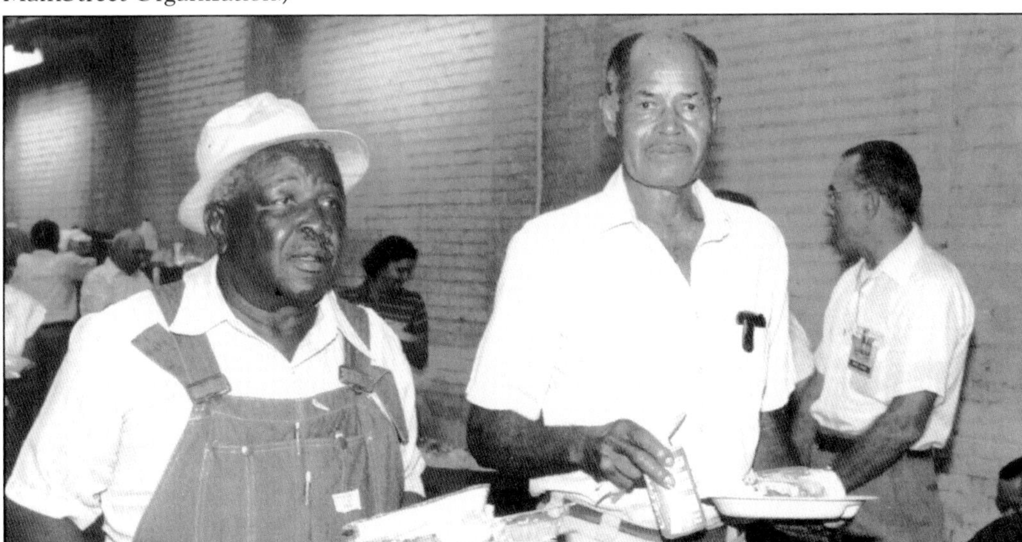

Bevelle held an annual barbecue and picnic with watermelon cuttings and homemade ice cream. Mose Martin (right) is the grandfather of Willie Carl Martin, who was asked by coach Bear Bryant to be the University of Alabama's first black football player in 1969. Willie Carl turned him down, but he went on to be a professional football player, returning years later to coach at his alma mater, Benjamin Russell High School. One of his football players was NFL wide receiver Terrell "T.O." Owens. Martin is currently an assistant coach at the University of Alabama. (Courtesy of Laura Oliver.)

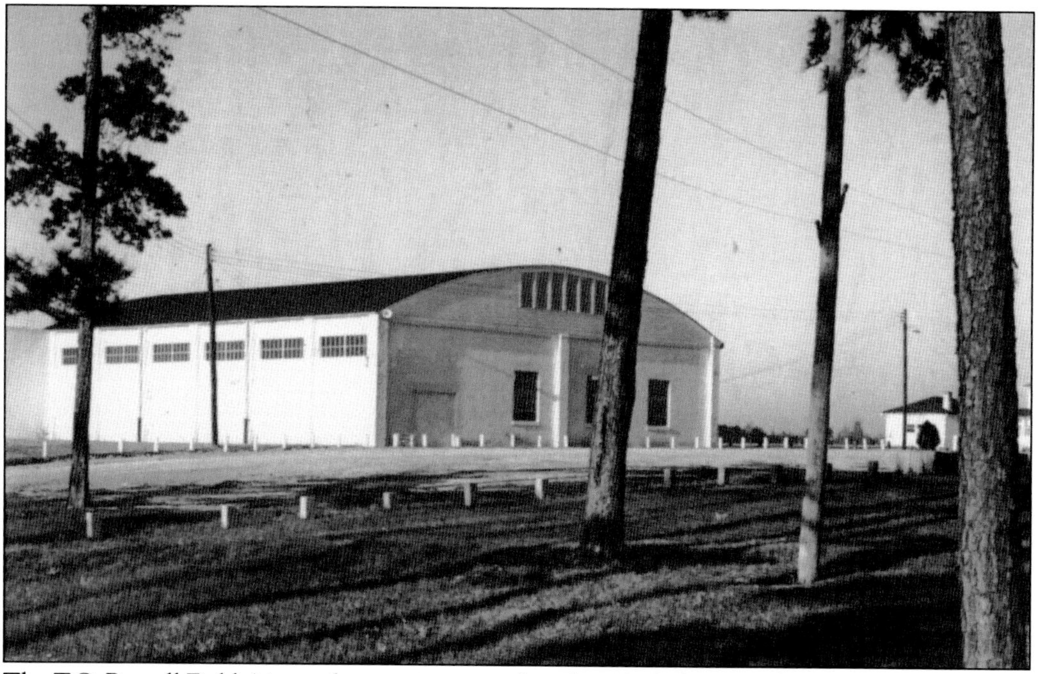

The T.C. Russell Field Airport hangar is pictured in this 1945 photograph. The airport was used by mill executives, local businessmen, and visitors to Alexander City. The airport also had a café that was a popular hangout for the high school kids, a swimming pool, and a covered pavilion. (Courtesy of Eleanor Carlisle.)

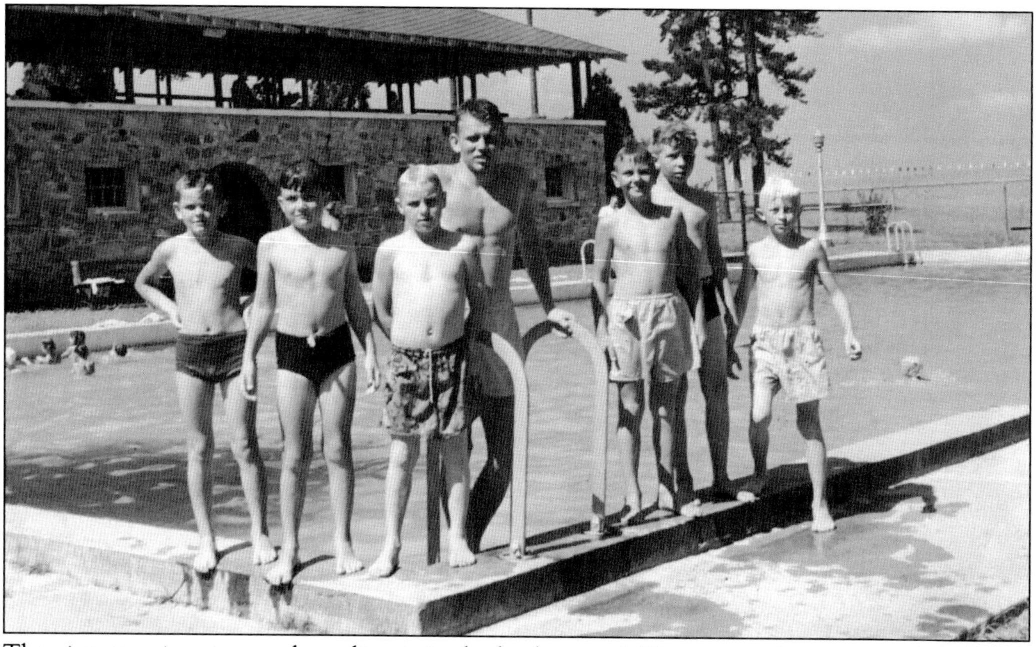

The airport swimming pool pavilion is in the background. The group of swimmers, from left to right, are Carlisle Towery, Billy Waites, David Carlisle, Taylor Headle (teacher), unidentified, Dwight Carlisle, and Glen "Cotton" Forbus. (Courtesy of MainStreet Organization.)

Charles "Red" Bailey (left) and coach Hamp Lyon observe children swimming. Coach Lyon was well known for building winning football teams. Retiring from teaching and coaching, Bailey was elected and served as mayor of Alexander City. He led the efforts to build a sports complex for recreational events that included a high school football field, tennis court, swimming pool, and baseball, and softball fields. (Courtesy of MainStreet Organization; photograph by Robert Graves.)

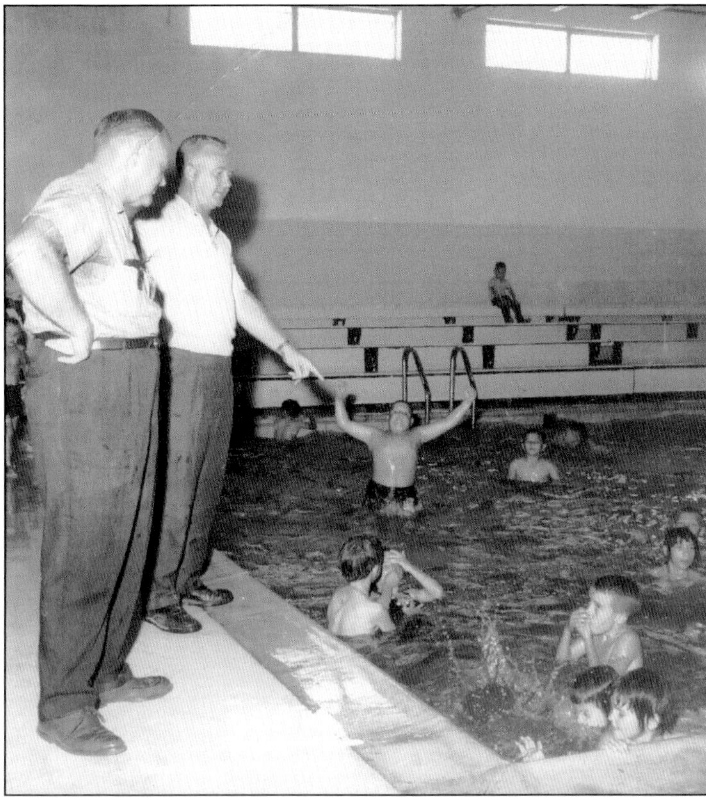

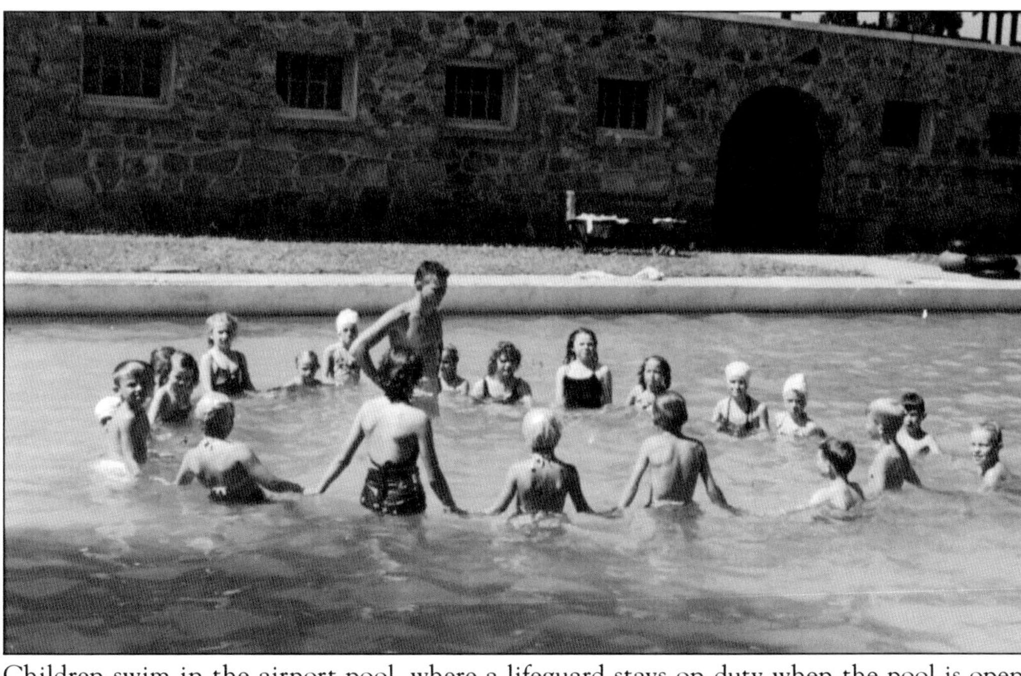

Children swim in the airport pool, where a lifeguard stays on duty when the pool is open. Swimming instructors were employed to provide lessons in the airport pool. (Courtesy of MainStreet Organization.)

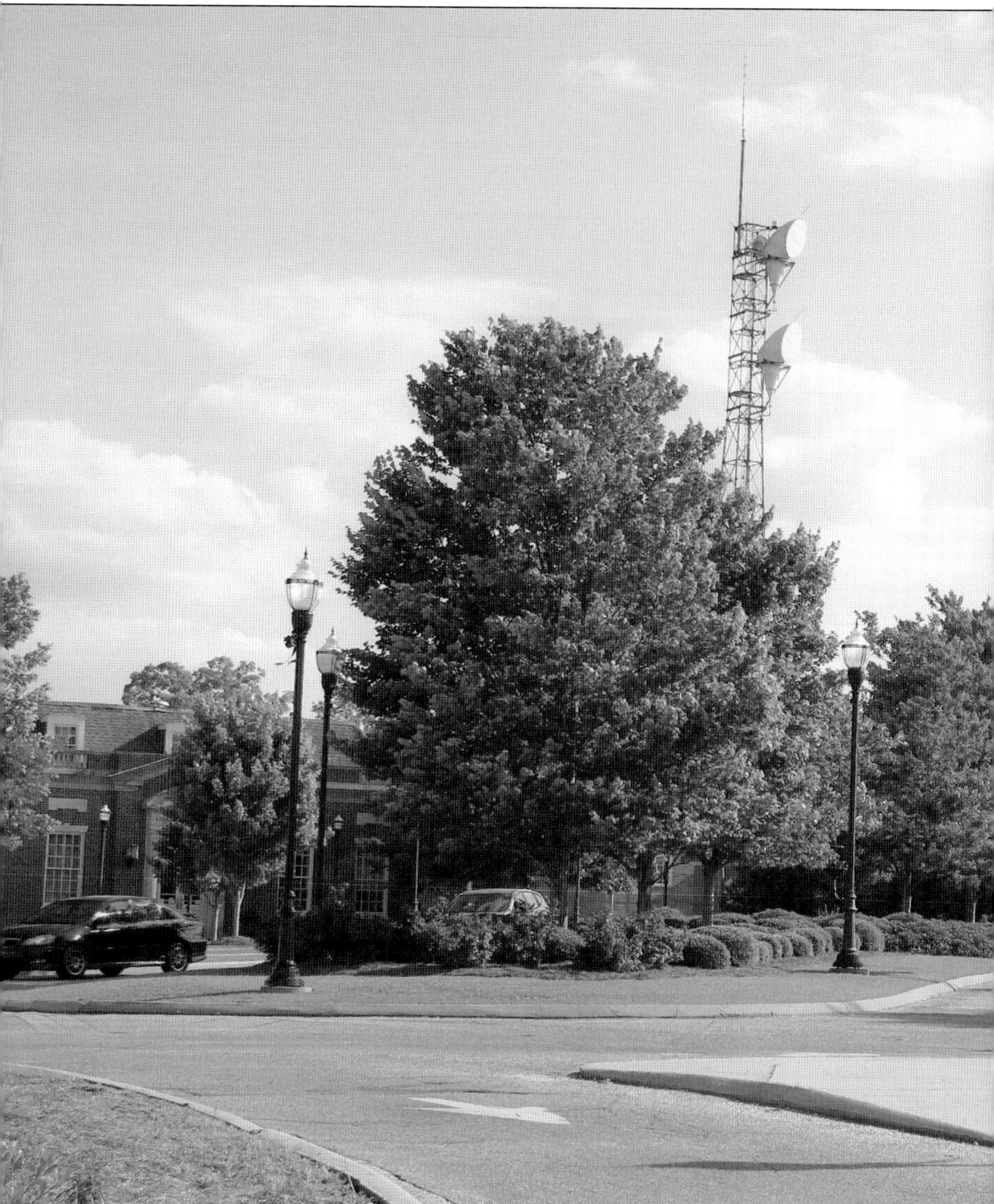

The Alexander City Court Square photograph shows the Alexander City municipal court building on the right, the First Baptist Church, the roundabout, and the Bud Porch Center for senior services. Barbara Young is Alexander City's first female mayor. Her husband, Tom F. Young,

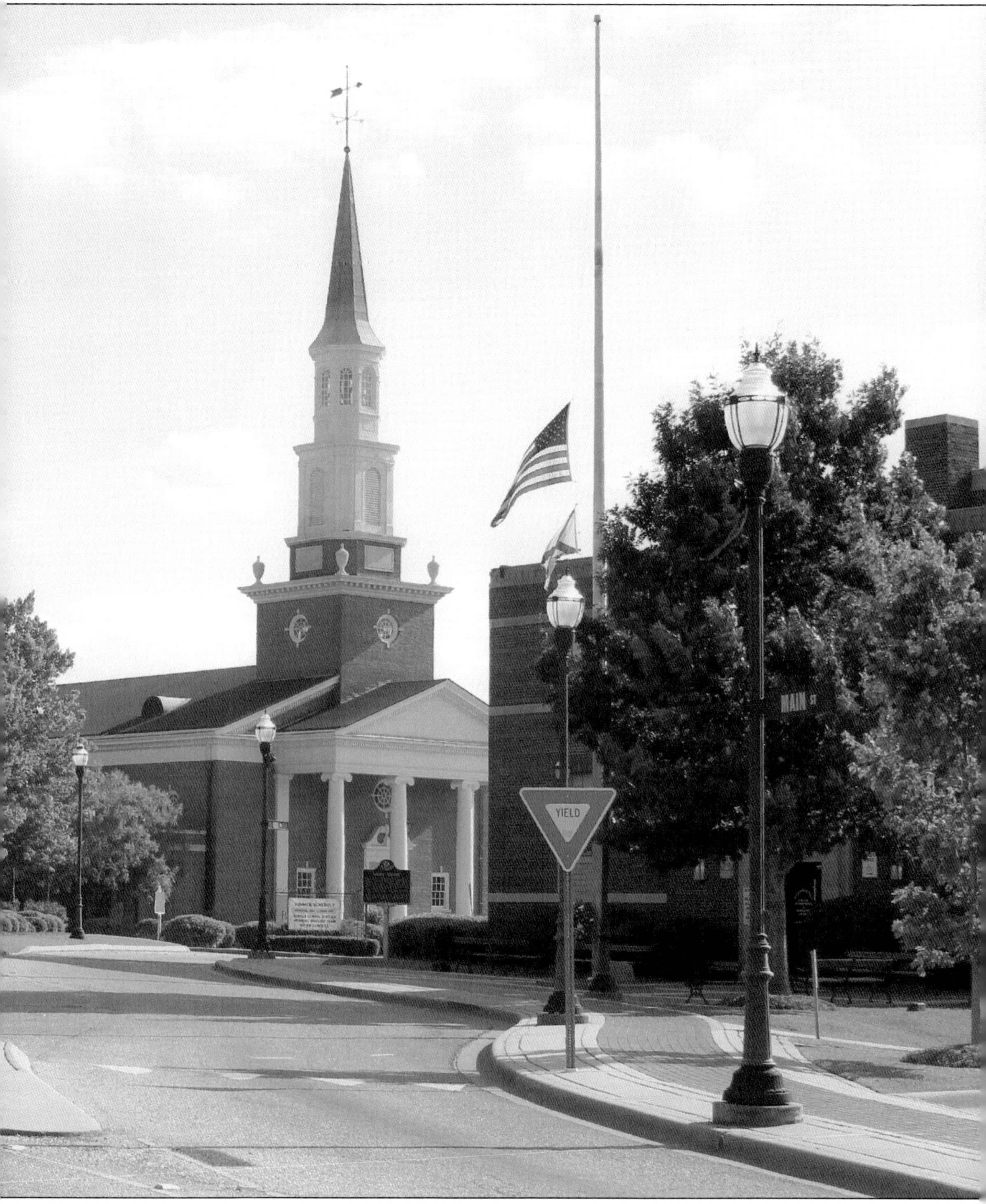

was a direct descendant of the city's founding family. (Courtesy of Peggy Walls; photograph by Tammy East.)

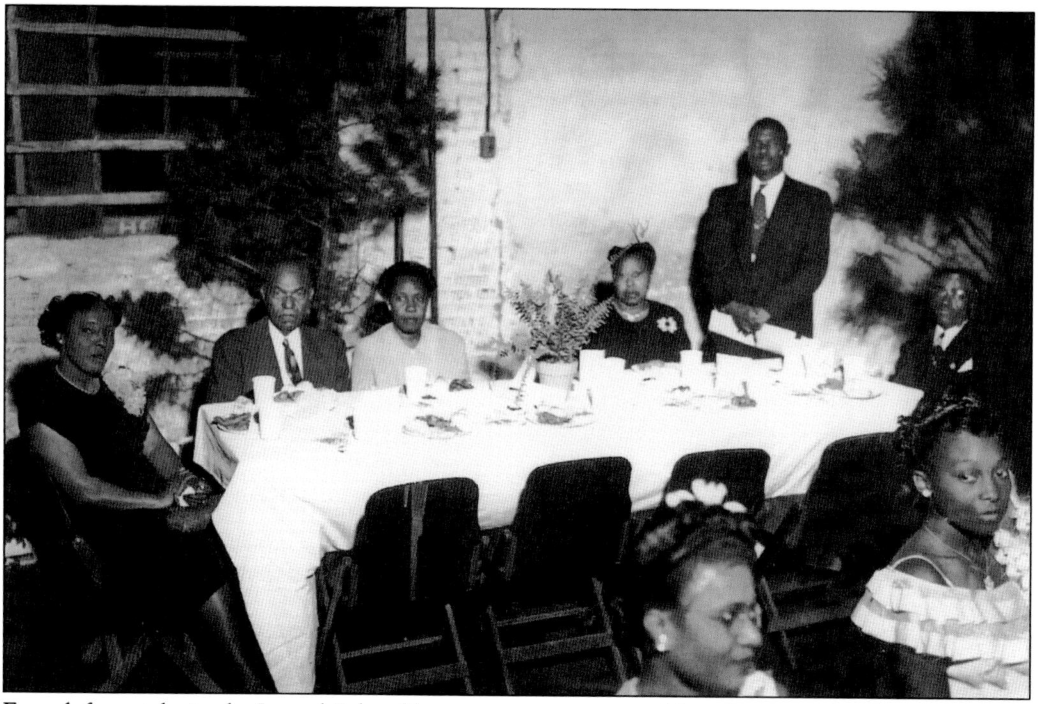

From left to right in the Laurel School banquet ceremony are Alma Corprew; Prof. William Jesse Darnell and his wife, Flora C. Darnell; unidentified; Burt Lowe; and Prof. N.H. Stephens. In the forefront are Ruth Stephens (left) and Margie Whatley. (Courtesy of Gwen Coley.)

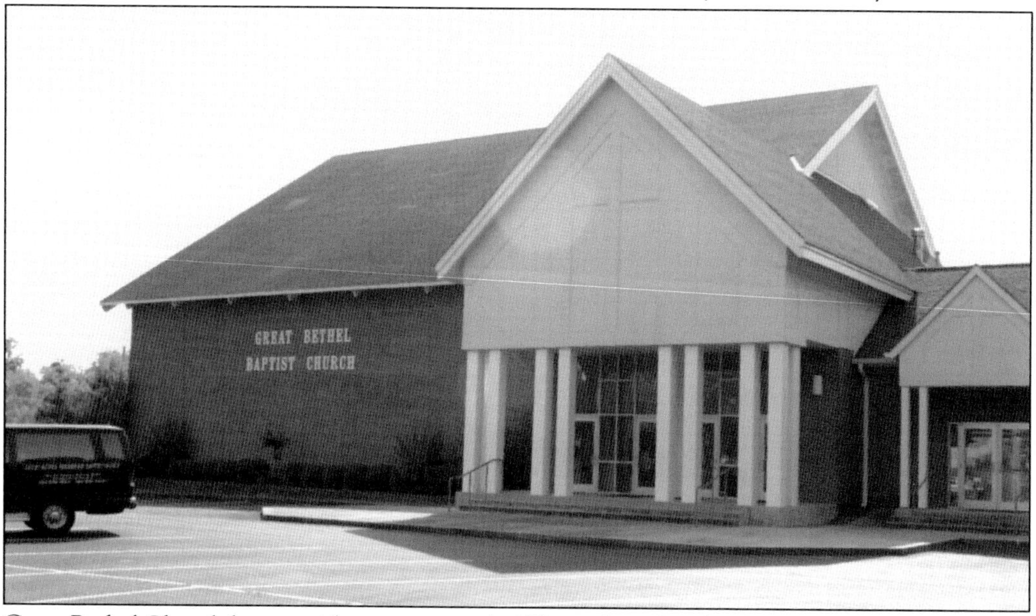

Great Bethel Church began with approximately 175 members. Under the guidance of Rev. Milton Nunn and other church leaders, the membership was multiplied many times over. In 1960, Reverend Nunn celebrated 43 years as the church pastor and leading businessman in the community. In his will, he left his possessions to promote the growth of the Great Bethel Church. (Courtesy of Peggy Walls; photograph by Tammy East.)

Nine

Hometown Places

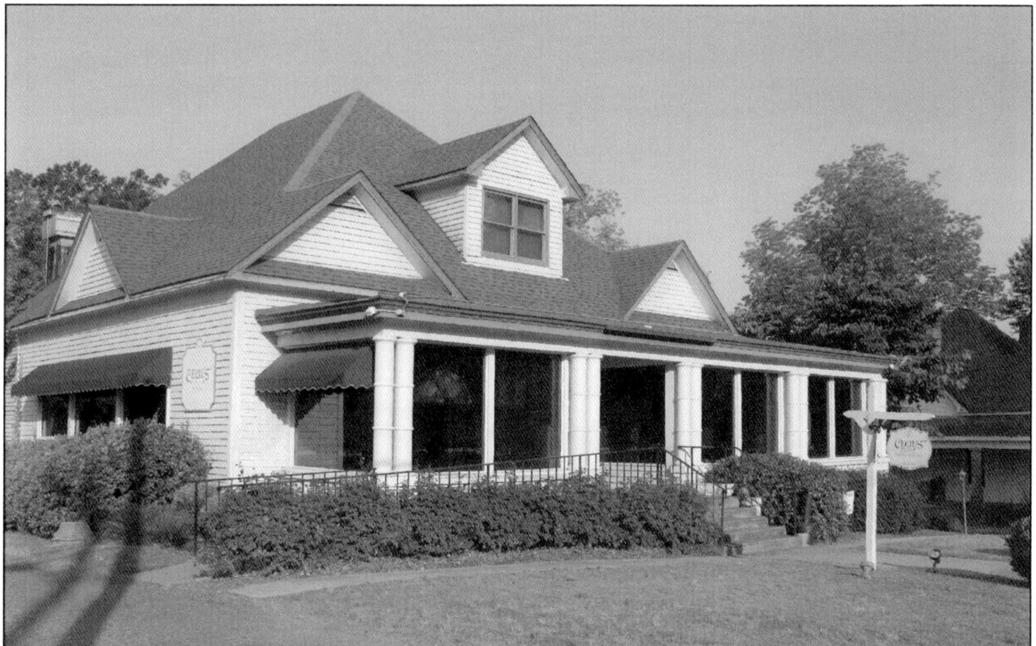

This structure on Green Street was erected in 1902 as a residential building, with its unique porch added in 1913. In 1943, the house was purchased by Dr. James Cameron for his family's residence, and in 1951, the building was converted to Dr. Cameron's medical office. In 1984, Cecil's Public House opened here; now owned by Bart and Stacy Jones, it is one of Alexander City's favorite eating establishments. (Courtesy of Peggy Walls; photograph by Tammy East.)

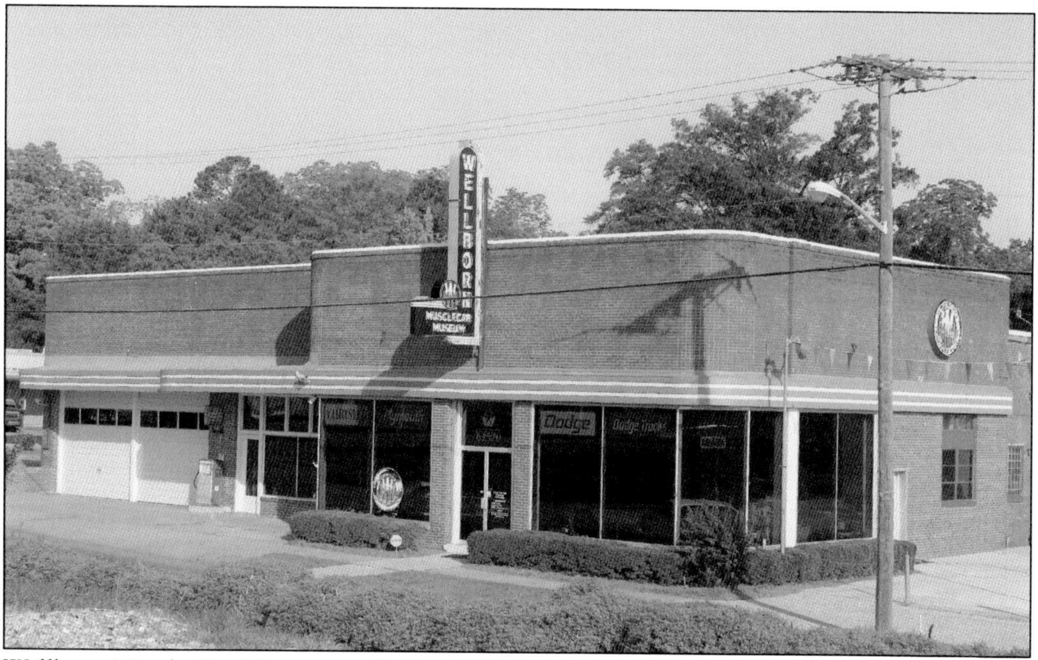

Wellborn Muscle Car Museum on Broad Street has a unique collection of muscle cars from the 1960s and 1970s. The museum has 60 cars on display, which include Mustangs, GTOs, Cudas, Chevelles, and Superbirds. Owners Tim and Pam Wellborn have one of the world's largest collections of Dodge Chargers. (Courtesy of Peggy Walls; photograph by Tammy East.)

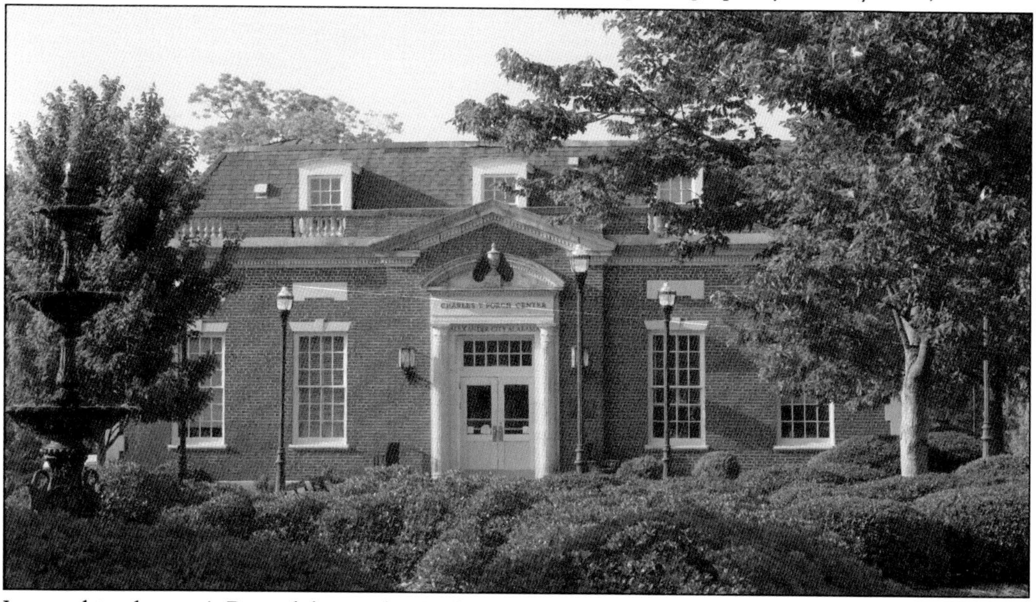

Located in the city's Roundabout, the Bud Porch Center is Alexander City's second post office site. The first post office was located on the corner of Main and Tallapoosa Streets and destroyed in the 1902 fire. Named in honor of longtime city clerk Charles "Bud" Porch, the building is now the home of Area Referral and Information Service for the Elderly, Inc., the Alabama State Department of Revenue, and the nutrition center for senior citizens. (Courtesy of Peggy Walls; photograph by Tammy East.)

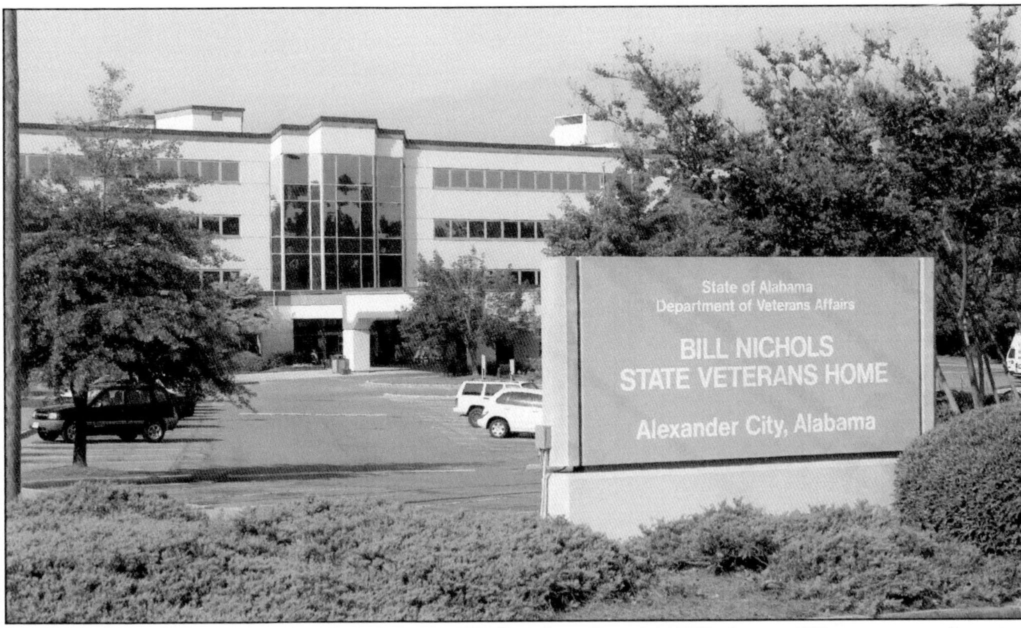

The Bill Nichols State Veterans Home on Elkahatchee Road, off Highway 280, is a senior housing community and care provider. The nursing home offers a 24-hour service for its resident veterans. It has been home to hundreds of veterans since opening in 1989. Alexander City is proud to have the first veterans' nursing home built in Alabama. (Courtesy of Peggy Walls; photograph by Tammy East.)

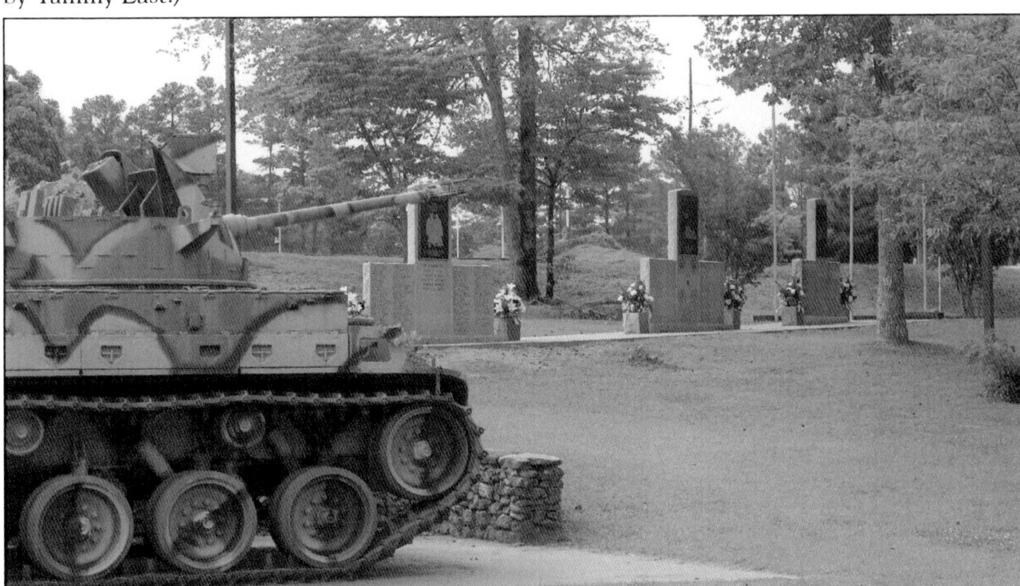

Alexander City Veterans Memorial Park is located in the Bailey Sportsplex on Highway 22 and is dedicated to veterans of all wars. The Confederate statue was removed from downtown Alexander City and placed in the park alongside an airplane, two tanks, a cross, and a cannon. Veterans of all wars and their families are honored in an annual Memorial Day program in May and a veterans' program in November each year in the park. (Courtesy of Peggy Walls; photograph by Tammy East.)

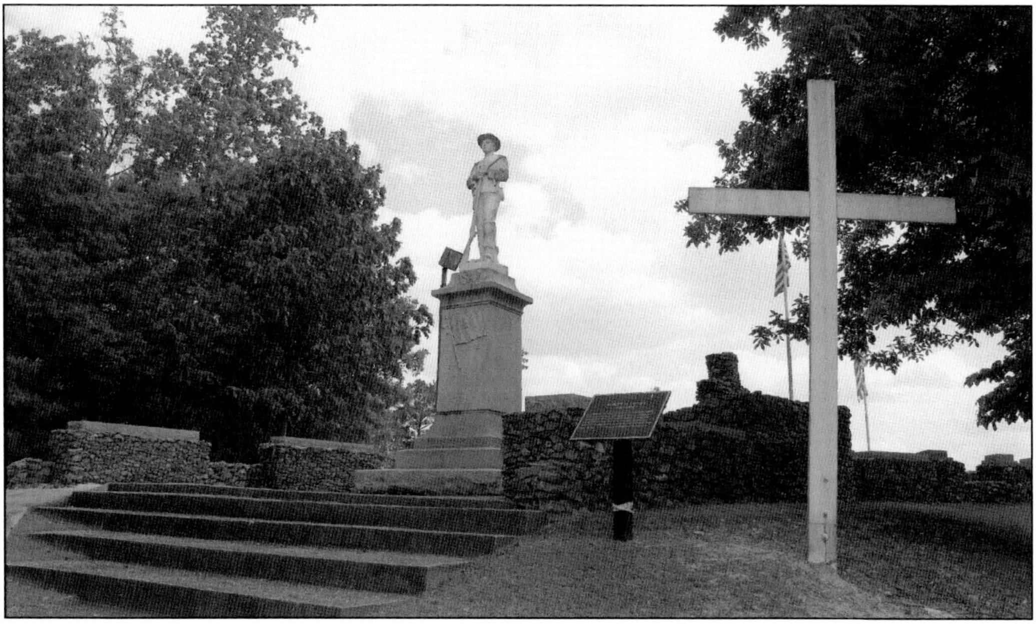

This statue was originally erected by the United Daughters of the Confederacy and given to Alexander City. Relocated from the center of downtown to the Alexander City Veterans Memorial Park, the Confederate statue was dedicated on January 11, 1992, by the Sons of the Confederate Veterans Camp 574. The statue represents all Confederate troops who fought in the Civil War. (Courtesy Peggy Walls; photograph by Tammy East.)

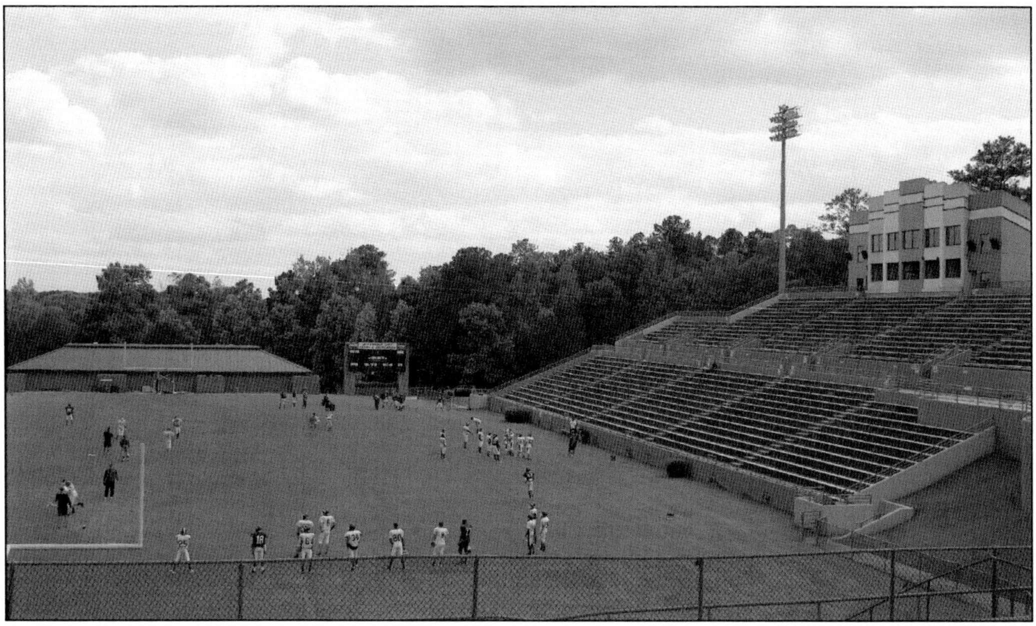

The Charles E. Bailey Sr. Sportsplex is a 212-acre public park with walking tracks. The football stadium is equal to that of a small college. During Friday night ball games, the lights can be seen and cheers heard from great distances. The park has a high sports appeal, with soccer fields, baseball fields, horse-riding arena, gymnasium, Senior Citizen Center, Veterans Park, and Imagination Station for small children. (Courtesy of Peggy Walls; photograph by Tammy East.)

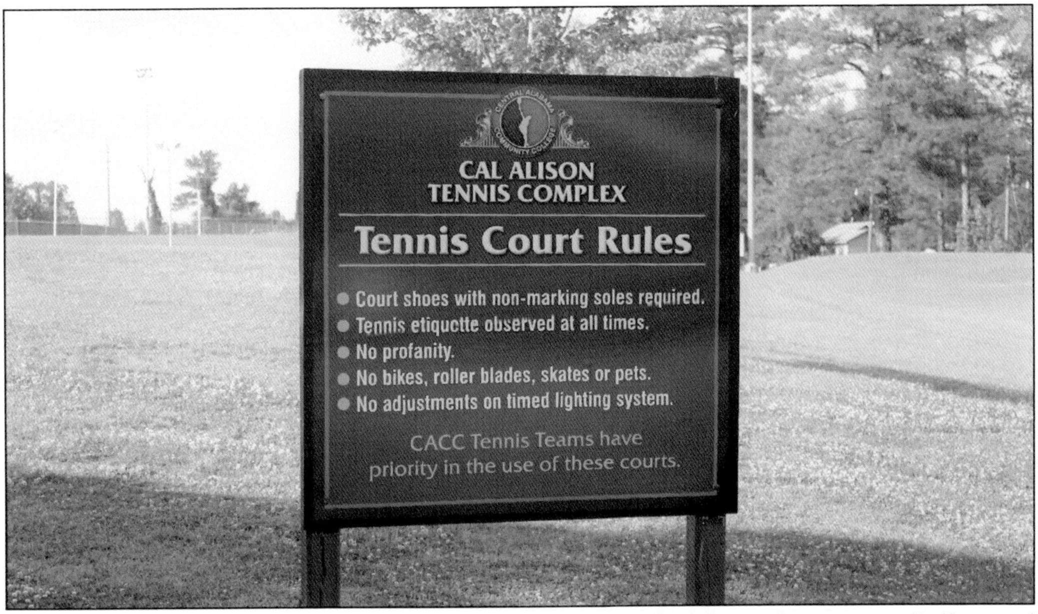

Cal Alison Tennis Court is located on the campus of Central Alabama Community College and named in honor of Cal Alison, who introduced tennis to the area. Cal and Elizabeth Russell Alison's daughter Roberta Alison Baumgardner was an outstanding tennis player and the first female athlete to attend the University of Alabama on an athletic scholarship. She was part of the first class inducted into Alabama Sports Hall of Fame. (Courtesy of Peggy Walls; photograph by Tammy East.)

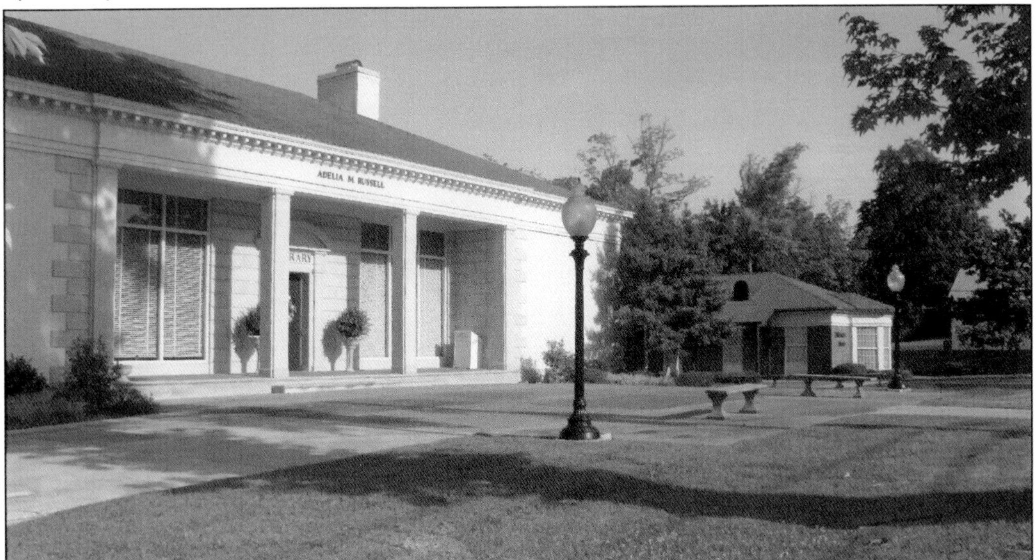

Alexander City's first public library was housed in one room in the old city hall, now the judicial building. In June 1965, the new library was constructed and dedicated as the Adelia M. Russell Library and opened on Church Street, one block from downtown. The construction of the three-story library was made possible through the efforts of many citizens. Mamie's Place, the first freestanding children's library in Alabama, was erected next door. (Courtesy of Peggy Walls; photograph by Tammy East.)

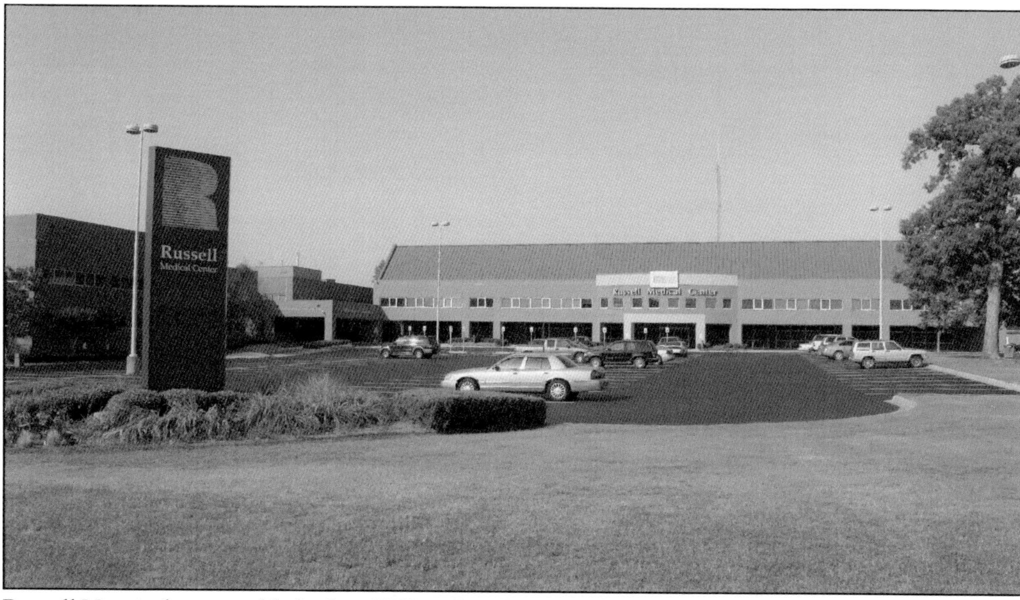

Russell Hospital was established in 1923 on Lee Street and moved in 1964 into the Russell Medical Center at its present location on Highway 280. The medical facilities include a cancer center and wound care center. In 2011, Thomson Reuters selected the hospital as one of the top 10 hospitals in the United States. That same year, Russell Hospital was recognized as one of six hospitals in the country to receive the Everest Award, citing the highest current performances and the fastest long-term improvements. (Courtesy of Peggy Walls; photograph by Tammy East.)

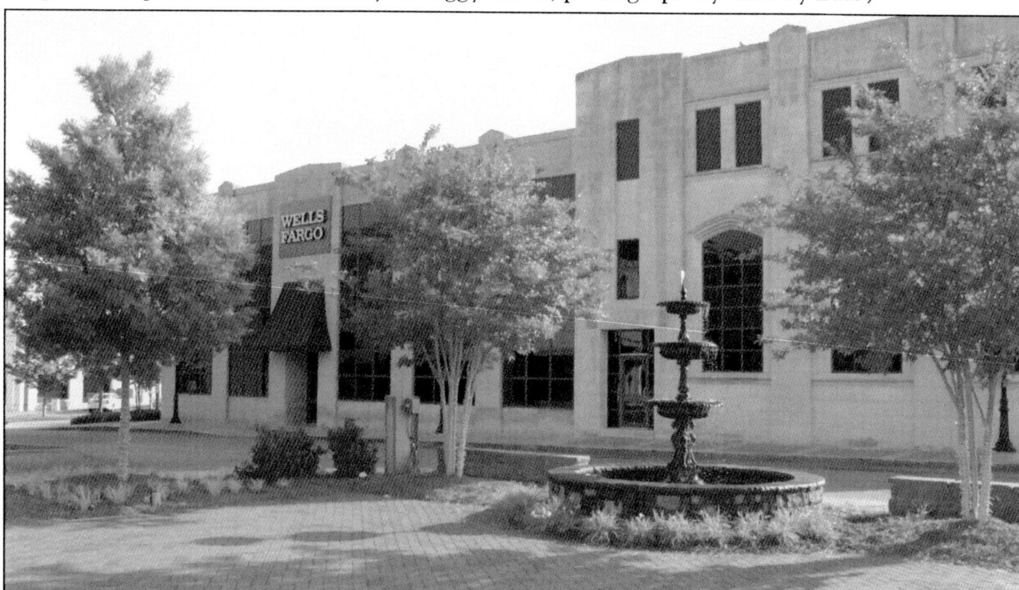

Alexander City Community Development, under the direction of Randy Thomas, sponsored the landscaping of a small park area across from Wells Fargo Bank, formerly Alexander City Bank. Robinson Iron crafted the black wrought-iron fountain that sits in the center of the Broad Street Plaza and the brick walkway. Jake's restaurant, operated by Jake and Trissie Mixon, is located in the old Fair Store building. (Courtesy of Peggy Walls; photograph by Tammy East.)

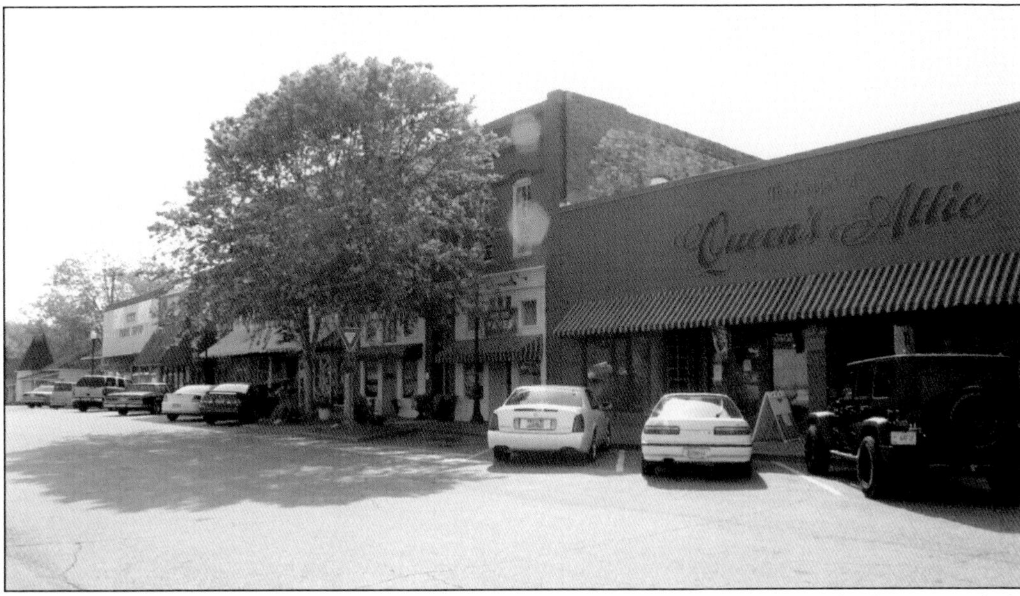

In 1892, Ed Duncan opened Duncan and Son's Furniture Store in what is now the location of The Shoppes of Queen's Attic. Rebuilt after the 1902 fire, the family business remained in operation until the 1980s. Following a more recent fire in the building, owner Larry Tuggle renovated the structure to resemble a stroll down a New Orleans Street. The building is available for parties and is home to an antique shop and Coffee and Cakes Café. (Courtesy of Peggy Walls; photograph by Tammy East.)

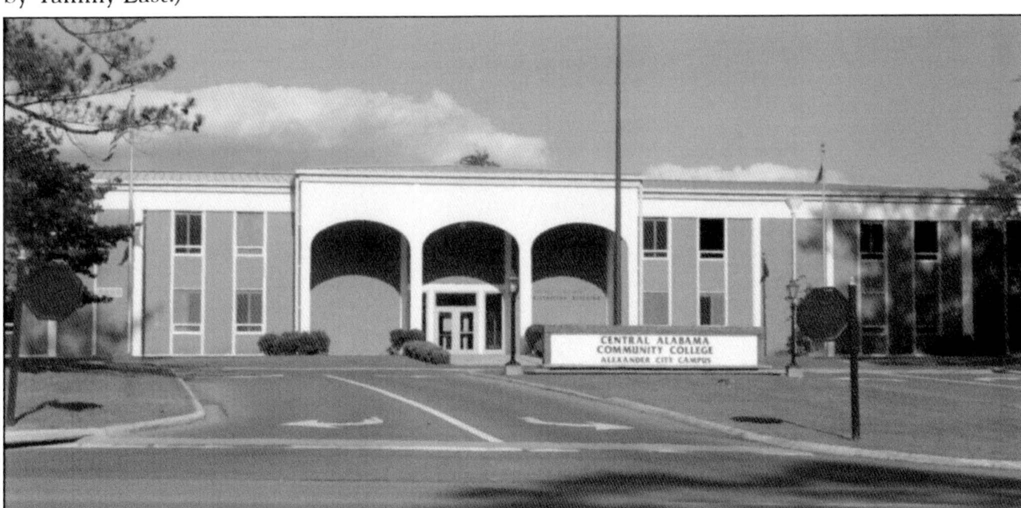

The Alabama State Board of Education created the Central Alabama Community College (CACC) on February 23, 1989, through consolidation of the Alexander City State Junior College and Nunnelly State Technical College. Preceding the establishment of CACC, beginning in 1964, the Alexander City Junior College served students in Tallapoosa County and surrounding areas. Classes were held in temporary housing until September 1966, when the college was moved to the current location. With an enrollment of over 2,000 students, CACC offers a two-year, postsecondary education in comprehensive studies. (Courtesy of Peggy Walls; photograph by Tammy East.)

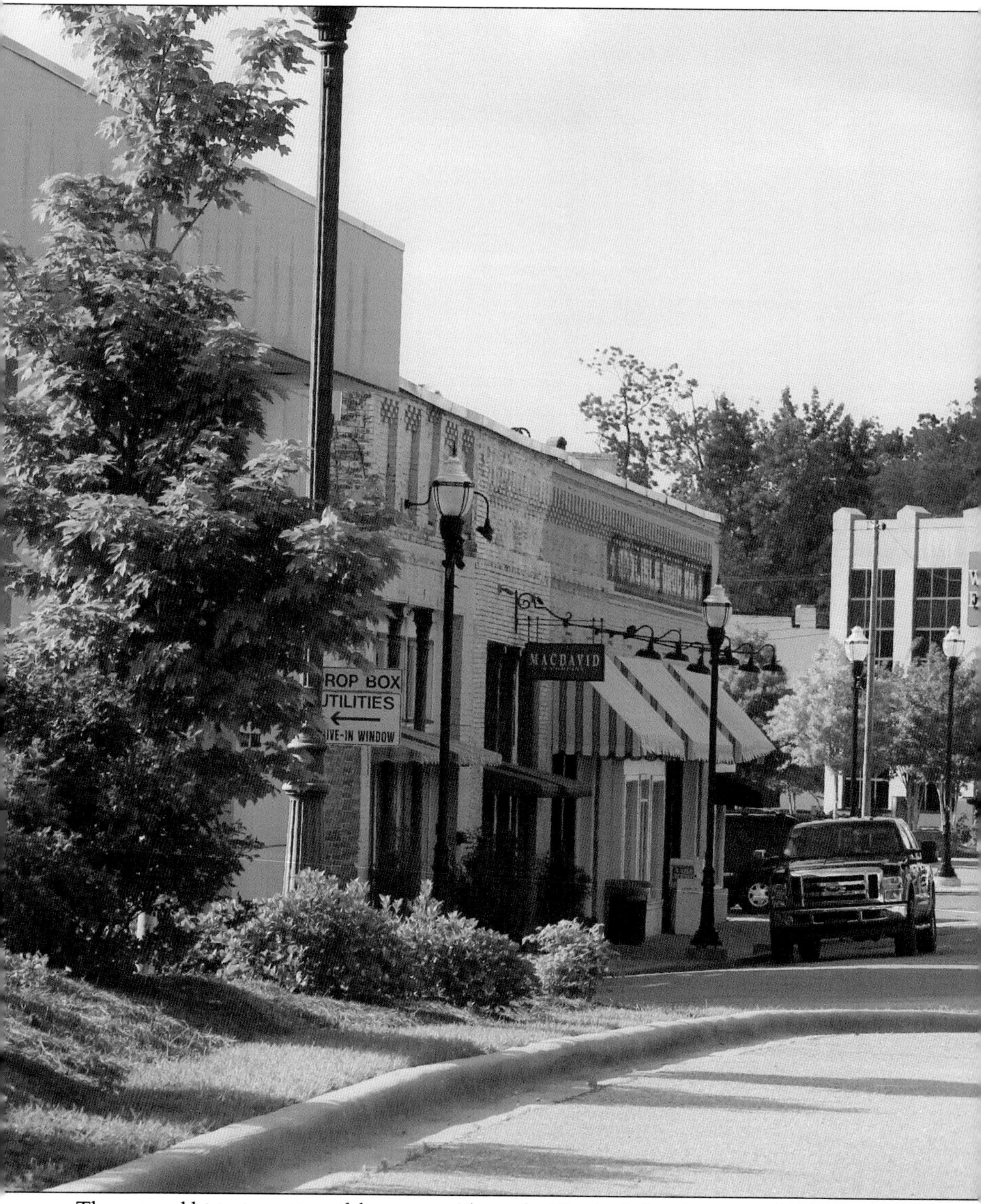

The restored historic section of downtown Alexander City includes the new and old. MacDavid & Co. is located beside the old Carlisle Drugstore. Founded in 1914, Carlisle has the old soda fountain still in place, where people stop by for lemon and limeades. People have gathered in front

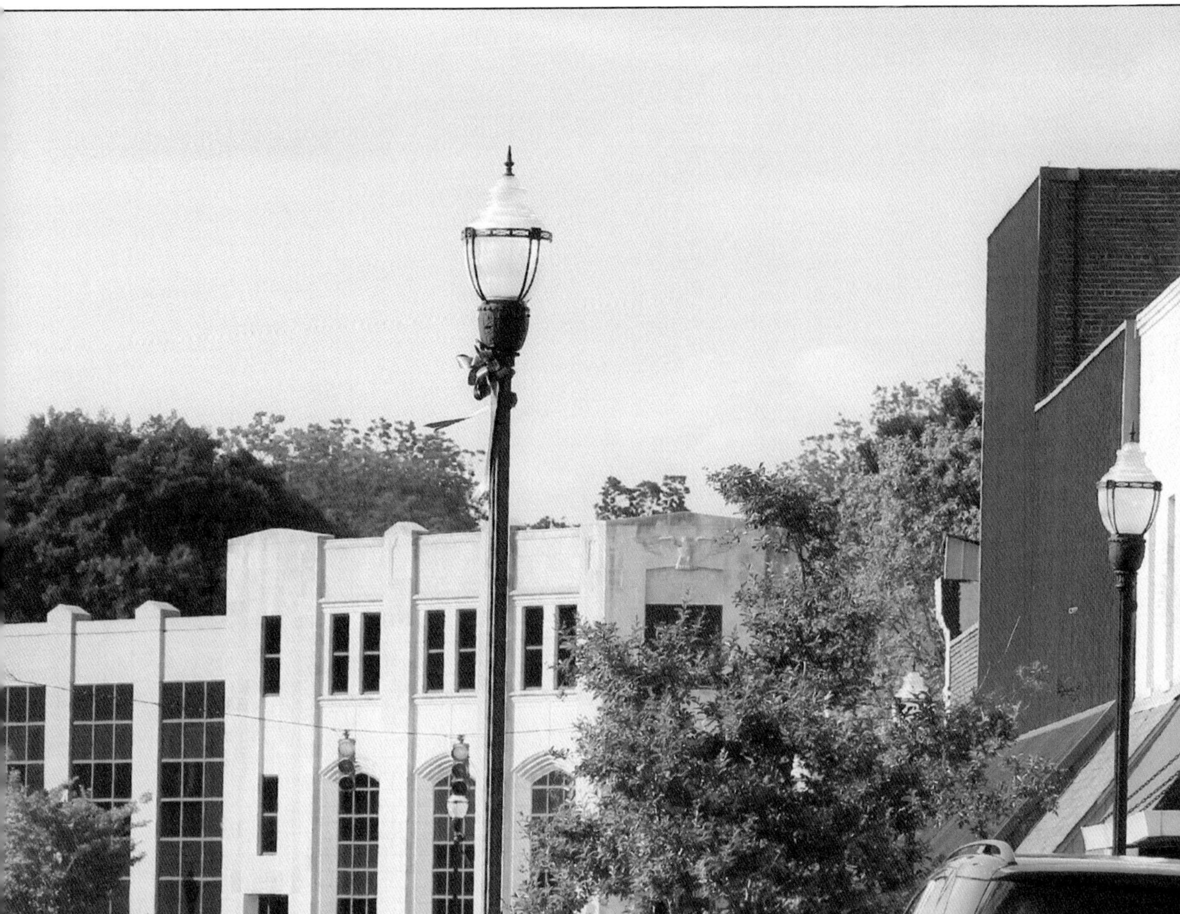

of Carlisle Drugstore for Christmas and homecoming parades for almost a century. (Courtesy of Peggy Walls; photograph by Tammy East.)

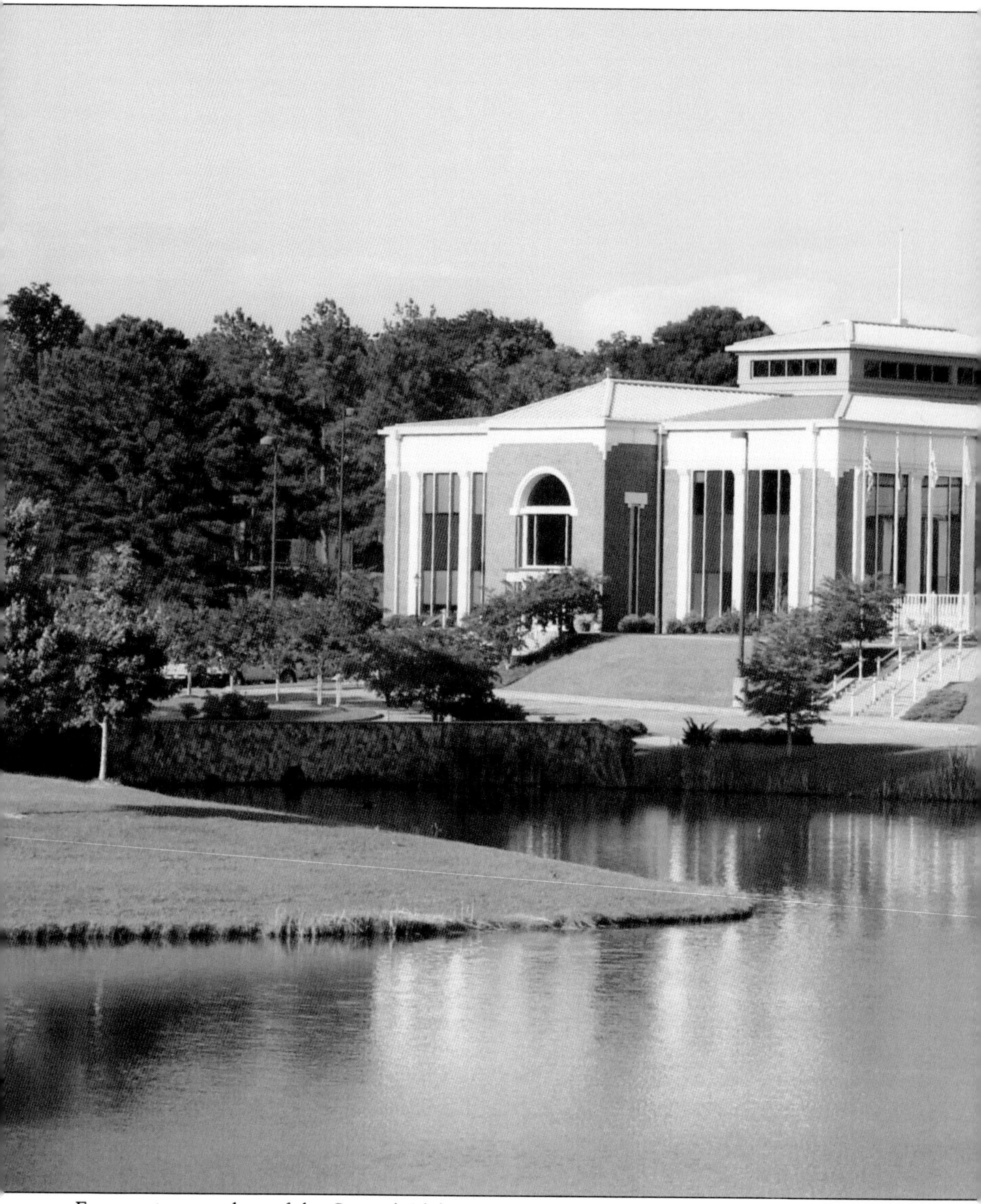

Former vice president of the Central Alabama Community College, Betty Carol Graham, was the 81st district state representative from 1994 to 2011. Graham was successful in her efforts to locate the technology center on the college campus. The Betty Carol Graham Center provides

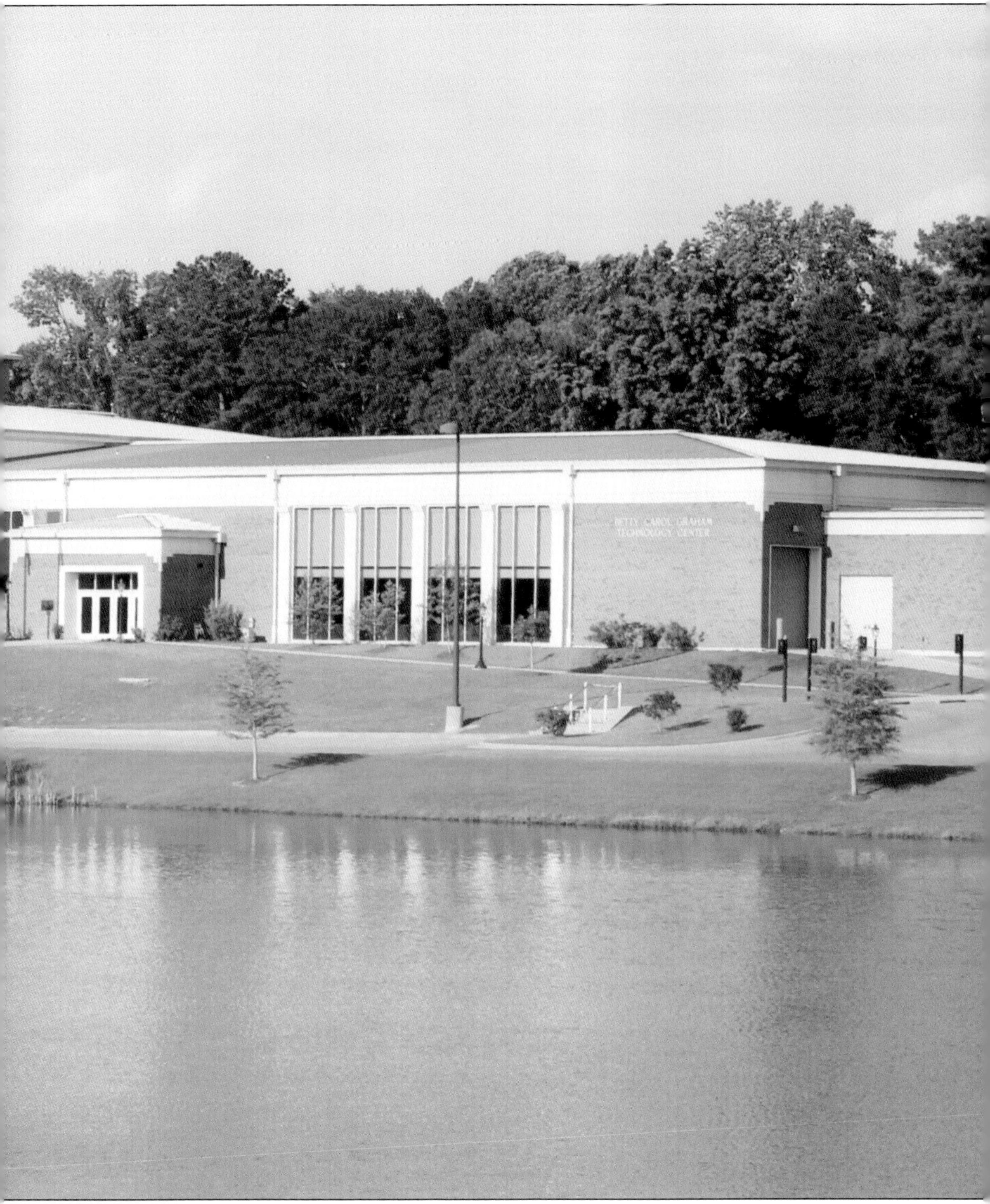

training and advanced studies for students in the city and from surrounding areas. (Courtesy of Peggy Walls; photograph by Tammy East.)

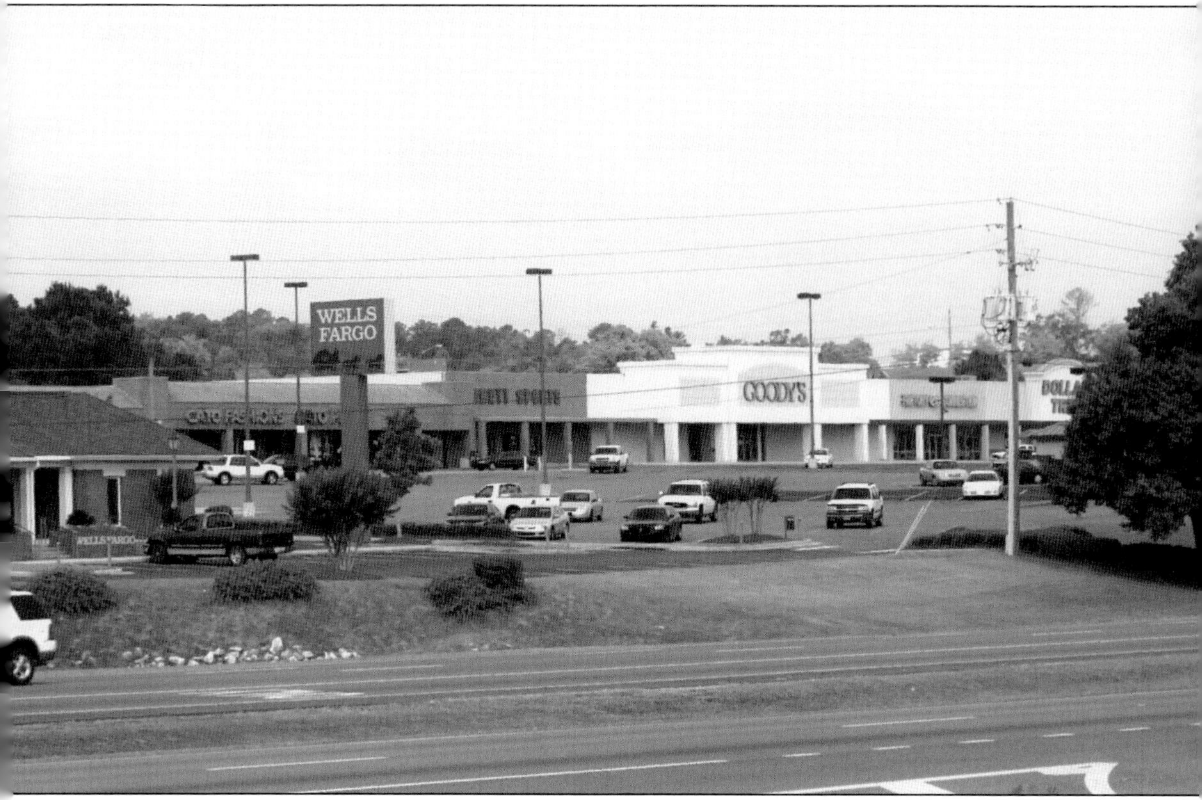

Highway 280 is a major four-lane thoroughfare from Birmingham, Alabama, to Columbus, Georgia. The highway renovation was completed in the 1990s. Average daily traffic from Elkahatchee Road to Airport Road is 25,000 cars per day, and from Airport Road to Highway 22 is 22,000 cars per day. Farther west and east, the traffic count is 15,000 to 17,000 cars. (Courtesy of Peggy Walls; photograph by Tammy East.)

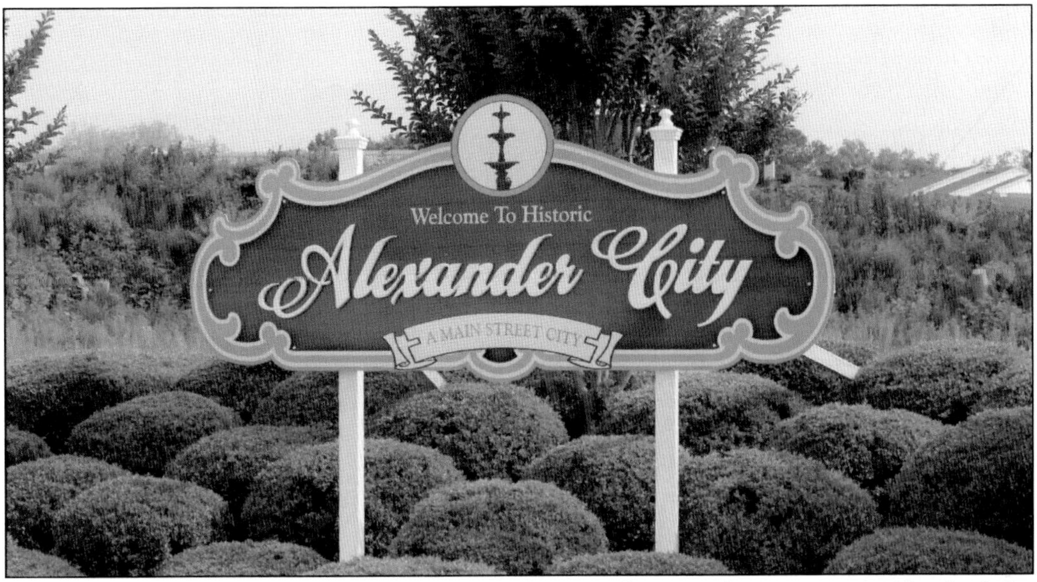

Alexander City is centrally located to Birmingham, Auburn, and Montgomery. Nearby Lake Martin has regular recreational events. The Wind Creek State Park, with camping facilities and swimming areas, spans 1,445 acres along Lake Martin. Art activities at Kowaliga include the Sarah Towery Art Colony and the Alexander City Jazz Festival downtown and at the Lake Martin Amphitheatre. The map highlights sites that appear on the National Register of Historical Places, shopping districts, and municipal buildings. (Above, courtesy of Peggy Walls, photograph by Tammy East; below, courtesy of Spring Hill Press, LLC.)

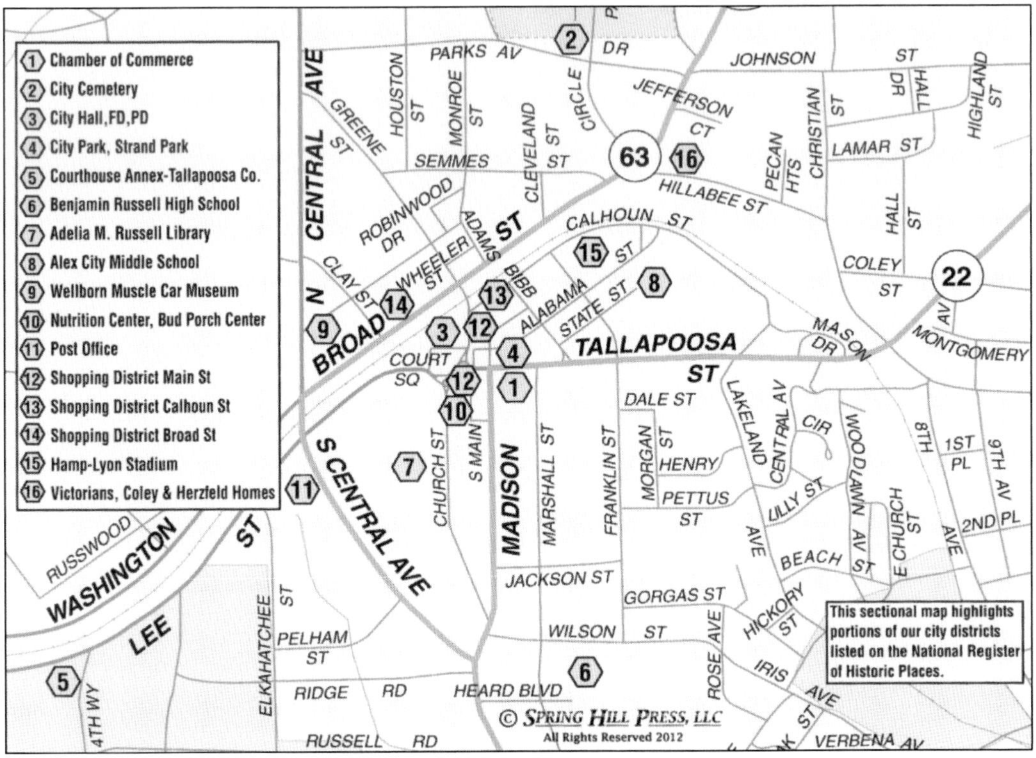

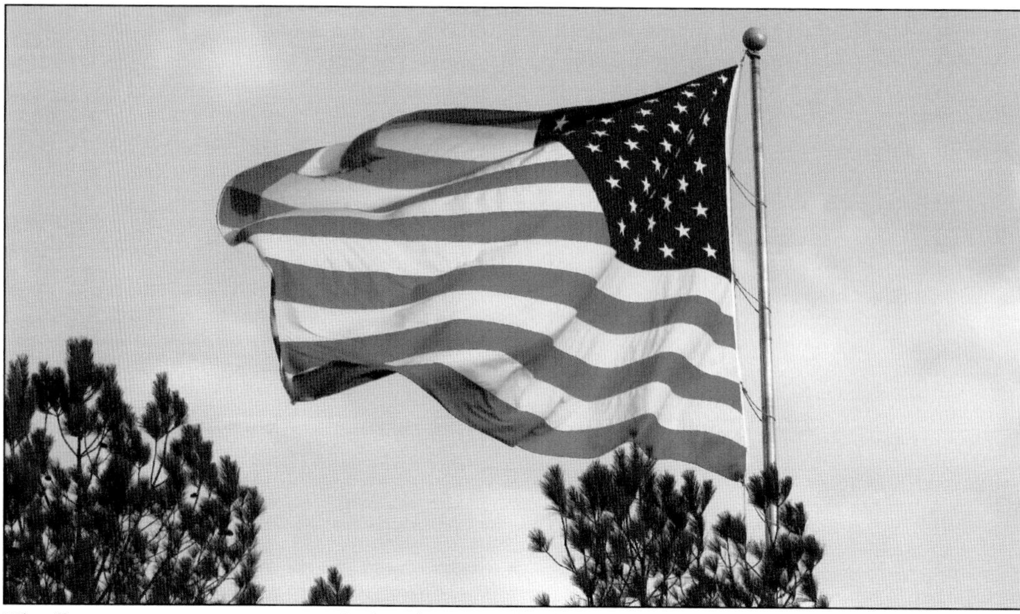

The flag serves as a patriotic symbol and as a marker for visitors who wish to travel into Alexander City. A turn on Highway 22 East will take the visitor through the Alexander City Court Square and on to New Site and the Horseshoe Bend area where the Indian Wars were fought in the early 1800s. (Courtesy of Peggy Walls; photograph by Tammy East.)

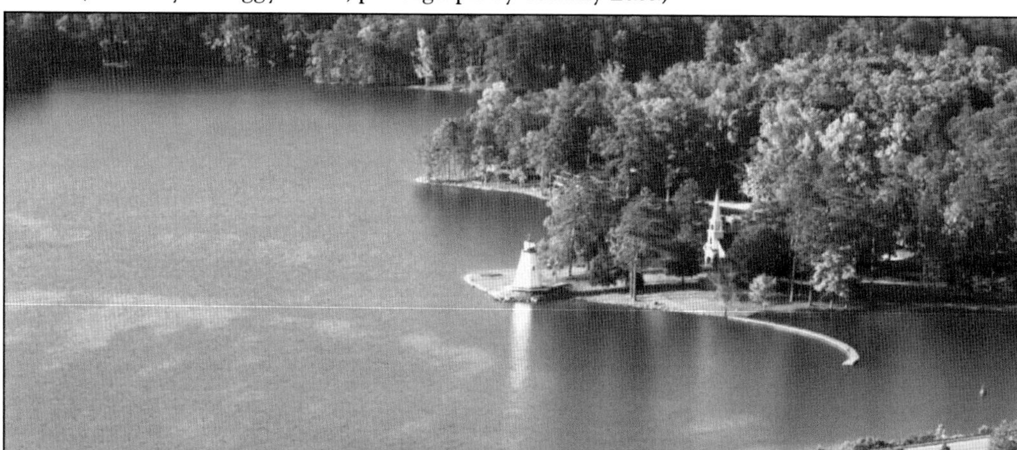

Across from the flag on Highway 280, Highway 63 South leads to the Children's Highway and Russell Cross Roads, Kowaliga Bridge, Sinclair Restaurant, and Children's Harbor. Ben and Luanne Russell created the lake harbor as a partner to the Children's Harbor Family Center at Birmingham Children's Hospital as a resort for children with special needs. The Children's Harbor Church and the Church in the Pines are popular wedding sites. From the early 19th century to the present, the Kowaliga area remains a favorite recreational site for visitors and Alexander City residents alike. (Courtesy of Russell Lands.)

BIBLIOGRAPHY

Frohsin, Ralph. *I'm Still Here: The Memories of Ralph Frohsin*. Self-published, 1991.

Kelley, Jennie Lee. "A History of Alexander City." In *Alexander City Centennial 1874–1974*. Alexander City, AL: Tallapoosa County Bicentennial Committee, 1974.

Saunders, Thomas Byron. "Alexander City, A New Century." In *125th Anniversary, Alexander City, Alabama*. Edited by Bob Saxon. Alexander City, AL: 125th Celebration Committee, 1998.

Saxon, Bob, ed. *125th Anniversary, Alexander City, Alabama*. Alexander City, AL: 125th Celebration Committee, 1998.

———, ed. *Tallapoosa County: A History*. Alexander City, AL: Tallapoosa County Bicentennial Committee, 1974.

Schaffer, Elizabeth D. *Lake Martin: Alabama's Crown Jewel*. Charleston, SC: Arcadia Publishing, 2003.

Schremser, Jewel D. *Avondale Mills*. Alexander City, AL: Tallapoosa County Bicentennial Committee, 1974.

Tallapoosa County Heritage Book Committee. *The Heritage of Tallapoosa County, Alabama*. Clanton, AL: Heritage Publishing Consultants, Inc., 2000.

Walls, Peggy. "Alexander City: 125 Years of Memories." Alexander City, AL: Russell Print Shop, 1998. Videocassette (VHS), 120 min.

———. "Gold Mining at Hog Mountain in the 1930s." *Alabama Review* 37 (1984): 202–220.

www.archives.alabama.gov/aha/markers.html

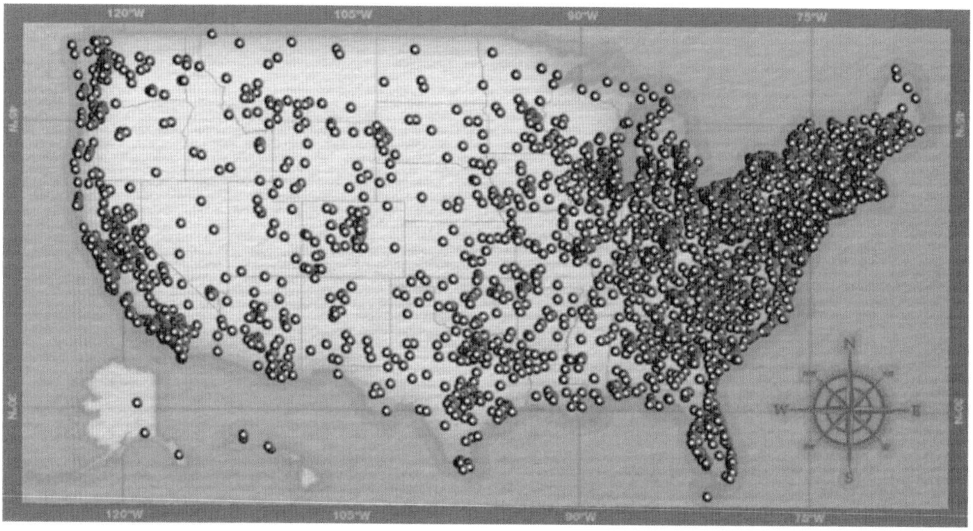